BETH CHATTO'S
GARDEN
NOTEBOOK

BETH CHATTO'S
GARDEN
NOTEBOOK

Illustrated by

Clare Roberts and Pamela Neighbour

J. M. Dent
London

First published 1988
This edition in paperback published 1993
Text © Beth Chatto 1988

Illustrations © Clare Roberts and Pamela Neighbour 1988

This book is set in 10/11½pt Pilgrim by
Gee Graphics Ltd, Crayford, Kent

Printed and bound in England by
Butler & Tanner Ltd, Frome and London for
J. M. Dent Ltd
The Orion Publishing Group
Orion House
5 Upper St Martin's Lane
London WC2H 9EA

Illustrations of plants are by Clare Roberts;
other illustrations are by Pamela Neighbour

British Library Cataloguing in Publication Data

Chatto, Beth
Beth Chatto's garden notebook.
1. Plants. Nurseries. Manuals
I. Title
635

ISBN 0-460-86095-X

CONTENTS

INTRODUCTION

IT ALWAYS seems extraordinary to me how many gardening books are written, bought, glanced at, and then placed on shelves to remain largely as decoration. There just is not enough time in our lives, even for enthusiasts, to sit down and read half the books we possess. Between us, my husband Andrew and I have shelves full of books, but comparatively few do we consult regularly. This is sad when one thinks of all the time, effort and loneliness that went into writing these books. They sit on our shelves like friends we rarely visit. Yet when I take one down, I seldom fail to read something of interest, something which makes me regretful I do not stay longer and look deeper into that particular author's mind.

When I was asked to write this book I was intrigued by the possibility of a different approach, but uncertain how far I could feasibly stray beyond the boundaries of the garden.

Two of my books, *The Dry Garden* and *The Damp Garden*, have told the story of making our garden from a piece of wasteland. *Plant Portraits* is a collection of short essays describing some of my favourite plants. A further book on the garden might well have become repetitive, tedious to write as well as to read. But this new approach was to be more personal. How personal? I had no clear idea of the content or form, but felt I was about to step out onto thin ice.

For many years I have kept several diaries. They have evolved from the small diary I used to keep when I first began the nursery. I would often look back into the previous year and be astonished to see we were within a day or so of taking exactly the same cuttings, or alternatively, be reminded that we should already have done something and had not. These simple but useful notes made me realise, as the nursery grew, that

1

we must make daily records of practically everything we did. Now we have a very comprehensive file kept by my head propagator, David Ward, of every process that takes place in the production of more than two thousand different kinds of plants. His propagating team, whether they are preparing and inserting cuttings or are potting seedlings, rooted cuttings or divisions from the field, all make their daily records, ready to be entered into the propagation file. This ensures the year-round routine of propagation, since the records of every plant are there, with many helpful details such as optimum timing, success rate – or failure, and any special comments relating to difficult plants. (There are, of course, other records kept connected with spraying, irrigation, and various technical matters to do with the smooth running of the nursery. These are in the hands of my technician, Keith Page.)

From my original diaries, there developed a personal file containing garden notes. Apart from my having to endure frozen fingers and feet, the keeping of this monthly record is a relatively simple task in winter when there is a limit to the number of flowers or fine foliage plants one can describe, but in March and April there is plenty to write about and by May I am overwhelmed. Each summer month could fill a book and there are far too many other things I must do. However, each year I make time to scribble a few descriptions, either of individual plants or families, or to write about an association or scene in the garden that came together well on a particular occasion. Rarely, if ever, does the exact scene reproduce itself. I have imprinted on my mind some scene where the light and balance of flowers, buds and foliage was memorable, and have never seen it so again.

It would be nice to keep Sundays for writing this garden notebook, but somehow there seem to be very few in the year that are free. Although the gardens are not open on Sundays there are often other commitments – to prepare a talk, write an article, finish a piece of planting that has been interrupted all week, or see my grandchildren. Sometimes I feel like doing nothing at all.

My third notebook is my private diary. In this I record the pleasures and problems that occur from day to day on the nursery and in the garden, together with a record of family events.

Visitors to the garden sometimes ask what training have I had? Why did I decide to make a nursery?

I have had no formal training in horticulture, but from the earliest days of my gardening career I was interested in the propagation of plants, teaching myself to produce plants for the garden from seeds and cuttings. I frequently sought help from books, but found basically that the knowledge of how and when came from constant practice and experience. Now after forty years as a gardener I am still learning, and shall do so to the end of my days.

The nursery began in a very small way. It was registered as 'Unusual

Plants' in 1967. Like many families before us, and since, we were going through a difficult time. My husband's health was very poor, our fruit farm had to be sold, leaving us with a few acres of wasteland in a hollow between two farms. It was waste because the soil was too poor for farming: dry stony gravel on the upper, south-facing slope, saturated black silt over clay in the hollow, with a spring-fed ditch running through the lowest level. This constant supply of running water, even during the longest period of drought, had attracted us twenty seven years ago, to build our home on the warm dry slope above it.

I was originally indebted to Mrs Pamela Underwood for sowing in my mind the thought that I might make a nursery of unusual plants. She was our neighbour when we lived in our first married home, (my mother-in-law's house) on the outskirts of Colchester. Pamela ran a nursery specialising in pinks and carnations, but was searching for something to take the place of carnations, the market in these being keenly competitive, with flowers coming in from Holland. Our garden collection of grey and silver plants appealed to her, particularly since they reminded her of childhood trips to Italy, where she had seen them wild on the hot hillsides. We were very glad to be able to help with plants and cuttings at the beginning of an enterprise which became well-known throughout the country.

When she decided to start the Colchester Flower Club in 1951 Pamela invited me to join as a founder member. (Colchester was the second such club to be founded, after Mrs Mary Pope had lead the way in Dorchester.) Like many other women in those dreary years of shortages and ration books, I was hungry for new contacts and ideas, and found my eyes opened to see plants in a new way. Perhaps as a painter must do – so I began to look at plants carefully and critically. I did not swallow all the ways of arranging them, but I went through most of the stages and learnt much that was to prove very useful in the future.

One of the friends I made among the club members was a charming old lady whose husband had travelled widely and collected beautiful objects, especially those from Japan. I admired these beautiful things and coveted her Japanese flower containers (I still have a fragile, but elegant basket she gave to me) ; best of all perhaps, I soaked up several books she lent me on Japanese flower arranging. These books influenced me in an indirect way, in my approach to garden design, as much as my husband's teaching on the natural association of plants. I have never had the slightest desire to make a Japanese garden in East Anglia, but I think I absorbed the basic principles of design, of the need to consider outline, scale and harmony, to create overall a sense of simplicity – even though that is not always easy to achieve.

Before long Mrs Underwood decided that I needed to be levered out of my cosy domestic life bringing up two small daughters and enjoying working in the garden. She telephoned to say that she had arranged for me to open a new flower club, to be its first speaker and demonstrator. My legs slowly gave way beneath me as I listened to her filling in the details, considerately omitting to tell me that the lady who was to receive me at this new club had been one of Constance Spry's best flower arrangers.

In those days I had not properly learned to drive the car. Suddenly I had that and a great deal more to learn. But on this first public occasion and many more to come, the garden saved me. Many of the flowers and leaves I used that day were unfamiliar to most of my audience. All this was about thirty-five years ago. Many of these plants are widely known today, but it is important to remember that the enthusiasm of women in flower arranging societies did much in their early days to encourage nurserymen to provide unusual plants.

For several years I travelled about the country, lecturing and demonstrating, showing plants from my garden. Many had come from the garden of my old friend Sir Cedric Morris, who, in the 'thirties, had inspired Constance Spry when she visited him, sending her back to London laden with armfuls of seedheads and many extraordinary flowers and leaves.

With this as my background it is not altogether surprising that I should have considered starting a nursery on my own to sell unusual plants, when I had met so many people who had asked me, 'Where did you get those lovely plants?'

I began with one girl to help me. Before the farm was wound up I had some help in making frames from railway sleepers, and clearing a small patch of wasteland. Harry Lambert, the youngest of Andrew's men, asked to join the new venture and has been with us ever since, helping to turn the wilderness into a garden.

Slowly visitors came, introduced primarily through the talks I gave in the surrounding towns and villages.

Then I issued my first catalogue, a simple typewritten affair – but I never thought of keeping one. I should be interested to see it now. In those days I had no idea the nursery and garden would ever become well-known.

There was a long probation period when I learnt that our ability to produce plants must be equal to the demand. Competent propagators cannot be produced overnight, nor assistants experienced to deal with the variety of questions that would be asked. Working closely with the staff in those early days I often heard my phrases floating round the nursery like a long-playing record.

As the garden matured and people came from further afield, there were suggestions for further publicity, even television. But at that time I think it might have destroyed us. We were not prepared to deal with such exposure. We needed the quiet years.

As the nursery grew I had to learn to delegate, to hand over the tasks I had enjoyed – and still enjoy, when it is not a waste of time for me to do them. Today I am training other members of staff to delegate, to teach new members their skills, so that they in turn can take more responsible positions.

Now, more than twenty years since the nursery began, we have a permanent staff of six men and eleven women, including the office staff. In summer from our neighbour's fruit farm come additional women who have been part of our team for many years. They arrive when the pruning of fruit trees is finished, and return when the fruit is ready to be picked. This fortunate arrangement keeps trained people and friends together. There are usually several part-time students during the summer months who come for practical experience before entering horticultural colleges.

When deciding what to put, or what not to put, into this notebook, I have been aware that not all will be of interest to every reader. Some passages will be skip-read while others, I hope, will be informative or relaxing.

If anyone is facing the need to begin a new life-style, I hope they may find encouragement, in the pages that follow, to 'take the plunge' with their particular inclination or talent.

Beth Chatto
Elmstead Market
1988

JANUARY

DARK mornings, short days, the precious light gone before four o'clock; January often feels the longest month in the year. But I seem now to have arrived at the age where dreary January sneaks by too fast. It might seem to be the ideal time to write a book, yet for me there are still too many temptations to dash off and do something outside rather than to sit down with pen and paper, to be disciplined and tidy-minded. All around is my garden and nursery, pulling me like a magnet to go outside and see what is happening. But if the weather is bad you may well be asking what on earth can be done in the depths of winter. With a team of enthusiasts turning up reliably every morning whatever the conditions, that is the question I must find answers for every year; but some winters are more tiresome than others. This one started like a lamb.

During a very enjoyable, mild December we were able to clean and clear up outside more thoroughly than we have done for several years. On the nursery the plastic tunnels were filled with anything which could be considered to be at risk, particularly the grey and silver plants; samples of anything which could be ill-spared or young newly potted plants which might perish in wind-frost – all were put under cover. A few really delicate creatures were given extra protection, draped with folds of old Netlon, the green, open-weave material we use to protect our shade-loving plants from too much strong sunlight in summer.

The temperature in the plastic tunnels, without heat, drops as low as it does outside, but the plants are kept dry. They do not suffer from alternate wetting and freezing which causes the death of so many plants and they are also protected from wind-frosts which are even more deadly. By protecting plants which we expect to be tender with extra packing – thick straw over the *Zantedeschia* (Arum lilies) ; bucketfuls of crushed bark or peat over plants whose roots or tubers will not stand freezing, such as *Schizostylis* and *Arum italicum* 'Pictum' – we can bring most things alive through our East Anglian winters.

Clearing up in winter

A cold, continental airstream suddenly hit me in my back as I stood making plans with Keith, my technician, on our first morning back to work after the Christmas-New Year break. We were full of plans: here a new tunnel needs to be erected, drainage must be improved in a low-lying part of our sales area and then new paving laid, the structure of our big Shade House will have to be rebuilt before the Netlon cover can be spread over it. As we talked, soft white feathers were suddenly shaken from the sky, and in moments, our heads and jackets whitened so we went for shelter into the packhouse. There, on the floor, was enough work to last for a week or more collected together before the Christmas break. Stacks of plants needing to be potted had been brought in and covered. The potting benches piled with compost were covered too, so work could be found, at least for a limited time.

Snow has been falling steadily and silently all day. Temperature about 30°F (−1°C). No wind. Beautiful views, 'like Switzerland', lie beyond the windows of our open-plan living room. The dark, shining surface of the ponds has vanished, completely frozen over. Everything seems to be lost in whiteness, except for groups of powdered conifers and evergreens. Deciduous trees and shrubs hold armfuls of snow. What can I find for my staff to do in such weather? I went out to see what might be done. Very little outside.

In the workshop several pairs of secateurs lie in pieces on a bench, being cleaned and repaired ready for pruning as soon as the weather improves. Trolleys need repairing. New pieces of metal must be welded to the base, new boards fixed across where old ones have rotted. Garden tools must be looked over, new handles fixed onto worn-down forks or spades which often feel so much better than brand new ones.

Renovating the tractor

The tractor and dumper truck, our two most valued old 'horses', have been waiting for this weather to be taken into care. Keith and David Plummer, an experienced mechanic recently made redundant who has now joined our team, treat these old faithfuls as though they were priceless antiques, reassuring me they will last for ever! Valves need to be ground, injectors cleaned, steering put in order, engines overhauled. I am not in the least mechanically gifted, but mysteries are being unravelled as I am kept well-informed and I am for ever grateful that my machinery and tools are in such good hands. While all these jobs get done quietly and efficiently, I know that often extra time and thought is needed to overcome problems caused by the change from imperial to metric measure. Adjustments have to be made so that new spare parts can fit into old machinery. We now have two welding plants, suited to different types of work. Most metalwork, whether it be repairs or building new equipment, can now be done in our workshop. There is scarcely a day in the year when Keith's wide-ranging expertise in practical matters, coupled with good humour, are not required by someone on the nursery.

Garden seats have to be cleaned and painted. Although we rarely have the time or inclination to sit on them, there are not enough for our visitors, who would like more. Garden furniture needs to be thoughtfully planned and carefully placed and in the past I have not given enough consideration to designing sheltered nooks for people; I thought only of making shelters for plants.

Pipes which have been thawed out and repaired are being relagged. As soon as the snow stops someone will be sent off with a long wooden rake to scrape it off the plastic tunnels and the evergreens which would be damaged by overloading. A check has to be made on ditches and overflow pipes to see that they are not blocked by sticks and debris which hold up the water and cause flooding. The rabbit-netting around the boundaries has to be checked.

Hundreds of bags and boxes of seed, collected from the garden during the summer and autumn, need to be sorted and sieved and then put into envelopes saved from the post, ready for sowing next month. It is a job I enjoy: delving into the piled-up cardboard boxes, tipping out large and small paper bags stuffed full of seed heads, wondering at the diversity of design in seed-cases, every one different. The seeds too are all shapes and sizes, some fine as dust, some almost as big as marbles, others fine papery scales – like fish scales. I particularly like the little round shining jet-black seeds of *Dictamnus albus* var. *purpureus*, the bright orange, pea-sized seed of *Iris foetidissima* and perhaps most beautiful of all, the blue-black 'pearls' of *Paeonia mlokosewitschii*, lying in their wrinkly, red, 'silk-lined' seed pods. Sorting my seeds often feels more exciting than opening Christmas presents because I have exactly what I want! Every screwed-up bag is a pleasant surprise, sometimes bringing a sigh of relief because we have harvested something badly needed, or something which rarely sets seed.

I still learn the hard way how not to do things, particularly when I find several large plastic shopping bags with black, slimy, unnamed

10

remains inside them. What treasure shall we be short of next season? Probably collected on a damp day, the stems and pods had rotted in the enclosed atmosphere. We collect all shapes and sizes of paper shopping bags during the year but leave plastic ones for the squashy fruits and berries that we must remember to sow before they become foul.

It is too cold to stand fiddling with seeds in the big draughty packhouse where the soil on the potting benches is frozen despite being covered. But a Calor-gas heater makes the staff rest room bearable and there a table is set up, all the piled up boxes brought in, with a wheelbarrow for rubbish. It will be a good job done, to have all the seed cleaned and ready for sowing. Each packet will be arranged in alphabetical order and then a typed list will be made for our records.

Sallyann Morris, who cleaned the seeds this year, took refuge from an icy day or two and tucked herself up in the office, carefully checking doubtful spelling before she made the labels to put into each packet, so that verified names will eventually go out onto the nursery. We use narrow 5 inch (12 cm) long plastic labels, a proper lettering nib which does not scratch and cause the ink to spread, and a special ink called Rotring (orange label) which bonds with the plastic. On different blocks of plants on the selling beds, much larger labels are attached to a metal stake with two brass split pins which we now have made for us. It may all sound time-consuming, and it is, but our labels last at least two years, until ultraviolet light causes the labels themselves to become brittle and to break.

Since before Christmas I have been nibbling, in odd moments, at my new catalogue. I try to write word pictures of plants which might make them irresistible. When I began the nursery twenty years ago, I issued a very small list with descriptions of plants, as I saw them, in place of photographs which I could not have afforded. My catalogue has grown with the nursery over the years but there are still no pretty pictures. I have not actually gone into the cost because, while I know they might help some readers, I myself, deep down, do not want to change. I am very attracted by good photographs in other catalogues but I find I easily forget them. It is the difference between watching television and listening to a good radio play. I can take the works of the best writers and gardeners, such as Vita Sackville-West, Graham S. Thomas or Christopher Lloyd, to bed and be lost till midnight, reading their thoughts and seeing their plants and gardens as a musician hears music reading a score.

The snow still lies deep, dry and powdery. At one time it was about 8 inches (20 cm) deep, plants and many bushes totally covered and huddled beneath the thick blanket, no distinction between borders and lawns, shallow steps obliterated. On the coldest night we recorded 21° of frost (i.e. 11°F, −12°C). Since then we have had some days of slight thaw, but frost returns every night. Long icicles hang in fringes over the windows. They look like deadly, gleaming weapons, two and three feet long. Will they all come down with a frightening crash? One which hangs from the office window measures 54 inches (137 cm), I wonder if it will make 60 inches (152 cm)!

Winter retreat by the wood-burning stove

After the heaviest snowfall Gerard Page cleared the drive with the big buck we have fixed to the back of the tractor. This is a heavy metal box, very useful for carting as it can be easily lifted or lowered to ground level. Just pushing the snow aside made walking and driving easier, but the quarter of a mile driveway remains whitened and icy long after the main road is clear, giving us an almost beleaguered feeling.

So much of one's time seems to be spent coping with the weather in winter. Dressing, to start with. So many layers have to be pulled on and off each time one goes out or comes in. Then the fires need attention. I have two wood-burning stoves (in the current fashion). Our low-lying, open-plan style house was designed with oil-fired central heating which seemed the obvious choice twenty-eight years ago. But now several of the radiators are turned off and the rest are only used to take off the chill and heat the water. For comfort we rely on the wood stoves, one in the office, the other in our living room. They are a joy to me. Maintaining them is far less trouble than an ordinary fire (which goes out when you leave it, and as I leave mine more than I sit by them, this is important). I have to admit too, that I love the primitive glowing heat. When I designed the office I arranged for big shelves to be recessed along part of the outside south-facing wall. Harry saws the wood and stacks the logs carefully on these shelves making a neat pattern of cut ends. We are fortunate to have a good source of wood from our neighbouring fruit farm. When old apple trees are pulled out they are sawn into trunks and branches and then they are stacked in great piles for at least two years for the sap to dry. As it is needed, the wood is sawn into small stove-sized logs using a circular saw driven by the tractor, and is then stacked in an outhouse, ready to fill the shelves.

I enjoy filling big baskets with the hard, heavy wood, feeling we shall be warmed again by stored-up energy from many past East Anglian summers.

There has been a ceiling of grey cloud over us for several days draining almost all colour from the scene. It is penny-plain, black, white and grey. My laurel bushes which usually make such a fresh, glowing-alive contrast to deciduous trees and shrubs, look tired, their leaves hang limp and bruised, especially where they have caught the full force of icy wind on their north-facing sides. So do many other shrubs which retain their leaves. The golden privet, *Ligustrum ovalifolium* 'Aureum' and the cream-edged privet, *L.o.* 'Argenteum' both look brown and withered. The grey-leafed *Senecio* which used to be called *S. greyii*, which we now call *Senecio* 'Dunedin Sunshine' (because it originated in a nursery of that name in Australia) has pathetically withered shoots dangling above the snow-cover which protects most of the bush.

Everywhere is very still, all living things suffering the pitiless winter weather, but from the warmth and protection of the house the scene is beautiful.

One morning soon after a fresh fall of snow, the sun shone, the sky was clear. Out I went to enjoy scenes and views that I have never experienced here before. Our usual inch or two of snow soon becomes patchy and messy but now, for the first time in twenty-eight years of making this garden, we had a thick eiderdown of snow, light and dry and sparkling. Above it stood the trees and shrubs I have planted during

A glimpse of a neighbouring farm through the west boundary

those years to provide screens and shelter, to create patterns against the sky and to enclose us from the surrounding acres of flat farmland.

The first thing I noticed as I watched my own boots sink below the blue-shadowed surface were the footprints of many other occupants of the garden. The mallard duck had left their heavy, plodding trails before flying off, hopefully, to some place where the water is not totally frozen over – probably to the salt marshes which are not far away. The large webless prints of moorhens, setting off in determined straight lines, were everywhere. Blackbirds, thrushes, robins and jackdaws were evident in a confused jumble of prints all around the house and buildings. I wish I could identify more of the strange little footmarks to be found in the snow. However, it is not difficult to recognise rabbits' long feet, crisscrossing an area we call 'The Wilderness', my last two acres of uncultivated land which is wired off from the garden with rabbit-proof netting. Here too I saw the prints of a fox together with a continuous hollow scraped in the soft snow. It was easy to imagine him dragging his kill back to some hideaway. Wing beats of alighting birds were left imprinted as blue-shadowed fans on the glittering whiteness.

But I was on my way to find *Lonicera × purpusii*. This is a winter-flowering shrub. It is not (in my garden) particularly decorative since the flowers are small for the size of the bush, but because they open in the depths of winter and because they are sweetly scented I make a point of going out to look for it on a rather out-of-the-way bank. I cut a twiggy bough and brought it into the house, wondering whether 21° of frost would have damaged it. But no, in the warmth of my room the pale green buds swelled and opened to small, palest-cream flowers with dangling yellow anthers. Their perfume now drifts gently towards me from the pot on my writing table.

Turning away from the honeysuckle bush my eye was caught by the beautiful coloured stems of various willows and dogwoods planted around one of the ponds. Their bright, enamelled stems glowed like firelight in the sun, brighter because of reflected light from the snow. The most vivid is *Salix alba* 'Chermesina', the Scarlet Willow. Its fresh, one-year-old shoots springing straight and clean from the base are brilliant orange-scarlet. Nearby were pollarded shrubs of *Salix gracilistyla* which had made 5-6 foot (153-183 cm) wands last summer, now shining olive-green.

Paler still are the knitting-needle-thick stems of *Cornus stolonifera* 'Flaviramea'. As the name suggests, this willow increases by underground shoots which can be a nuisance in small gardens, but it is invaluable for stabilising soggy banks beside water. *Cornus alba* is the Red-barked Dogwood. All its forms have crimson stems, but *Cornus alba* 'Sibirica' has the brightest, though less vigorous shoots.

The longest, straightest shoots will only be obtained by regular pruning. I always find it painful to make the decision to cut my shrubby willows. One day I am dwarfed by bosky, well-grown shrubs and then, next time I pass by I am looking down on sawn-off stumps. I feel bad to have deliberately destroyed all that strong, beautiful growth. Yet I know that if I am patient and endure a few weeks of bareness in spring (when they seem to be slow to break new buds) the results will eventually be worthwhile. The stout stocks and established root systems will thrust up the best-coloured, straightest, and sometimes incredibly long shoots. If left unpruned for several years there will be a tangled framework of dark, weathered branches with only a fringe of short, one-year-old, coloured shoots glowing round the edge. This can still look attractive on shrubs which have grown to form small trees, showing arcs of colour as they push high above mixed plantings.

'How often do you prune your willows?', you may ask. It varies. We have to consider the vigour of different varieties and also of course, the amount of time we have to spare. We do not always do what is ideal. If you can manage it, I think it is probably best to prune every year in February, removing about half the shoots, leaving the youngest, brightest looking stems. Some we prune every two years, others we leave longer, but not too long. I once left *Salix elaeagnos* (*rosmarinifolia*) for several years. With long, fluttering, grey leaves, white-backed on purple stems, they made superb specimens. I was loath to touch them but eventually found we had to restrain them from smothering other good things. Faced with the huge framework in winter how hard dare I cut? Gingerly I went round, saw in hand, cutting off vast pieces but leaving, to my mind, an acceptable framework. Along came a young member of staff who, not before consultation, confidently took the saw and slaughtered my framework almost to the ground.

I knew in theory he was right but I just hadn't the courage. Would it

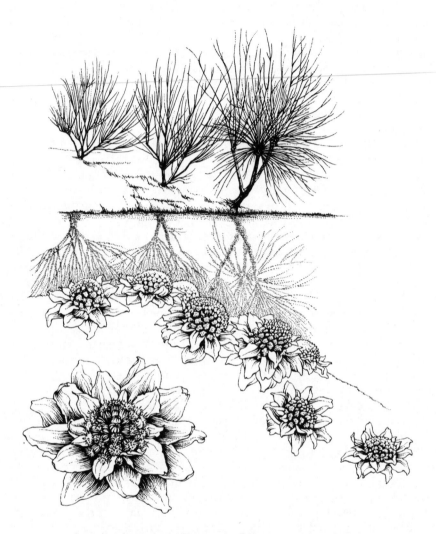

Petasites japonicus 'Giganteus' flowers open in February
beneath *Salix elaeagnos*

be too great a shock to the system? Well, they were slow to start, but by
the end of the season they looked magnificent. However, this ruthless-
ness could not be applied to just any shrub; most must be pruned back
gradually if they have grown out of hand. A group which always
reassures me as I look out of the west window of my house is dominated
by a vast native oak, possibly two hundred years old, which has dark
blocks of holly nestling behind its furrowed trunk together with laurels
and yellow-berried *Pyracantha* which I added for interest to the native

16

originals. To link this fine old farm tree to the pond which lies between it and the house, all surrounded now by sweeps of mown grass, I planted a Weeping Willow, *Salix × chrysocoma*. Now, visually, from the house, they are joined. The oak, dark and rugged, forms a bastion at this corner of the garden, supporting and sheltering the willow which hangs its long, pale yellow strands right to the frozen surface of the pond.

In great contrast are the curly corkscrew twigs and branches of *Salix matsudana* 'Tortuosa'. This willow eventually makes a fairly large tree in heavy or wet soil. In drier conditions it grows more slowly, making smaller, yet graceful, heads of silvery-fawn twigs and looking its best, I think, leafless in winter sunlight, when every polished curving surface shines as if it were wet. I walked across to look at *Salix × erythroflex-uosa* whose habit is similar, but whose branches and twigs are tinted warm orange-yellow.

Planted near the shrubby willows, on the higher, drier parts of the pondside banks, are several forms of *Phormium*. The great green-leafed *Phormium tenax* still supported stiff, stout stems, soaring 10-12 feet high and carrying clusters of blackish-brown seed pods the size and shape of small bananas, now split open and empty, their shining jet-black seeds spilt to the ground; good food for some starving birds, I hope.

Strategically placed in the garden are several different coloured-leafed forms of *Phormium*. They can be found in soft shades of rose-red and brown, bright yellow and green; more imposing than any of those in my climatic conditions, are the great purple-leafed specimens. It would be lovely to see them uncovered all winter since there is nothing else evergreen remotely like them, but I dare not leave them unprotected. Average winters would do little harm, but once I had fine specimens cut to ground level. They recovered from below ground but took two years or more to rebuild their former splendour. This year in late November we took no chances. Several strong, tall bamboo canes were thrust firmly into the ground around the clumps and tied at the top. Dry straw was tucked among the base of the leaves and then a large piece of polythene (bought by the roll from horticultural sundriesmen) was fastened wigwam-fashion over the canes and straw, leaving a space at top and bottom for ventilation. The straw base can sometimes encourage another hazard: water voles (recalling Ratty of *The Wind in the Willows*) and mice find it a most congenial winter residence with larder combined. One spring we wondered why several shoots had toppled over. Investigation showed their plump starchy leaf bases had been eaten away.

Looking across the white, open spaces, with undulating borders and lawns simplified and united by the snow blanket, I was thankful for the enclosing groups of shrubs, some deciduous, some evergreen, with fine trees above them outlined against the sky and lifting my spirits in this flat farmland of Essex, as do mountains elsewhere.

Although they are deciduous two of the most lovely winter outlines in my garden are formed by bog-loving conifers, the Dawn Cypress, *Metasequoia glyptostroboides* and the Swamp Cypress, *Taxodium distichum*. They make narrow, pyramidal shapes, as elegant and necessary as Gothic spires to the architecture of a town. I walked close up to the bole of my biggest *Metasequoia* and saw how its great trunk emerged from the ground in a twisting, almost spiralling shape which caused the bark to split into long silvery-green flakes (the green caused by algae in the damp air) and show the warm pinky-brown living bark beneath. Looking up, I saw the young upturned twigs of the same warm colour forming a curving, curling edge to the narrow, pyramidal outline.

Going across to a group of Swamp Cypress, I noticed their trunks were smoother and although each tree forms an attractive spire in the landscape the fine twigs are straight, so the trees look more reserved, less exuberant than the Dawn Cypress. Isolated in a wide open area of snow-covered grass, stands my oldest *Betula jacquemontii* a Himalayan Birch. What a sight, in brilliant sunshine, in this whitened landscape! From the main ivory-coloured trunk break six lesser trunks, to divide and redivide, creating a vast fan of branches shining white against the cold, blue winter sky, lightly dusted here and there with emerald green algae. Almost to the very tips the branches are bone-white, and then they suddenly break into a soft halo of warm brown twigs still dripping with seed-bearing catkins. Not too far away sits *Magnolia grandiflora* comfortably clothed to the ground, a magnificent dome of rich, glossy leaves. Standing beneath it I looked up to see the bright, copper-coloured undersides, slightly puckered and glistening.

Holly and ivy are the basic images of many Christmas cards; symbols of life carrying on when much else appears dead, or has vanished beneath the frozen surface. I would almost go so far as to say they should be in every garden, but perhaps I should substitute 'something evergreen' instead of being so specific. Not everyone has the room, or the right conditions for large-growing evergreens. I am thinking of laurels and rhododendrons in particular. But hollies can be found in all shapes and sizes, many are plain, but no less handsome, while several are variegated. There are seven pages of holly (*Ilex*) in Messrs Hilliers' *Manual of Trees and Shrubs* to tempt the reader, and a walk among the Holly Collection at Kew Gardens will certainly fire the imagination. Some will be difficult to obtain but nurserymen will be pleased to propagate more unusual plants if enough of us ask for them.

The fashion for planting too many depressed, congested or even constipated-looking dwarf conifers all together in one small space does not appeal to me. Probably I should appreciate some of them individually if they were used in conjunction with other trees or shrubs to create a balanced design, but distorted-looking specimens will always have an uncomfortable effect.

Trees, shrubs and plants look best, not massed together tightly as a collection, but each planted to be seen to individual advantage and at the same time each contributing to the group. So, choosing and placing winter evergreens is important. I remember several years ago, after we had started the garden here at Elmstead Market, suddenly feeling very dissatisfied with a group of shrubs which I had not faulted when they were full of leaf (and, for a few weeks, blossom) during the summer. But now, leafless and with nothing distinguished about their habit of growth, the whole patch looked muddled, formless and lifeless. By removing some of it, planting a holly and *Mahonia* among the rest together with vigorous sheaves of the evergreen *Iris foetidissima* 'Citrina' nearby and patches of small-leafed ivies as ground cover, the picture became much more interesting in winter and now forms a better background to the summer carnival which passes before it.

On my wintry walk I stopped to look at a solid clay bank which was formed by the creation of the neighbouring farm reservoir about thirty years ago. It is very steep and for almost twenty-five years had remained practically bare, too inhospitable even for native weeds. Then I thought of ivy. I selected several forms of *Hedera helix*, our native species. Some have very small crinkled leaves, others have rounded leaves gently curling. Another has almost goffered edges. One has leaves so finely cut they resemble the feet of a bird. All are green, some touched with bronze. None are variegated. With a barrow-load of compost below me (several barrow loads were eventually needed) I climbed the steep bank and made holes as deep as I could, sloping them outwards so that they would not become waterlogged wells. I filled them with compost and firmed well-rooted plants into every space, about 3 feet (91 cm) apart. Now this curving stretch of bank, shaded overhead by a Weeping Willow with a narrow path at its base, is a wall of green and is beautiful to look at every day of the year.

Just think of the unsightly places which could be transformed with ivy. There are many different varieties, from large-leafed kinds which can clothe the side of a house, or make a great circular carpet beneath the sweeping branches of a fine tree where few other things would survive, to the many small-leafed kinds, both plain and variegated, which can be used to climb, to make trailing carpets on the ground and over such awkward objects as manhole covers. (In Germany I saw most attractively designed manhole covers. They were round with a castellated pattern round the edge looking like stepping stones in a paved walk. I saw similar ones in the forecourt of a garage so they were not the crazy dream of a no-expense-spared designer. Our builders and architects drop hideous rectangular lids just anywhere, it seems, and these are impossible to line up with any garden design.)

If you look out of your favourite window now, are you satisfied with the view? Does it lack design? Would a small-leafed, narrowly-pyramidal holly do anything for it, and how many plants can you see which remain green – or grey, or bronze – throughout the winter, furnishing the bare soil at ground level?

I left my low-lying Damp Garden, passed by several huge feathery stands of fine-leafed bamboo, *Arundinaria nitida*, and the broader-leafed *Arundinaria japonica*, both noisy at dusk with quarrelsome sounding birds settling themselves in much needed shelter after a day's meagre foraging. I always marvel at the energy expended on so much chattering!

Rounding a corner I came face to face with *Viburnum tinus* 'Eve Price' sitting in a snow-buried carpet of dwarf periwinkle, *Vinca minor* 'Bowles's Variety'. There she was, massed with pink-tinted flower buds, the leaves on her young shoots reddened with cold. *Viburnum tinus* is another of those taken-for-granted, background-furniture type of plants. Never a blaze of glory, thank goodness, but never boring either. There are several forms available: *Viburnum t.* 'Lucidum' has larger, more glossy evergreen leaves with slightly bigger, but less pink flowers than *Viburnum tinus* itself; 'Eve Price' is the most compact and most densely smothered with flower clusters. They put up with our average winters with no serious damage, but it is prudent to place them where they do not have to face the most bitter wind-frosts.

In the cold sunlight I admired the bulky masses of *Pinus radiata* and contemplated the low sweeping branches of *Pinus ponderosa*. Just one specimen of this pine adds unimagined grandeur – wherever there is room to contain it. A grand old tree-man, Douglas Doyle-Jones, gave me my seedling about twenty-five years ago. He had planted one many years previously and allowed it to do what it would in his woodland garden. From about halfway up its cinnamon-coloured trunk drooping boughs had spread out, clothed with clusters of long needles at the ends of the branchlets like huge radiator brushes. They eventually touched the ground and then, continuing to grow, curved upwards, covering a vast area of rough-mown grass. I shall never forget the sight. And that was in my mind as I stood looking and wondering which boughs to cut off, since I cannot spare half that space around my tree. I was encouraged to do something about it by the memory of a visit to a garden in Portland, Oregon, where I saw some huge and ancient specimens which had been sympathetically pruned to allow a garden to develop beneath them. Further along, I stopped to touch the long, pale fawn-coloured strings of seed pods hanging from the slender green branches of *Acer negundo* 'Variegatum' which I had noticed, but not had time to enjoy since the leaves fell. In the distance, looking almost like a tree in blossom is the pink-fruited Mountain Ash, *Sorbus hupehensis* 'Rosea'. When we first bought it, it was called *Sorbus oligodonta*. It is still, in midwinter, laden with drooping clusters of pink and white berries.

During the drought of last summer I felt anxious about *Mahonia aquifolium* 'Moseri' which I think I have planted in too open a situation. It makes a much smaller shrub than *Mahonia aquifolium*. Its young leaves in spring are at first almost translucent bronze-red, then pale lemon turning to green as they mature. But now every leaf is brilliant cherry-red – another little 'bonfire' with the blue-green needles of Scots Pine as a background. I think I shall move it to a tiny woodland area where it will have semi-shade to protect those thin-textured leaves.

For a companion it will have *Rubus thibetanus*. This is a very pretty, reasonably well-mannered bramble from Western China. It makes a thicket about 4 feet (122 cm) high. In summer we enjoy the dainty, much-divided leaves, greyish-green above, felted-white beneath. In winter, when leafless, the stands of pale, bloom-coated stems stand out against a dark background. To keep it tidy and to encourage clean, fresh growth, it is wise to cut off the old stems at ground level in early spring. If not, you will have a confused jumble spoiling the effect of young canes.

From my kitchen window I can see, in the far distance, what appears to be a low cloud of smoke near the base of some very ancient, knotty willows. The effect is made by a colony of *Rubus cockburnianus* which grows much taller than *R. thibetanus*. Well over 6 feet (183 cm), the arching purplish stems are vividly overlaid with white bloom. Inter-tangling, they create a large silvery-white 'bird-cage'. I have planted several together to form a large group – charming in the wild garden, almost magical when caught by low rays of the sun on a late January afternoon.

By now I had reached the large reservoir at the end of the garden into which overflows the water from our ponds and underground springs. About twelve years ago the reservoir was enlarged by our neighbour to irrigate his fruit farm. Happily, I was allowed to plant the perimeter on the farm side as well as on my own. The hazards of this enterprise I have described in *The Damp Garden*. Now the view was fixed in a cruel, icy grasp. The large expanse of water was entirely frozen over, solid enough to bear my weight. But the surrounding sunlit scene filled me with delight. Before I get carried away I should mention that I was inspired to plant around this reservoir after seeing only one photograph of the waterside at Sheffield Park. I have since visited this superb garden of trees and shrubs and know how many light years I fall short of the artist who planned and planted it; space, as well as talent and experience in dealing with trees on that scale, being limited in my case. But it is always good to be inspired by the best, and in my very simple adaptation I begin to enjoy the plantings round the reservoir.

With the sun behind me I could see how the coloured-stemmed willows had matured, making me feel I must plant more. *Salix matsudana* 'Sekka' with shining mahogany stems, makes big unwieldy shrubs, ideal to tumble down the steep clay banks. Some have stems joined together and flattened in a curious way as though pressed with a flat iron, fanning out to make the curving pieces much valued by flower-arrangers.

A *Sasa veitchii* beneath a weeping willow

I have planted several bamboos around the reservoir. One of the most effective in winter is *Sasa veitchii*. It makes low thickets, 2-3 feet (61-91 cm) high of purplish-green canes furnished all summer with wide-bladed, rich green leaves. In autumn the colour is withdrawn from the edges leaving a creamy-white margin of varying width. This variegated effect, which is in fact a kind of withering, is very handsome all winter, remaining until we cut down the old canes in spring to make way for fresh young growth. If a few stems of winter foliage are cut and put in a cool place to dry, the leaves remain in perfect state, slightly curled, but very acceptable for large dried arrangements, with more 'life' than pressed-flat foliage. However, I must warn that the plant is very invasive. Its thick, strong shoots are designed to thrust underground, ideal to stabilise steep clay banks or colonise a wild area, but they must be confined, or left out altogether, in a small garden. Young birches already show white trunks with polished purple twigs carrying next year's catkins. Well above the water-line, hollies and × *Cupressocyparis leylandii*, the Leyland Cypress, make welcome breaks of evergreen. I stopped by a strong growing tree with thick twigs and large, pointed, polished buds and rubbed one between my fingers to smell the richly aromatic scent of balsam. The tree is *Populus trichocarpa*, one of the tallest and fastest growing of balsam poplars. In not so many weeks' time, when the snow will be forgotten but while spring still seems far ahead, we shall, one morning, all unawares, catch that scent on a warm southern breeze, released across the garden just as the fat buds are swelling and bursting. Looking across the reservoir I can see my neighbour's land sloping up beyond our growing screen of trees and shrubs. All is tidily set out with young fruit trees on a grid pattern. Beside each tree a golden bale of straw has been set on the snow, waiting till the frost has melted before it is spread as a weed-suppressing, moisture-holding mulch. While this fruit farm is a strictly commercial undertaking, not planted for effect, I am grateful for such a pleasing contrast to my garden; for its well-managed orderliness and, I hope, for its continuity.

Today, from the kitchen window I watched a fieldfare pecking vigorously at a half-rotted Bramley apple. His feathers were so fluffed up against the cold he looked almost spherical. Through my binoculars I could clearly see his soft grey head and rump and the darkly spotted 'waistcoat' outlining his white chest and underside. You might mistake fieldfares for missel thrushes (they are related) but in October, before we have caught sight of them, we hear a familiar 'chuck, chuck' in the orchards and know these winter visitors have arrived from further north

Fieldfare feasting on a Bramley apple

in time to clear up fallen apples. As I watched, I saw him hop onto a low branch and delicately pick shining orange seeds from the drooping pods of *Iris foetidissima* 'Citrina'. Some fell onto the snow, so down he plumped, to pick up every one.

A sudden flurry of movement and there was a grey squirrel, who immediately seized the half-eaten Bramley and sat holding it in his little black paws, with bushy tail fluffed out over his head like a sheltering umbrella.

Grey squirrel

Next, a hen pheasant stalked into view. She scraped about, half-hidden beneath a bush, leaves and litter flying around her, when, within seconds it seemed, she emerged holding a large, bright green caterpillar which quickly vanished into her crop.

Every evening during the cold spell I have watched a cock pheasant strutting around the house, glowing like some bright garden ornament left over from the summer. A bowl of scraps goes out every morning until the hard time has passed.

A large basin of turkey dripping has sat since Christmas in my cold larder, discomforting me. For several years I have rarely used animal fat and have almost lost the appetite for it, but puritanical upbringing dies hard and I could not completely dismiss the thought that this flavoursome dripping might come in useful to 'start a soup'. Out it came, was melted down and poured over a great washbowl of flaked oats, packets of cereal left over from grandchildrens' holidays and other bits and pieces. It has been such a relief to see it all disappearing where it was most needed. Jackdaws, and sparrows by the dozen, tuck in single-mindedly, while ridiculous blackbirds waste far too much time and energy chasing each other away. While no one was looking a thrush hopped in nervously, driven by dire need. I was glad to see a redwing close at hand. As he fed I could easily see the rusty-red patches beneath his wings, and the finely-pencilled golden 'eyebrow' over each eye, his other distinguishing mark.

Blue tits, great tits and greenfinches teetered on the boughs of *Magnolia* × *soulangiana* waiting to take their turn at a bag of nuts.

I went into the garden to see what was providing food for those creatures too shy to come to the house. Hungry birds, pecking out every live bud on certain shrubs, had left behind confetti-like showers of scales on the snow. This means there will be little spring blossom on *Prunus subhirtella*, nor will I pick long yellow boughs of *Forsythia*. We had sprayed with repellant and thrown black cotton reels back and forth across the flowering cherry, but bullfinches are not easily deterred in quiet country gardens. I feel very cross with them, remembering how pretty my little tree can look if it is spared, but what else can they eat? Except my neighbour's pear buds of course!

The catkins I noticed earlier on *Betula jacquemontii* have been raided, and fruit on every holly, *Pyracantha*, *Rosa glauca* (*R. rubrifolia*) and most of the barberries have gone. Strangely, the bright red berries on *Skimmia japonica* are never eaten, and the hedge of *Cotoneaster lacteus* at the top of the drive has not been touched. These are always left till last, so they cannot be very appetising.

I found that every twig of *Genista pilosa* sticking out of the snow has been chewed off, making me feel relieved we have covered our stocks of *Dianthus*; long strips of wire netting were rolled over them and tucked under to make a cage against the wretched rabbits. These pests have slipped into the garden during the summer when any of several gates may have been left open. (It is not always convenient to hop off a tractor each time you pass through.) It will take a gun and a couple of dogs to dislodge them.

As though someone had turned on a vast convector-heater, a warm airstream suddenly blew up from the southwest and winter vanished overnight. The icicles disappeared without a sound. Indoors the rest of the month seemed to be taken up with preparing our catalogue for printing. When we receive any kind of catalogue through the post, most of us seldom think of the headaches and problems involved. But with the experience of producing our own I begin to think plant catalogues have more pitfalls than most. Every dot and comma, let alone correct nomenclature or accurate spelling, must all be presented to the printer in a clear and reasonably tidy copy. We have just spent weeks it seems, with floor and table stacked with reference books checking every name, and been taken aback several times to find that we have been incorrectly spelling something we took for granted we knew! In other cases there have been name changes by botanical committees who decree these things. It is not always easy to keep up with the latest pronouncements; there is the fairly complicated procedure concerning presentation of Latin names and common names. A system has evolved whereby Latin names are usually in italics, or in bold type. Cultivars or hybrids are put in single inverted commas. (Had you noticed they were not double?). English garden names have capitals but no inverted commas – and so on. Capital letters have to be carefully considered and used consistently throughout the text.

It may sound fairly obvious (and it is, once you know what you are doing) but it requires a fair level of concentration to keep all these balls in the air at the same time. Next comes the new price list to be considered. More consultations, this time with other growers' catalogues, discussions on availability, on scarcity value. Some plants are very slow, or just plain difficult to propagate.

We also have an ex-directory catalogue. This includes many plants which we propagate in too small quantities to be publicised, but among our pots delighted enthusiasts sometimes find just the plant that they have been seeking.

Tonight the sun set at 4.30 p.m. I stood at the west window and watched the low red horizon stretching beyond the whole length of our boundary behind a black screen of hawthorn, oak and willow, all in carved silhouette. A long-legged heron flew up and flapped heavily across the ponds which are now restored to shimmering blackness by the thaw, reflecting the different patterns of trees and pale amber light from the sky. The thinnest silver rind of new moon was drifting among violet puffs of cloud.

It was the first time in this new year that I had felt inside me the upward surge of a new season beginning. There are many weeks to come which may be wintry, but the light is coming back stronger and longer every day.

From time to time, we need to reconsider our methods of running the garden and nursery. Sometimes change is welcomed by everyone because it can be seen to be a benefit. The work involved is tolerated, even enjoyed, when the results can be seen to be advantageous. But sometimes, the prospect of change hovers uncomfortably. I know I should be initiating new projects but am reluctant to start. To jog along comfortably is pleasant, but gardens and nurseries are never entirely the same from one year to the next. Little changes are constantly being made. Big changes are disturbing and have to be considered over a period of time.

Several members of my staff and I have recently attended talks given by other nurserymen and we came away with much to mull over. Most of these talks are given by people who produce plants on a wholesale basis. We have to pick up useful bits of information without being knocked sideways by feelings of insufficiency.

It is easy to feel outclassed by large-scale commercial enterprises, but we have to strive for professional efficiency in our own field producing a very wide range of unusual, and sometimes difficult, plants in an individual garden-nursery context.

The grandfather clock

28

FEBRUARY

THIS morning I awoke to hear the grandfather clock striking 4 a.m. and was immediately alert, all my present commitments feverishly chasing themselves through my head. Apart from a garden I have foolishly agreed to plan, there is the Chelsea Flower Show nudging more and more insistently as the weeks rush towards May. Usually I have a nucleus of large plants and shrubs in containers which provide an established-looking background. The sudden severe weather in January has killed off several of my old plants. I have no frost-free place large enough to protect them all; in normal winters a plastic covered tunnel has been sufficient.

Another commitment is this notebook which has been fermenting in my mind for several months. I would like to write it, to record some of the ups and downs of a nursery garden, but my one fear is not finding time to write decently. Even keeping up a scrappy diary becomes difficult as the sap rises.

Then there is Kazuyoshi Watanabe, a Japanese student who is arriving tomorrow. Some weeks ago I received a letter from him asking if he could come for work-experience with me. In the past I have had several such applications from students in Germany, Holland, Belgium and France, but I did not think I could cope adequately with them as I was still much engaged teaching my own young staff. Every day on the nursery is different. Because we grow such a wide range of plants it is not possible to have long runs of routine work. All regular members of staff must eventually be able to think and act for themselves.

I was not really in need of a new job but two factors influenced my decision to accept this young student. In recent years I have received much kindness and warm hospitality from plantspeople, both in Europe and the United States, which I should like to repay in some way. Then, coincidentally, a week or so before Kazu's letter arrived, I had a visit from a young Dutchman who had just returned from a year spent working on a nursery in Japan. His enthusiasm for Japan and Japanese plants impressed me. I felt I should take a chance and accept this totally new experience on the nursery for us all. I hoped that we would all have something to give him, and there could be much we might learn from him. I always hate writing letters of rejection, thinking of the feelings of the young person who must be disappointed. But taking a complete stranger into our fold is a risky thing to do. Some of us are nervous with strangers who speak our own tongue, but when there is a language barrier it is even more disconcerting. There is also the problem of accommodation. Ours is not a good area for people willing and able to take lodgers. Anyone who can has probably already rented a room to a student from Essex University, which is quite near to us. So I have decided to give him a room myself until something can be sorted out. (At times like this I wish I had a large old house with attic bedrooms which I could convert for students, such as I have sometimes seen on my travels. But in rational mood I know I should not care for the burden of keeping the fabric of such houses intact.)

I am hoping that one of my staff will help me out as temporary host to Kazu by 14 February when my grandson Thomas, aged four and a half years, will go into Norwich Hospital for an operation on his spine. Thomas was born with fused joints (not all, but too many), which means, as his mother, Mary, says, that his architecture is all wrong. But he is a stout-hearted little fellow with a very lively brain. Already he has endured and survived two major operations. It is painful to think of the suffering which must lie ahead, yet I pray he will have a life to develop the strong character he already possesses.

All these thoughts suddenly propelled me out of bed, tense and withdrawn. As soon as I was dressed I stepped outside to take deep breaths to calm my thoughts, when suddenly I caught my first sight of a carpet of yellow aconites, clustered under the autumn-flowering cherry. They seemed to have popped up overnight. All at once I could see it was a lovely morning, the garden was coming to life again, the long season of daily delights was beginning. A few pink-flushed Christmas roses (*Helleborus niger*) had opened nearby while the green and ivory marbled leaves of *Arum italicum* 'Pictum' stood fresh and undamaged all around. When the ground is frozen hard they collapse like limp rags, stuck to the surface of the soil.

The little *Narcissus* which has been named *N.* 'Cedric Morris' (after my dear old friend and mentor) is in full flower. The late Sir Cedric Morris brought this unique little daffodil home from Spain more than thirty years ago. It always shows a flower or two for Christmas,

Narcissus minor 'Cedric Morris' always shows a flower
or two for Christmas

continuing to bloom well into March. It is a perfectly formed lemon-yellow trumpet daffodil, the stem about 12 inches (30 cm) tall. The trumpet is about the size of a thimble. I could see the large red buds of *Paeonia mlokosewitschii* just breaking the surface of the soil. I shall enjoy the unfolding, mahogany-tinted young foliage long before the flowers appear in May. Without being aware of it, I was drawn out of my futile fretting by these early treasures.

I have a lovely form of the Spring Snowflake, *Leucojum vernum* 'Wagneri'. It is sometimes mistaken for a snowdrop, but it is quite distinct. Each stem carries a pair of large, green-tipped white flowers which hang like shallow lampshades. One stem has already opened two perfect flowers, while others beside it wait impatiently, each upturned bud showing at ground level, held closely between the strong green blades of emerging leaves. The snowdrops, it seems to me, are late this year. There are a few in flower, but you have to look for them.

Fine clumps of the dark plum-shades of the Lenten Rose (*Helleborus orientalis*) are full of fat buds. I must wait until all the different coloured forms of this plant are in bloom before I try to describe them. *Helleborus atrorubens*, of which I have only a few plants, has been in

31

flower for several weeks. Despite the January cold its flowers are perfect, three or four blooms of soft rosy-purple nodding on each short, dark stem. Unlike the Lenten Rose, this hellebore does not keep its old leaves during the winter and the flowers come before new leaves have emerged. (During the winter we go round the nursery stock beds and garden cutting off all the leaves of *Helleborus orientalis* to prevent the spread of black patches of mould (Botrytis) which spreads from the leaves to the flower stems and buds. It does not seem to harm the plant if kept in check, but it can destroy a lovely display of healthy blossom.)

In February sunshine I can stand close against large evergreen bushes of *Skimmia japonica* 'Rubella'. This is a selected male form of the female bushes near the house which are loaded with inedible red berries. The male form is, I think, at its loveliest now, covered with upright clusters of seed-pearl-sized buds which glisten slightly and are of an indescribable but lovely shade of warm brownish-red. The upturned glossy leaves have red veins on their backs, while the young stems are red too.

The Spring Snowflake, *Leucojum vernum* 'Wagneri'

32

Helleborus corsicus, snowdrops and *Arum italicum* 'Pictum'
beneath a silver birch

Beneath a warm sheltering wall I picked a few buds of *Iris unguicularis* 'Walter Butt'. Although we have several forms, including the white version of this lovely Algerian Iris, I think 'Walter Butt' is my favourite. It is so free-flowering and has a delicious scent, reminding me of primroses. Not all of them are scented.

Among the casualties of last month was our cock pheasant. Rosemary Shelley, my secretary, on one of her lunchtime walks found the remains of a wing hidden behind the heathers, almost certainly left behind by a fox. One Sunday morning several years ago, my husband Andrew and I had the dubious, yet breathless pleasure of watching from the house as a fox rummaged in a heap of garden waste on the edge of the garden. He carried something partway across the lawn, stopped, presumably to eat it, then went back for more. From the house we watched this procedure for some considerable time, guessing that he had found a nest of duck eggs. Since then I have inherited very good binoculars from my father, but the fox has not returned in daylight. Many years ago one of my brothers watched a vixen playing with her cubs in the hollow where my water gardens now lie.

As I went on my rounds, making a list of jobs to be done, I was followed by the clear, repetitive song of a thrush perched high up in a white-berried Mountain Ash.

Here is the kind of work sheet I make on my regular rounds of the nursery and garden:

On the West Boundary: Prune shrubs.
Clear out variegated Archangel (*Lamiastrum*). Clear out ivy.
Enlarge the cyclamen bed under the Great Oak.
Reshape the bed under *Paulownia tomentosa*.
Put peat blocks to soak in stream bed. (They are as hard and dry as blocks of wood.)
Divide and make stock of:
Trollius europaeus 'Alabaster', a lovely, pale-cream form.
Ranunculus aconitifolius 'Flore Pleno' – the double white Fair Maids of France.
Cut down the end poplar along our entrance drive to make room for lorries bringing nursery supplies to turn into 'The Wilderness' which is being cleared and prepared for new stock beds.
Dig out bamboos which flowered last year and are now obviously dead.
When the land is dry enough, dig a 'T' shaped drain to take surplus water off one end of the Wet Nursery.
Propagation:
Split and pot special forms of *Bergenia*.
Mark all clumps of *Narcissus* 'Cedric Morris', to be able to find them later for propagation.

Divide *Hacquetia epipactis* and pot under shelter ready to plant out for stock when established. *Hacquetia* is a curiously pretty plant forming low mounds of flowers in very early spring. They are daisy-like in shape. Their large green 'petals' are really bracts, with centres filled with clusters of tiny, bright yellow true flowers.

Divide *Hepatica nobilis*. This very large mountain anemone has rich blue flowers as big as a ten-penny piece. I found it in an old Suffolk vicarage garden and would not vouch for this name.

All these oddments of jobs are outside the general run of nursery work but involve plants which need to be increased for the future. I also made a note to remind someone to go round the nursery and garden to cut off all the leaves of *Epimedium*. If this is left too late there is a risk of cutting off the flower stems as well. If it is not done at all you scarcely see the delicate flowers hidden among last year's leaves.

Hacquetia epipactis is a curiously pretty plant in winter

Epimedium × *versicolor* 'Sulphureum' makes a particularly good display with quite tall sprays of palest yellow flowers.

During the past week we have had some absurdly mild days, such a sudden contrast to the freezing temperatures of January. One day we recorded a maximum of 58°F (14°C) – a day for shirt sleeves. Can winter have come and gone so briefly? Somehow I doubt it.

Keith and Gerard are busy laying concrete slabs to make paths in the selling area for Shade Plants. (In summer this area is covered with a large Netlon cover, fastened over a permanent framework. When they have completed this section, all the selling areas will be divided into long narrow beds wide enough to stretch across comfortably.) The beds will be separated by these little paths which make walking and wheeling trolleys so much easier. They are laid in sand and so can be easily dismantled if necessary. Susan Taylor and Lesley Hills are filling in the pots behind them, glad for milder weather to get all their beds neatly blocked up, everything in alphabetical order before the packing of orders starts again. Melanie is making identification labels, a large one for each separate block of plants. We just do not have time to label every plant, but we supply small labels for visitors to write their own, together with trolleys to cart their plants to the pack-house. If anyone needs labels to be written we are usually willing to do this, but if we have a coach party with everyone queueing up at the same time to do their shopping it is simply not possible.

Spent the day designing a client's border, a job I enjoy but should refuse since I seem to have enough jobs to last three lifetimes. At first I tackled this one with despair rather than enthusiasm as I had been given so little information – just a long curving border relating to nothing. But gradually I became absorbed. I hope it will give the owner the oppor-tunity to see plants grouped according to height, bulk and texture as well as colour, so that he may eventually use the underlying principles and make the garden his own.

Several days ago Stephen May, one of my propagators, had an accident. A holly branch brushed across his eye scratching the cornea. He was taken off to the Casualty Ward at Colchester Hospital where he was treated and is now making a complete recovery. This incident made me aware of an omission which I should have covered long ago: an Accident Record Book. Now we have one.

Facing a misty, drizzly, dreary day, I decided I must make a start on preparations for Chelsea. I spent most of the day sorting and throwing out corpses of old plants which have given good service at past shows: large mature plants of *Santolina*, *Ballota*, *Salvia* and *Cistus*. (Such a horrid smell, the smell of rotted plants.) The cold has been too much for them, but smaller, younger plants have survived, unscathed, in similar conditions. In the propagating house, where it is warmer, I cut out shabby canes from tall bamboos and lightly pruned several fine specimens of *Pittosporum* which make useful height among my Mediter-ranean plants. It would be a luxury to have a complete house made of the same material as the propagating house to protect my overwintered Chelsea plants. This latest addition to our nursery buildings is constructed in a rigid, double-walled plastic, called polycarbonate, which looks rather like clear corrugated cardboard. It is attached to a strong tubular frame. We are keeping temperature records of this house, to compare them with the maximum and minimum temperatures inside the single-skin tunnels and also outside in the open. These records, and the performance of plants and cuttings in the propagating house, show that it warms up more quickly and retains heat longer than the other tunnels. Without doubt, it has lengthened our propagating season without additional heat, except for the soil-warming cables which are buried in the sand on top of the benches that support trays, boxes or pots of cuttings.

I do not force plants which would be out of season by Chelsea time, but I do find it helps to pot a few things which are very slow to start by putting them on a gentle heat to encourage root action. Such plants include grasses, which I hope will be taller by the end of May than they would become outside, and ferns which are sometimes scarcely unfurled by May after our typically cold springs.

The propagating house is taller and wider than the other tunnels, so we remove some of the staging at one end to make room for sheltering some of our taller and more vulnerable show plants like the bamboos and the pittosporums.

After heaving and emptying large pots, wheeling away the rubbish to a compost heap or bonfire, I felt a little weary by teatime, my first day of outside work since Christmas.

During the evening I had a telephone call from my elder daughter, Diana, who lives at Castle Donnington, to inform me that Lucy, her six-year-old, had just developed chicken pox and that Emily, aged four, would undoubtedly follow suit. She had planned to bring these little ones to spend a week at her sister Mary's house in Southwold – and to look after Mary's second boy, Jeremy, while she was with Thomas at Norwich Hospital. My plan was to go as relief to Diana in ten days' time, but now I must go in three, and one of the interim days – tomorrow – I must spend in London with my publisher.

Caught the 9.15 a.m. to London and Welbeck Street. Here were assembled almost all of the paintings and drawings for *Plant Portraits*. This book began as a series of vignettes written for the *Telegraph Magazine* colour supplement. When it was decided to publish them in book form changes had to be made. New artists were chosen for the illustrations. Each essay had to be increased by about a hundred words. That is not very much, but somehow the additional 'copy' had to be knitted-in so that the joins were not too obvious. It is a thrill to see the galley-proofs of something which you have written and rewritten by hand, some of it several times, before it is typed. (I once tried to teach myself to type, but was too impatient, too inaccurate. I am used to thinking with a pen in my hand without the clatter of machinery.)

When the manuscript is typed by my secretary, Rosie, it is easier for me to read – days, even weeks after it has been written, when I can take a more detached view. Then there will be more pruning and alterations, often to make the sound, as well as the sense, flow more easily.

Malcolm Gerratt, one of the directors of Messrs Dent & Son, greeted me with a welcome cup of coffee and then took me to meet my editor, who is preparing *Plant Portraits* for the printer. On a very large table were paintings, pencil sketches and pen and ink drawings (made by two different artists), which I had longed to see since they will be so important to this new book. There were more than a hundred to look at. Some plants had obviously caught the mind and the imagination of the artists more than others; many of the illustrations made me gasp with pleasure. What a sin it would be if too much of this glowing quality were to be lost in the printing. So much time, concentration and stamina has gone into this joint effort. Seeing the manuscript in galley proofs and the illustrations mounted and assembled, it is an exciting, almost unreal, moment.

When it was first suggested to me that the weekly portraits might be published in book form I had thought it would be a slight thing, but the quality of the illustrations has lifted it immeasurably. Now I long to see the book bound in covers. We spent the rest of the day sorting out many details, some of them small but all necessary if we are to avoid embarrassing errors in the finished printing.

Winter has returned, as surreptitiously as it came in January. The past ten days have been, on the whole, surprisingly mild. But today began with strong chilling winds which, by coffee time, brought waves of snow showers across the green garden. By lunchtime the view from my office window was shrouded in white once more. I had started the day determined to go outside to arrange a work programme for while I am away, possibly for three weeks, looking after my grandson. But Rosie checked me speeding through the office. Could I spare a moment? There was a problem. While I had been in London the day before she had been investigating the legal requirements concerning our Japanese student. She discovered it will take eight weeks to obtain the necessary work-permit. (He came to us from Eire where such a permit was not required.) Until we have this document we must not employ Kazu, either paid or unpaid, without risk of prosecution. He may be my guest, to observe only. Quickly we had a council. What could be done? Certainly we could not have him hanging around watching others work. He comes from a nursery family in Japan and is used to working with his hands. 'What about a language school?' said Rosie. Several phone calls were made, even including one to a travel agency, in case he had to go back to Tokyo. Soon we had a list of options to put before him. In the middle of this two ladies appeared to discuss the final details concerning a luncheon talk I am giving in March to aid a school for autistic children. Despite the snowstorm outside, I was warmed by the friendliness of my visitors and by feeling part of the communal effort to help children and parents in need. I felt I was in good hands and that everything would be well organised. Anyone who gives talks has a fund of funny and unfunny stories concerning mismanaged meetings. These are invariably the result of inexperience so it is a great relief when you realise nothing has been overlooked.

At lunchtime Kazu, who has been with us for a week, came in shuddering with cold. I opened up the wood-burning stove and served hot soup. When he was warm, inside and out, I presented our morning's problems and possible solutions. He took it stoically until it sunk in that he must not work at all! Opening and shutting his hands he asked how could he not work for eight weeks! Returning to Tokyo was not considered for a moment. The Language School sounded a good idea. He had enough savings to cover the expense. Suddenly it didn't seem such a bad Friday after all. We rang the Language School and made an appointment for them to see him. By the end of his course Kazu will feel much more at home with the language and, I hope, with all of us.

At last I was free to see the outside staff to arrange what could be done if the wintry conditions persisted. Susan reminded me that the Shade House cover needed to be restitched. Trolleys and barrows could be painted. The outside lavatories could be painted inside if the paint did not freeze! In the workshop there was still plenty of work repairing machinery. Back in the office I arranged for money matters to be taken care of; it doesn't do to disappear and leave the staff without means to buy what they need to finish a job.

Fridays usually end with shopping in Wivenhoe, a large village alongside the river Colne about three miles away. Kazu came with me, in and out of old-fashioned shops, the modernised Co-op, and finally in and out of several cottages to see friends before I left for Southwold.

Then we went home to make supper.

Over thirty years ago I read an article describing how the 'Staff of Life' was made, listing many unrecognisable chemicals added to maintain freshness, to assist the rising and to make the whole process of bread-making more reliable and faster. Among the additives I could recognise were chalk and bleach! There was also a chemical called Agene, which has since been banned. The article ended by saying 'on no account give white bread to your dogs – it could kill them'. Appalled, I wondered why I should give it to my family. I remembered my childhood in a small village in northwest Essex where my brothers and I often watched our friend and neighbour, the baker, pull sweet-smelling crusty loaves, all shapes and sizes, out of deep ovens with his long wooden spatula. We had sat on top of the wheat sheaves as the harvest was taken through the village into the farmyards and then to the mill on the river to be ground into flour. In the farmyards I loved the smell of animal feedstuffs, and always thought how appetising was the smell of great buckets of pig food as it slopped into their troughs. Only much later have I realised that they were being fed crushed whole grains. Disturbed by the article, I suddenly made a decision. No more bought bread, I told the young delivery girl. Laughing, she said she would be back in a week's time to see how I was getting on. More than thirty years later I still bake bread and so do my daughters, although when I began they were small schoolgirls who wailed that they wanted to be like other people and eat factory bread. Fortunately, today it is not a nine-days wonder either to make, or eat, wholemeal bread. It is as easy to make as scones and nothing fills the house with a more appetising smell. About once a month I spend part of Sunday making bread and cookies; they keep like new in the freezer.

Breadmaking

Because I have been involved with farming and fruit growing and know a little of the way food is produced commercially I tend to be suspicious of much of it. There are so many sides to the subject. As the population has expanded more and more food must be produced at a price people can afford. Pests and diseases which formerly reduced many of the crops cannot now be tolerated, so we have become used to seeing perfect fruit and vegetables in the supermarkets; so perfect that they sometimes look and taste like plastic. We are assured that all chemicals have been well tested before use on crops, but I cannot help feeling disturbed about long-term effects and am always shocked to see anyone eat fruit or salad without washing it.

When I was first married I was delighted to have a large vegetable garden. It was wartime; I was teaching in a local country school and the headmaster also put me in charge of the allotments where we produced vegetables for the school kitchens. Being a young woman straight out of college, I was not immediately accepted in what is traditionally regarded in the country as a man's place. 'Moi Dad don't do it loike that, Miss', was a frequent observation. I suggested we could wait to see if there was any difference in the results. Possibly not. A year or two more and some of these rebellious young sparks would be disagreeing just as vigorously with their fathers. Among those boys was a round-faced, dark haired, young enthusiast, just ten years younger than I was. Ten years ago, after a varied career in engineering and market gardening, he came to ask me if I could find a place for him. It was Keith, who now runs his own department on my nursery. Pupil and teacher roles are now reversed, certainly as far as engineering is concerned!

My interest in unusual plants began with unusual vegetables. Forty years ago it was not easy to find seed of uncommon vegetables. I was introduced to them by Sir Cedric Morris and his friend Arthur Lett-Haines, who was an inventive cook. These two men were artists of merit; since their deaths Cedric has been given a posthumous exhibition in the spring of 1984 at the Tate Gallery and Lett a smaller, but imposing retrospective show, which ran concurrently at the Redfern Gallery in Cork Street. But more important perhaps, for their friends, they were bon-viveurs. During the twenties and thirties they lived among poets, painters and writers in this country and in Paris. They travelled. I knew them for the last thirty years of their eventful lives and, like many people who visited Benton End in Suffolk, I felt touched by a kind of magic. They were not at all conventional teachers but together they provided an atmosphere in which seeds of talent grew. Their style ranged from deceptive simplicity to alarming sophistication. Their humour was usually naughty but never embarrassing; their lifetime's experiences generated both wisdom and sometimes childlike naivety, while their monumental arguments made me tremble with apprehension. All of this opened my eyes and, at times, boggled my mind. Lett was a painter of dreams, a poet and innovator. Cedric was both a painter and a gardener. His garden became a mecca for plantsmen long before unusual plants were generally accessible. In all the years I visited the garden at Benton End, I should be sure to see, on every visit, some plant or bulb I had never seen before. At its peak I think it was the finest collection of plants and bulbs in the country and all of it grown personally by Cedric. I would exclaim at drifts of rare bulbs, at the abundance of so many things I did not possess, or only had in penny numbers. 'Scatter the seed' he would say giving me handfuls – and I did, but I also had to learn his patience, to tend the seedlings sometimes as long as seven years before they flowered. When he was over ninety years old and almost blind, I saw Cedric Morris on his knees, weeding among his treasures.

Just as inspiring was Lett's cooking, exciting to taste and exotic to look at. He was a friend of Elizabeth David and as her books were published I read them hungrily and cooked my way through most of them. Cedric gave me a little type-written catalogue produced by Kathleen Hunter who was, I think, a protégée of Eleanor Sinclair Rohde who wrote *Uncommon Vegetables* and *A Garden of Herbs*, two of her books which have influenced me. In this catalogue I found many unusual vegetables listed, most of which can be found today in commercial seed catalogues. There were purple-podded runner beans, avocado, avocadello marrows and scorzonera which I think is almost as delicious as the French artichoke. There was broad-veined chard and sorrel for soups and sauces. Seakale I had inherited from my father-in-law, but Lett gave me a new idea for using it. In early spring, before the new shoots emerge, you put large buckets or pots over the crowns, putting a piece of tile or stones over any holes in the bottom of the pots to shut out the light. Some time during late March or April the blanched stems will be ready to cut, cook and eat like asparagus, with melted butter. It does not taste like asparagus but has its own special flavour and texture. One cold spring evening I cut seakale for Lett. To my surprise he cut off the crumpled leaves at the top of the stems and scattered them into a salad we were making. They looked very appetising, bleached various shades of orange-pink and purple, and they tasted deliciously crisp and crunchy. These days, I rarely throw away those early saladings from the garden. Since my family grew up and left home, time spent on the vegetable garden has become less, but it has never been abandoned. I learnt from another friend to make better use of my time and space in this area of the garden. Most of us do not need long rows of cabbage or lettuce, nor twenty cauliflowers which all come at once. Short rows, or even small blocks of things like lettuce, especially the cut-and-come-again type of lettuce, keep us in salad all summer and rarely go to seed. I have learnt a lot from Joy Larkcom's books and her articles in the Royal Horticultural Society's Journal. Two years ago we met for the first time, and now when she visits me we always make for the vegetable garden, to see how her gifts of unusual seeds are progressing.

This revitalised interest has brought me now almost to the point of becoming a vegetarian. I still enjoy the occasional good dish made with meat or fish but also take pleasure in making varied salad and vegetable dishes which do not leave me feeling deprived. I realise how fortunate I am to have land on which to grow vegetables when many people have no option but to buy everything they eat.

After taking Kazu to the Language School I set off for Southwold. The radio had reported many roads blocked in Norfolk and Suffolk. Suffolk schools were closed. Anxiety expressed about my driving ability was perhaps more than usually justified. But while care was needed, the sense of drama quickly evaporated. As I drove north-east, I saw the snowfall had been heavier than in Essex, but the main roads were cleared leaving single track lanes between six- to eight-foot (2-3 m) piles of snow. Strong winds had blown powder-dry snow across the flat open expanses of ploughed fields to form carved and convoluted drapes and drifts against hedges and ditches. The small side roads still had a surface of packed ice but I arrived safely at my daughter's house without having done anything noticeably foolish.

It takes a little while to adapt from being a nurserywoman to being a Grandma. I am much less practised at the latter. My first engagement was to be shown the way to a morning school, walking across the town, led by Jeremy, almost three, who was to be my companion for the next few weeks. It was a bitterly dry-cold morning, the pavements slippery with packed ice; but the snow on South Green leading to the school was deep enough to bury a little boy's legs. We opened a latched gate into a pretty bricked and cobbled yard, with last summer's plant pots ranged round the walls looking empty and forlorn.

When I returned from school Mary, with Thomas, aged five, was ready to drive to Norwich hospital. Thomas anticipated his stay in hospital with enthusiasm. It is for him a familiar place with friendly, familiar people and an Aladdin's cave of a toy room. The rest of my day was spent sorting out a new routine.

It is Valentine's Day, the day of Thomas's operation. His back will be opened and a rod attached, from top to bottom of his spine, to prevent the curvature becoming intolerable. Will he stand the anaesthetic? On two previous occasions his heart has stopped for four minutes. A day of tension and prayer. For Mary and her husband Alastair another day of waiting and walking the streets of Norwich. I walk along the seashore. It is very cold with a strong north-east wind whipping creamy foam on top of churned coffee-coloured waves. They break over bright sand and shining piles of shingle. There is no sun, but a pale bowl of grey sky contrasts with all the pastel shades of brown. Gulls rise and fall along the edge of the receding waves. Pray for Thomas, his apple-red cheeks and his lively mind.

Dark-eyed Jeremy needed his share of loving. With sleeves pushed up his chubby arms he helped me to make a crumble topping to cover thin slices of huge Bramley apples I had found in an outhouse. His parents are returning home tonight and I try imagine how they will feel; what on earth they might feel like eating, whatever the news. Finally, I made a mixed vegetable hot-pot which could be reduced to a thin soup if they had no appetite at all. I watched the clock, knowing that many good friends, both near and far, were with us in thought. There must be news by four o'clock. With just a few minutes to go the telephone rang, and Mary's voice, high with relief, said, 'He's all right, in intensive care, full of drips and tubes, but with colour in his face – thank God!' Jeremy and I returned to the kitchen to give thanks and make bread, that most soothing of occupations. Within an hour his parents were home, pale with exhaustion but comforted by Jeremy's delight in having them back. For the next few days we jumped every time the phone rang, but we gradually accepted that Thomas was safe. Soon he was taken off the support machine and, though weak, was again his usual articulate self. He has surprised everyone, even the medical team to whom we owe so much, by his strong recovery. But he must lie immobile, on his back, for three weeks. Parents of small children who spend many weeks – even months – in hospital, suffer in a way we cannot imagine if we have not had such an experience. The grinding weariness of boredom, unhelped by the relief of routine occupations, the sickening guilt because they feel bored trying to entertain their own sick child – all this has to be lived through, following long months of tension beforehand.

At home, Jeremy and I got on with the job of getting to know each other and kept the household running smoothly. Every day, wrapped in scarves, boots and 'glubbs', we tramped the slippery pavements past gardens blanketed with frozen snow. Southwold is a small, attractive town. To be able to walk only a few hundred yards, either to the beach or the shopping square, is a novelty for me. Jeremy's friendly 'hellos' were returned by assistants in shops and by workmen up ladders; most of them enquired after Thomas. Before long a stream of cards and little presents, or of pictures painted by his classmates, was being collected and taken to the hospital. Thomas and his family belong to this community. Its members had shared our anxiety, and now shared our relief.

At daybreak, with the little Siamese cat curled under my chin, I turned on my radio and was startled to hear the announcer give the date and to discover there were only eight more days left in February. With a shock, I realised I must pull myself together and catch up with my notebook. There will be little enough time when I return home. Through wintry weather we have lost several weeks of work outdoors. Once this weather breaks there will be an avalanche of jobs which need to be done before plants start into growth again.

I spent the day making preparations for Mary to come home from the hospital for a weekend's rest. I was determined there would be nothing left to do – that we should both relax, without my fussing around like an over-anxious hen. She arrived in the dark, drawn with weariness, but gradually revived like a wilted flower put into water, thankful to be in her own home. Next morning, leaving her to her own kitchen, I sank into a deep armchair to write a letter. Moments later a head popped round the door and commented wryly that there were jobs to be done . . . like cooking! Astonished, I shot up to find her taking pallid parcels out of the deep freeze. Grandma had turned off the wrong switch! I looked into the emptied freezer and saw my job. Picking up a bucket and cup, I baled out the bloodied ice water. 'It's purple isn't it', said Jeremy brightly, standing on a chair, 'like my Ribena!' (We have been practising colours!) My vegetarian instincts grew even stronger as his mother opened damp parcels of prime pork, but we have to be practical. Once it was well-washed and dried, and most of the revolting white fat removed, the prospect of cooking so much meat in a variety of ways was not without interest. The best pieces were put in the oven to roast. The rest I cut into cubes while Mary went shopping for a few oddments we required. By the end of the afternoon the house smelled like Christmas and we had pork with cider, and juniper berries – pork with coriander and ginger, and pork with red wine, peppers and garlic. What seemed like a disaster had been resolved and we had many meals prepared which could help in the weeks ahead. It had not been the relaxed day I had envisaged but it had been fun working together.

For the next two weeks temperatures were scarcely above freezing during the day, with hard frosts at night. Then suddenly, as in January, the thaw came. Alternately, we had bright sun with mild temperatures and then chilling fogs.

In Mary's small, enclosed garden we found a creamy-white Lenten Rose in flower, several primroses and a clump of snowdrops in bud. Plants of *Euphorbia wulfenii*, which looked so shrivelled in the frost, had recovered. In her vegetable garden Mary searched for emerging spears of *Narcissus* bulbs in the rough grass beneath an old Bramley tree and ancient knotty pear trees. Red broad-beans (the seeds are red), which Joy Larkcom originally gave to me, are just through, undamaged. (Mine were sown earlier, and lost, in January – we must sow some more.) Garlic leaves are four inches high and her purple sprouting-broccoli look promising. Seed potatoes lie in trays in the little bedroom high under the roof – next door to mine where I have lain cosily these past three weeks, listening in the darkness to the sea pounding the shingle.

Several days later I ignored the domestic round and spent the morning writing, with Pushkin, Mary's neurotic Siamese cat, squeezed into the back of my chair while Jeremy was happily absorbed on the floor in his own world of farmyards and space invaders. With little breaks for drinks, or a game of hide-and-seek, we all three passed the time to our mutual satisfaction.

A brewery dray in Southwold

After lunch we pulled on layers of clothing and walked to the beach. The entire length, as far as the eye could see, was strewn with indestructable waste, tumbled in a continuous band beneath the sea wall as if it had been left waiting there to be sucked up by the local council's giant hoover! If only it could have been. There must have been thousands of plastic containers. Many were milk cartons, with labels in Dutch, German and English, thrown, I presumed, from passing ships. There were large rolls of nylon string and rope in all thicknesses and colours, interlaced with great bundles of seaweed, all woven together by the recent wind-driven seas. Coloured bits of glass, smoothed and polished by churning shingle, wickedly sharp broken bottles, odd shoes and empty clusters of cuttle-fish eggs – all were examined until, driven by the cutting east wind, we left the beach and climbed the steep slope to South Green where a row of black, icy cold cannons face out to sea. These had to be climbed and straddled before we could walk across the seared brown grass, back into the town and home. We passed a few large and imposing houses standing rather aloof on South Green and thankfully sought shelter in the little side streets where every house is different, tightly packed together like sweets in different coloured wrappings. Bricks of mellow-red, or pale yellow London clay, give a solid, settled feeling to the street, while pink, blue and white-washed walls stand out clean and prim, even on foggy mornings. Scooped red pantiles shelter many of the cottages which have quaintly irregular roof-scapes, some low and flat, while others soar to pointed gables. We stopped to admire the huge grey and white Percheron horses which pull the green and red painted drays to and from the brewery which dominates the centre of the town. Great tubs of spent hops steam in the yard, just too far away to be reasonably transported to my garden for compost.

A huge Wych Elm stands in a large grass plot, the meeting point of several small roads. The tree is remarkable for its beautiful shape, flattened like a gigantic mushroom. More brewery buildings surround it on two sides while the third is bordered by a row of neat little cottages. For several days we smiled to an old man who sat at his window, watching the world pass by. Then his chair was empty. Was he ill or had he been a visitor using a holiday cottage?

A peacock on a hay wagon

At the end of the road is the lighthouse, immaculately white from top to bottom. We watched the big blue bus turn round in the square, raced to the red pillar box and then we were home at our own green front door.

Unknowingly, we had carried sticky black oil waste on our shoes, soon revealed as black smears on the carpets. Next morning I bought eucalyptus oil and, with a piece of clean cloth, easily removed the ugly stains without leaving a trace. Later I learnt that a special oil is sold in most seaside towns for this local hazard but I think it worth knowing that eucalyptus oil is good for removing tar-stains brought in from the street. I found this hint in an old book, *Labour Saving Hints and Ideas*, inherited from my mother-in-law. One of the most useful things I have learnt from this book has been how to remove fruit stains from table linen. (Tablecloths are not so generally used nowadays, but I well remember the horror I felt as a child seeing dark purple plum juices seeping into the crisp white cloth and later the ugly grey stain, which took weeks of bleaching on green grass to fade.) From this book I learnt a magical way of dealing with spilt wine or fruit. Lift the stained area over a large basin or bowl and pull the cloth tight like a drum. Pour over it boiling water from the kettle. You will see the stain vanish completely.

Now we have reached the end of February, the evenings are light till nearly six o'clock.

'Uncle' Jonathan collected us to go and see his farm, a child's story-book farm. Calves suckled our fingers, peacocks drooped from the high sides of wagons, bantams peered down from the roof-top level of hay bales. A magnificent cockerel, a Moran cock, with long arching silvery plumes, strutted like a lord among his wives. The pigs were fed, the noise hysterical as they waited for their turn for malted barley grains and yeast to flow through the system of pipework to their troughs. We were given warm fresh eggs and saw the smoke-house where Jonathan smoked the herring we have been eating. After fishing them out of the sea he hangs them over hot smoke which curls up from a pit of smouldering oak leaves and saw-dust.

Dozy pigs

We drove home in the dusk, past mud-splattered piles of frozen snow loitering still on shaded banks. Time for supper and bath. Postman Pat was waiting for us to read his adventures. Daddy had gone to the 'hosstable' to see Mummy and 'my friend Thomas'. Before the light was out, heavy eyelids were sealed in sweet sleep.

MARCH

I HAD looked forward so much to being home again, to the little spurts of pleasure that would come as I walked round to see what had happened while I had been away. Instead, to my dismay, I felt empty and thoroughly defused. Little things seemed monumental problems. I felt peeved to see all the flowers on the big cyclamen in my sitting-room lying flat on the table (and felt ashamed of my intolerance when I found little welcoming bowls of winter blooms by my chair and bedside). It is commendable not to overwater, but large plants transpire an amazing amount of water, especially if the day suddenly turns warm. Lifting the pot to judge the weight is still a good way to tell how dry the contents may be, especially with present-day soil-less potting mediums. A primarily peat-based compost will feel very light if it is dry.

Next morning, with aching head and snivelling nose, I thought it prudent to look sideways at the day's problems. Then as I became involved it was soon apparent that much work had been well done and I went round to say so.

Taking a look at the garden in thin drizzle, I saw that several crocuses showed waiting buds: both the dark purple and pale lilac forms of *Crocus tomasinianus*; rich blue of *C. sieberi*; pale forms of *C. chrysanthus* and little *C. susianus* – the Cloth of Gold crocus, its outer petals marked with dark purplish-brown feathering. A good form of *Iris histrioides* made a patch of royal blue among silver-grey foliage.

The snowdrops were well up at last, forming strong clumps and drifts where I have moved and divided them in the past. Some must be moved again before they have finished flowering. In the damp, chill air they are looking very downcast.

Now I am having nightmares about my Chelsea exhibit. How shall I fill my alloted space 30 ft × 20 ft (10 m × 6 m), having lost almost all my established trees and shrubs in pots during the hard winter weather? These had taken several years of continual care to produce and have formed backgrounds to several of my displays.

It helps with the jitters to be up and dressed, so out I go early to face the day's demands. (Sometimes after a long day answering endless questions, the early morning problems almost resolve themselves. Perhaps coping with little things stretches the mind to deal with something bigger.)

After a week of wondering how I could possibly exhibit miserably small plants on such a disproportionately large stand, I suddenly pulled myself together, determined we would show somehow, even though the display would have to be different. I signed the form confirming our intention to exhibit and organised hotel accommodation for myself and my staff during our stay in London. We were committed. Now began the long task of gathering plants together for the show. Armed with the previous year's show list, I usually start by containerising plants which I know need most time to become established to be at their best by the middle of May. Since my exhibit relies primarily on foliage plants, I do not need artificial warmth and light to produce flowers out of season, such as lilies and delphiniums. But I do need undamaged foliage and a few flowers in season to provide interest and sparkle. The shelter of plastic tunnels is usually enough to keep soft spring foliage protected from late frosts or drying east winds.

I like to put most of my plants into strong black plastic bags, called Fablo pots, obtainable in many sizes. The horticultural fashion has changed, however, to the 'use of square rigid pots. These look fine in orderly rows on the nursery, but are useless to me when showing. With soft pliable containers I can butt several plants together to make them look like one well-established clump.

Impatient to get on, I suddenly found that my stock of Fablo pots was run down and most of the sizes that I needed were missing. Telephoning suppliers on such occasions rarely saves time, so I jumped into the car and drove out to mine, only to find that they were sold out of just the sizes that I needed; stocks were being run down, etc., etc. Almost spitting blood with exasperation, I drove on to see a friend who runs a very efficient tree and shrub nursery. (Sometimes I can help him with unusual cuttings.) He laughed at my predicament, asked what sizes were missing and climbed into a loft to hand me down what was needed. Then he sat me down in his office with a cup of coffee while he found the address of his supplier. Now I have laid in stock large enough, I hope, to last my showing days. (How many more Chelseas shall I do, I wonder?)

When I started my nursery, just twenty years ago, I felt sure there was a market for unusual plants – but how to find customers? I soon discovered that small advertisements from an unknown supplier were worse than useless. Advertising 'unusual plants' in those days mainly brought requests for catalogues from owners of small greenhouses who hoped I would supply exotics like Pitcher plants, Bonzai trees or Gloriosa lilies. My few typed catalogues of hardy garden plants were obviously ending up in wastepaper baskets. So I decided to renew my contacts with the flower-arranging societies, women's institutes – any group, indeed, where two or three might gather together and be interested in something different for their gardens.

For several years, while we strove to improve our knowledge and skill in producing plants, I drove up and down the country with a van full of foliage and flowers, demonstrating flower-arranging and extolling the lasting value of our plants in the garden. Many of the trips took me two, sometimes three, days away from the nursery: one to pick and prepare the material; the second to drive the often long distance, though occasionally it was just a quick dash after a day's work at home. If I had to stay away for a night, there was a third day to return, tidy away the left-overs and carefully store my containers. I enjoyed these trips very much, travelling through the country and meeting many enthusiastic people, but they were a time- and energy-consuming way of developing the business. Weekends had to be spent catching up with jobs left undone – primarily propagating cuttings which would suddenly have shot up like beanstalks and, of course, we had no regular secretarial aid to handle the office work at that stage.

But we were growing; gradually more staff were being trained to take my place on the propagating bench. In turn, it was the ability to produce plants reliably that promoted the need for better publicity to sell them and meet our wages bill.

This was the thrust I needed to take me to London; to make the decision to show at the Royal Horticultural Society's Hall in Westminster. It had been a very mild winter – and at that time the RHS held its first fortnightly show in January – the garden seemed full of early spring flowers and the nursery carried a good stock of Lenten Rose (*Helleborus orientalis*) in full bloom. With courage born of innocence, I dug splendid flowering clumps of hellebores, purple-leaved *Tellima grandiflora*, variegated *Iris foetidissima*, pink and blue pulmonarias and other simple garden plants to set down beside the glories of Messrs. Rochfords exotic house-plants and the flowering trees of Messrs. Hillier of Winchester. In our packhouse I made a mock group to see how it might look, then packed all the plants into my faithful van and set off for a new adventure. On 28 January 1975, I arrived at the hall, a total stranger to the other exhibitors. But I was soon put at ease by their kind helpfulness and by that of the RHS staff. By the end of the day I had made a little winter garden on my exhibition site. Next morning, to my astonishment, I found that I had been awarded the RHS Silver Flora medal. No other medal, not even the coveted 'Gold' at Chelsea, has given me the same pang of pure delight.

Encouraged by the response of public and press, I put up several more RHS exhibits and eventually arrived at the Chelsea Flower Show. A new phase in my career was about to begin: far less time became available to prepare talks and make long journeys to deliver them; in some ways this was a matter of regret for me. I had so much enjoyed meeting people and illustrating my talks with live material. Today, the few talks I give are mostly for charity; perhaps for a hospital or a school for handicapped children. Occasionally I go further afield. An invitation to talk in Dublin has been followed by three lecture-tours in the United States over the past three years.

Visiting photographers

Now my talks are illustrated with colour slides taken in the garden and nursery over many seasons by talented friends and professional photographers. I do not take photographs myself; I am often told that I ought to and indeed I should like to learn the art, but as I can never find enough time to write about my plants I do not see, as yet, how I could take up another enthusiasm and practise it well. So photography is left to members of my staff and to visitors, who are sometimes kind enough to send me slides. Gradually I have evolved a system of labelling and storing my slides so that I can readily find the ones I need. For each different area of the garden, such as the Dry Garden, the Damp Garden or the Cool Garden, I have separate slide boxes, both of views and plant portraits or groups within those areas. Each slide is named or described briefly, and a green spot is stuck to the appropriate corner so that a carousel can be loaded without slides being upside-down or back-to-front in the feed-channel. For the initial slide selection I use a small view-finder, putting the chosen slides into a carrier so that I can view them in sequence in my Kindermann projector. This has a small screen which pulls out of the lid of the unit, showing a picture about the size of an exercise book. Here I can judge the quality of each slide and, by pushing through thirty-five in a sequence, can tell if they follow smoothly the theme of my talk.

This month we have not yet had half a day which could be called spring-like and the month is more than half gone. Frost whitens the grass most mornings and sudden squalls of snow or sleet-showers keep the crocuses tightly closed. The first day of spring was blown in on a blizzard, driving veils of snow across the nursery, to the despair of the girls trying to pick-up and pack orders. It has been a frustrating month for everyone on the land, particularly after the damaging weather in January and February. Now, as certain plants fail to come to life, we are beginning to realise how many plants ordered and paid for have been lost. It is depressing for us, as well as for our customers, not to be able to complete orders, because plants which were well-cared for and healthy last summer have not survived. The weather is much to blame, but not entirely. Over the years I have found that a mixture of peat and sand with a slow-release fertiliser incorporated into it, has been satisfactory for our plants in containers, combined with foliar-feed sprays put on every ten days or so during the growing months. The mixture we put in our pots is a key factor. For many years we have bought ours from a local supplier, but the management changed and problems arose. The worst was the amount of annual meadow-grass which appeared, especially maddening in pots of small plants like alpines. We changed our supplier but landed ourselves with worse troubles; too many pots have had to be burnt because of infestations of bracken and sorrel! But more damaging has been lack of sufficient drainage in the compost. Many of our plants, especially the drought-resisting types – and others too, which will not tolerate having wet necks – need a much grittier compost. We have said so, of course, but have not been able to obtain the appropriate mixture. Most large commercial growers use potting machines which are quickly worn out if too much grit scours their insides, so the standard commercial mixtures lack the good drainage we require. This, I fear, has been the cause of some of our losses this winter. So I am much occupied with investigating how to make our own potting composts, suited to the different types of plants we grow.

In the potting shed

It is not just a matter of spending x-thousand pounds on a mixer and assuming all our potting problems will fade away; on the contrary, it would be so much easier to pay for a large container of the stuff, ready-mixed, to be dumped on our yard as has been done in the past.

Now space has to be found, preferably near to the potting area, where the mixture can be made. A concrete floor must be laid to keep everything clean and weed-free. Electricity must probably be brought to the site to power the machine – unless it uses diesel. But the main concern is: what type of machine? Contacts have to be made and time found to visit other growers and suppliers to evolve something which will eventually meet our needs. Meanwhile we are improving the design of our potting benches, so there will be more room on either side of the potter to lay out plants and cuttings comfortably on the one hand and trays of filled pots on the other.

By the middle of this month I was creeping about with an attack of 'Spring back'. This malady is well-known to gardeners, being acute stiffness and soreness in the muscles of the lower back. The lazy east wind ('lazy', say East Anglians, because it goes through you instead of round) combined with bending and lifting heavy trays of Chelsea plants had caught me out after too many weeks spent mostly indoors. I am occupied for much of each day collecting plants together; some are dug as extra-fine clumps from the garden or stock-beds and others are taken from the nursery. All are put under shelter to encourage growth for the big show. But never have I seen my Chelsea plants looking so wretched, so reluctant to move. 'Ah! But a warm spell at Easter will find you fretting that they will become too advanced', I tell myself. Maybe. But today the potting compost is full of frozen lumps; the plastic tunnels are covered with rumpled slides of snow and my hands ache with cold yet again. Feeling as reluctant as my plants, with aches and pains everywhere, I retreat to the office and to the comfort of its wood-burning stove.

Yet this is typical 'getting-ready-for-Chelsea' weather; all over the country, exhibiting nurserymen will be counting the weeks and watching thermometers. But whatever the weather, it will be wrong for someone. An early heatwave, followed by sudden sneaky frosts in the first half of May, can result in blackened foliage and blossom overnight. But by Chelsea week, however lethal the weather may have been, there will be no sign of the panics and heartaches of the preceding months. Years of experience, patiently developed skills and practised juggling produce the show, even if it may not always be quite what the exhibitor originally intended.

One year, tense as a drum but trying to play it down, I was both comforted and disconcerted when one of the most experienced exhibitors in the country told me that he was not worth living with the last few weeks before Chelsea. This event, I have found, is never in any sense a routine; each year there are different problems; each year we have to strive to earn the privilege of showing at the finest flower-show in the world.

It is always refreshing to go out and make changes in the garden. I am revitalised as I make plans for next week, next year, or many years ahead. For too long, certain parts of the garden have lain in abeyance, waiting to be redesigned. Sometimes changes are needed to make the garden more labour-saving. Or an area may be grassed over to create a more restful effect. But most enjoyable are the spaces I clear to make homes for more plants and to create new groupings, possibly with introductions I have not grown before. Ideally, every square foot of soil should contribute to the design, but making good use of the soil is easier to write about than to achieve. The garden is large and intricately planted, and although I have help, I must consider the time available for maintenance. However, maintenance is easier and more pleasurable if I have planned and planted with forethought.

I do not enjoy planning when I am frozen to the marrow, but a slight easing of the ferocious east wind encouraged me to collect several long hosepipes, a couple of border-forks and a bucket of split canes. Beneath the Great Oak, I wanted to enlarge a bed of cyclamens and improve the line of the grass path leading to this site. A hosepipe held firm at one end between the prongs of a fork pushed well into the ground can be pulled smoothly into gentle curves and then the final line is held on either side with a few split canes pushed into the soil.

Neighbouring borders may need their curves realigning, so that all blend together harmoniously. Long shallow curves are pleasing to the eye and less irritating for the lawnmower. If the hosepipe cannot be left in position I make a cut on either side of the pipe with a half-moon edging blade and remove the narrow strip of turf with a fork, leaving my new edge marked in the grass.

Sometimes I dream of having several acres of established woodland where I could find suitable homes for choice shade-loving plants. I imagine great clumps of *Trillium*, *Cypripedium* and other treasures which need shade and moisture. But then I should not be living in Essex, where woodlands are few and far between, where rainfall is minimal and where few shallow-rooted plants are able to stand severe root-competition in summer drought.

On the edge of our garden is a small copse, not much more than a group of young oaks but large enough to create a little leafy walk in summer. I have recently begun to experiment here, to see which plants and bulbs will survive and perhaps naturalise in the thin grass around and under these trees. Once again I have indicated a slightly winding path with hosepipes to show the mower which part I would like to keep cut. The rest of the grass will be left until the foliage of flowering plants has died down, then it will be scythed when necessary or mown with the Hayter. I am not yet certain how I shall treat this additional feature in the garden. Over the past two years composted garden refuse, spent potting soil and the remains of vast bonfires have all been spread over the area to help improve the basic soil, which tends to be poor and gravelly. Out of these dressings have germinated *Aquilegia*, *Thalictrum* and *Digitalis* among the most suitable plants. *Verbascum pulverulentum*, with its huge rosettes of grey-white felted leaves was among the unsuitables which have been removed. Despite the poor gravel subsoil, the Lenten Roses (*Helleborus orientalis*) planted two to three years ago have made quite good plants and I should like to add more. Drifts of snowdrops and small flowered species of *Narcissus* are already making an encouraging display. Despite cold winds I have been putting out pot-grown plants of the blue-flowered forms of our native wood anemone, *Anemone nemorosa* 'Robinsoniana' and *A.n.* 'Allenii'. From elsewhere in the garden I have lifted large clumps of *Erythronium dens canis*, the charming Dog's Tooth Violet. (Although easy to remember, this always strikes me as a silly name. The flowers in no way resemble violets; they look more like fluttering, narrow petalled cyclamens, in soft, rosy-mauve with protruding grey-blue anthers, standing above smooth oval leaves marbled in chocolate-brown and jade-green.) Both flowers and leaves are very fleeting, coming early but disappearing all too quickly. Yet they are exquisitely beautiful and of such fragile wax-like texture.

Dog's Tooth Violet (*Erythronium dens canis*) in the woodland garden

It is the roots which suggest the name Dog's Tooth; when dug, they appear as bundles of narrow creamy-white, pointed corms – very like the pointed teeth of a dog. While they are still in full flower and leaf, I have been carefully dividing these bundles and planting them in little groups – sometimes close, sometimes scattered, along the edge of my shady walk. I have seen these erythroniums studding short turf in the Pyrenees and on high alpine mountains, in full sun. But every afternoon awesome purple and black clouds massed overhead and torrential thunderstorms drenched the tight turf. In English gardens they seem to thrive almost anywhere, but I find that a little shade and shelter protects the flowers and helps them last longer. By the time the floor of my woodland becomes shaded and dry I hope that all my spring-flowering bulbs will have completed their cycle and died down naturally. Among the Dog's Tooth Violets I have planted another delicate little treasure, *Corydalis solida*, which flowers at much the same time. Its soft clusters of bluish-lilac flowers are held just above finely-cut waxy blue leaves. When it has set seed the whole plant disintegrates and disappears without trace. But beneath light, leaf-mould soil are little tubers shaped like small new potatoes, slightly flattened and yellow in colour; they are easily identified if one happens to dig up a clump by mistake.

Surely epimediums would do well between the bulbs beneath the trees? I must try some. With their dense clusters of underground rhizomes they can survive relatively dry and shady conditions. Their low mounds of heart-shaped foliage look delicate in spring when sunlight filters through their beautiful rust-red and pale green patterned leaves, but they stengthen as they mature to leathery green forms and gradually, over a number of years, become very successful colonisers. Here there are too many clumps of Soft Grass (*Holcus mollis*), which quickly make tussocky plants, each large enough to fill a small wheelbarrow. So I shall dig out most of these – they are easily dislodged when young – and perhaps replace them with different forms of *Epimedium*.

It will take a few years, and much trial and error, to see which plants thrive, or better still, naturalise – that is, spread themselves without help from me. Different kinds of *Symphytum* are already there, with croziers of little funnel-shaped flowers in yellow and orange or pink and blue. *Symphytum caucasicum* is perhaps the most handsome in flower, with tall sprays of pure sky-blue flowers, but it can be a nuisance in a mixed border where it spreads far too successfully.

It will be interesting to see how I cope with shade-tolerating perennials in this new garden experiment as well as spring and autumn bulbs. Several forms of Autumn Crocus (*Colchicum*) are already there. With bulbs alone, the area could be mown after all their foliage had died down, towards the end of June or early in July. Perhaps some of my perennials could be scythed down later, as happens in the hayfields of Switzerland in July. But I can hear at least one of my gardening friends

60

chuckling and saying I shall be lucky if it is not a mess of nettles and
brambles in two years' time. He may be right. There is no such thing as
'Wild Gardening'; the hand of the gardener must always be caring and
selective to keep order over unruly and unwelcome invaders. Already I
see and remove young seedling blackberry and elderberry bushes from
beneath the trees where I am sure they have been dropped as seeds by
birds sitting on the branches above. They will no doubt continue their
thoughtless sowing.

On Friday evenings I generally attend to my houseplants. Recently, I
have reduced the number and variety I once kept to comparatively few,
and I feel that my rooms would look lifeless and unfurnished without
them.
     We built the house in 1960. It is a low-lying, split-level building
bedded into the warm gravel bank overlooking, on the west side, a
hollow now filled with ponds and water-gardens. Large floor-to-ceiling
windows frame wide views of the gardens and allow good light indoors
for large plants, helping to create the illusion that house and garden are
one.
     A huge *Sparmannia africana* fills one corner where one can sit
beneath the green shade of large, heart-shaped, woolly-textured leaves.
The heavily branched shrub almost touches the polished wood ceiling,
which slopes down dramatically over the whole living area from the
open hall above. This South African shrub usually produces large heads
of fluffy, creamy-white flowers in late winter, but last summer I had to
curb its enthusiasm so that we might live comfortably together and the
subsequent growth did not have enough time left during the summer
months to produce flower buds.
     In the hall, on the upper level of the house, a white-painted brick wall
runs alongside the glass-fronted entrance and is hung from floor to
ceiling with *Rhoicissus rhomboidea* planted in a narrow bed at the foot
of the wall. This white painted wall and the bed beneath extends
outside, beyond the glass entrance, to become the side wall of our
garage. There it is clothed with another vine-like plant, *Parthenocissus
henryana*, whose long stems of beautifully figured, dark green and
brown leaves, strangely marked with contrasting silvery-white veins,
become a glowing curtain of crimson and red in autumn. Inside the
house, the *Rhoicissus* can be seen from the sitting room below, looking
up and across the dining room which is separated from the sitting room
by a low divider. At the end of the dining table another tall window has
a narrow strip of dark tiles beneath, on which stands *Begonia haageana*.
This too has made a handsome plant, 5 feet (1.5 m) tall and 3 feet (1 m)
across. Its many branching stems are supported by canes carefully
concealed within the plant. Large-pointed, deeply-wrinkled leaves are
red-veined above and red-flushed beneath, while both sides are covered

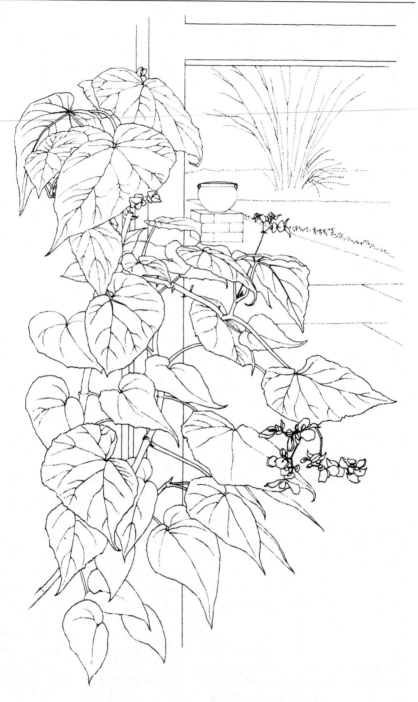

One of the house plants, *Begonia haageana*

with soft bristly hairs. Flowers are produced throughout the year on tall, fuzzy red stems, which carry large open clusters of round white flowers speckled with short, rose-red hairs. Beside this spectacular plant crouches the equally attractive *Begonia erythrophylla*, given to me many years ago by a Dutch garden designer. This plant produces low-growing furry rhizomes which curve over the edge of a large low pot, all totally concealed by a wealth of shining, smooth green leaves, almost circular in shape. In spring, elegant sprays of small, shell-pink flowers appear.

Since the New Year, a large rose-pink cyclamen has sat by one of the sitting-room windows on a small round table. During the winter it has warmed our spirits with over a hundred blooms and it is still looking fresh and full of flower at the end of March. For those who despair of keeping cyclamens in good heart, I should say the temperature in this room seldom goes above 65°F except near the wood-burning stove. The large open living-space affords this temperate heat, both by night and day, which suits plants well, but I am sure that it feels fresh to visitors used to small rooms snugly closed.

By the end of the sofa stands a low table which, for weeks, carried a pale pink flowering *Azalea indica*. While the ponds were frozen-over I kept a bucket of pond-water inside the house with which to water this plant, plunging the peat-filled pot into the bucket until bubbles ceased to form. When the plant showed signs of making new growth (and most of the flowers were over) I put it into a small, frost-free greenhouse, where it would have overhead light, to encourage new flower buds for next year. Another bucket of pond-water is to hand beneath the greenhouse bench to prevent the lime-hating *Azalea* being watered with tap-water which contains chalk.

In place of this *Azalea*, the sitting-room now has a good specimen of *Jasminum polyanthum*. This plant is not hardy, except in the mildest localities, but it can be a delight in a conservatory. It needs good top-light to produce long sprays of pink-flushed pointed buds, which open as starry white flowers, filling the room with sweet scent.

All of these house-plants are watered according to need. Waterers, I sometimes think, are born, not made. Plants can be left to collapse with thirst before their plight is noticed, or else left to drown when the container, in which their pot is standing, is left for days, half full of water. Large pots sometimes need to be stood in a large bowl, or bucket of water, to soak the root ball thoroughly and then they should be left to drain before being returned to their cache-pot or saucer. When I have been round my house and office with a large watering can, which spares too many trips to the tap, I go back later to check that all the water has been absorbed. If any is left, I take two washing bowls, lift the large flower pots from their containers, and stand each one in turn in one of the bowls, then tip the spare water into the second and mop up the splashes.

About once a month, or every six weeks, each plant is given a small dressing of slow-release fertiliser. This is essential to promote fresh growth and fine healthy foliage. Regular trimming and training is also necessary to keep the plants the right size and shape for their environment. Long, lanky, unsupported plants do not create a restful atmosphere. Now, with March almost gone, I look forward to bringing in little posies of fresh flowers and foliage from the garden. Some of the pot plants which have given us so much pleasure through the long winter months will be rested outside, or in the greenhouse, where they will be repotted, or started afresh, from cuttings.

APRIL

STINGING showers of sleet and rain bedevilled us almost to the last day of March. Then, miraculously, April arrived on a warm stream of air from the south. I drove to Kew Gardens to spend the day with the assistant curator, Brian Halliwell, and to give a talk to the Kew Mutual Improvement Society in the evening. The sun shone – it almost felt like summer – but the great and stately trees of Kew showed no sign of bud burst. Beneath them pale daffodils rippled across high, grassy mounds. I was pleased to see *Prunus mume*, the Japanese Apricot, in flower. (I had read about it but never seen it.) Obtainable in white and in shades of pink, with both single and double flowers, it smells of almonds and makes a graceful-looking light tree. By pruning hard some of the branches, strong, straight shoots are encouraged which are studded with flowers the following spring.

I much enjoyed the day; seeing all kinds of treasures, talking endlessly about plants, and none of us needing to make excuses for doing so. It is very stimulating to have such an opportunity to share knowledge and experience of plants and to hear new opinions, not to mention the widening of horizons which comes from seeing plants new to cultivation. Several pages of notebook were filled with new names and old names updated.

I almost forgot that I had a job to do. But, after a delicious and fortifying meal, cooked by Brian (who had entertained me all day), we made our way to the lecture theatre where we sat through a remarkably short Annual General Meeting. Then I heard my name announced as the speaker. This is always a frightening moment. With heart thudding, I walked to the platform and turned to face the rows of pale faces which swam up before me, almost to the ceiling, on tiered seating. But by the end of the evening the anonymous faces had become responsive person-alities, encouraging me by their warmth and enthusiasm. I had taken them with me back through the twenty-eight years in which we have made the garden from a wilderness, showing the difficulties and failures, as well as some of the successes. Feeling as though I had drunk champagne, I drove home through the glitter of night-time London, in a fine mood to be impressed by the dark and stately architecture, theatrically lit, softened and screened by shadows and black tracery of bare trees. Finding my way along the embankment and out through the more prosaic East End, I joined the twentieth-century late-night traffic and allowed myself to be brought down to earth.

Almost overnight, the scene has changed. The Chelsea plants are growing at last. Already some have to be moved from the plastic tunnel, which quickly becomes very warm on sunny days, into the cooler net-covered Shade House. Yet another area, sheltered from wind but open to the sky, is needed where plants sufficiently advanced can be allowed to grow naturally. Many of these have silver or golden foliage which loses its brightness if kept under any kind of cover. So, I spend some time of every day in the weeks running up to Chelsea checking to see that plants are progressing enough, but not too much. As the weather veers from warm to cold and to warm again, I often find myself moving plants back and forth to try to achieve what I need. It probably sounds silly, but it is maddening how quickly a plant will come into flower when you hope to hold it back, and equally frustrating to see how slowly it moves when you are longing to see the buds open. But my small manipulations are slight compared with those of nurserymen who, with expertise, use heat and artificial lighting to produce perfect blooms out of season.

Some of the bushy background plants like *Ballota pseudodictamnus* and *Santolina chamaecyparissus* already need to be carefully pruned. They have suddenly doubled in size, but if left would become lank and floppy in the sheltered tunnel. They will eventually make comfortably bun-shaped plants about the size of a lavender bush. To keep them in good shape and ensure plenty of young growth at the right time, I carefully tip every shoot now, about five weeks before the show. If it is done later there would not be time for the plants to be at their best. Both have very attractive woolly-grey foliage.

The velvety leaves of the various coloured forms of sage, *Salvia officinalis*, already look attractive, especially the variegated form whose young tip leaves are purple and pink, edged with cream. *Salvia argentea* is not bushy, but makes low rosettes of large, rounded leaves so thickly furred with silky hairs, both back and front, they could almost be used as powder-puffs.

I have prepared over a thousand plants, bulbs and small shrubs for my Chelsea exhibit. Not all will be used. Some may be past their best, others may not be good enough to show. During the last few weeks of preparation other things which I see when passing back and forth across the nursery and garden may be added.

I do not make a drawn plan of what I will do but in my mind I have a picture of the kind of groupings I shall make. As the garden here consists of very contrasting areas – the dry 'Mediterranean Garden', or the water gardens – so does my exhibit. My Chelsea exhibit is perhaps a microcosm of the garden. One section is designed around a small pool; this is simply made by bending a strip of hardboard, about 6 inches (15 cm) wide, into a simple oval shape, fixing it with wooden pegs and laying heavy-gauge black plastic-sheeting over it. To hide the plastic, curving pieces of bark stripped from trees in a local timber yard are placed around the 'pond' and any visible cracks are filled in with bright moss. Behind the pool I make a small vertical group of Silver Birch, a feathery bamboo and perhaps a variegated dogwood to suggest a landscape. Plants which need damp conditions are grouped closest to the 'pool'. Further away, on the shady side of the trees, are plants for cool conditions, while the opposite end of the exhibit is kept open as if it were a dry, sunlit site, with an upright juniper and dramatic foliage plants to set the scene for drought-loving plants.

Above all it is the contrast of form and texture, and the subtle variations in colour of foliage which I enjoy putting together. As with a flower arrangement, it can never be repeated exactly. Each year it varies a little. New combinations spring to mind as I work with the plants, building a picture. Building is the right word. When we arrive after our sixty-mile journey, we find our numbered site looking as flat and empty as a tennis court. We take two days bringing up the plants in large, closed vans. My task is to supervise the unloading of trolleys so that boxes and trays of plants are not dumped just anywhere, but will be put roughly near the group in which they belong. (A lot of time and energy can be wasted, looking for plants you know are there but cannot find.) As the trolley loads come in we have to be careful not to overflow onto anyone else's standing ground. I am always relieved when I find myself next to a rose exhibitor who will not usually arrive to stage until Sunday, because I can then spread my boxes a little more, have room to manoeuvre, and get them emptied and out of the way in time.

The first few hours of making the stand tend to be nerve-wracking. I begin by grouping the few trees and shrubs in each main section. Then I position the 'pond' so that I can create a bank-effect behind it. Pots often have to be lifted and stood on boxes, pots, trays, or bricks to get the right effect. Every bit of artifice has to be concealed, no pot or container must be visible, all must look as if it were growing naturally. We cover the constructions with old netting and florist's moss; finally pulverised bark, such as we use to mulch our borders in the garden, is spread on the surface. When the exhibit is complete the flat site has gone and a small undulating 'garden' has taken its place. Plants look better if they appear to grow on different levels.

Once the nucleus of each group is established, I tend to finish one section at a time, feeling myself into the atmosphere of a bog garden or dry garden group. As progress is slowly made, pots are carefully watered, camouflage is secured, and labels put into place. My young staff are there to help and humour me and learn what goes on behind the scenes at Chelsea. They will stand on each corner and confidently answer a thousand questions from visitors before the show is over.

Easter was early this year, at the end of the first week in April. Easter Saturday morning was mild and spring-like, just right for planting. I loaded a trolley with dwarf cyclamens to plant in the newly enlarged bed beneath the Great Oak. They are mostly three and four years old, grown from seed which was collected from the parent plants already established in the same bed. Usually in July, we look for the bursting seed-pods filled with little round brown seeds, but this past year or two the pods have been emptied, robbed by ants perhaps, or mice? But if I part the marbled leaves of the old plants in early spring I usually find plenty of tiny, single-leafed seedlings clustered on top of the old corm. I am always puzzled by this, since they cannot hope to do much more than subsist in the shallow layers of leaf mould collected there. We lift them out carefully and plant them in shallow boxes to grow on for a couple of years before they are planted individually into pots. From this you can conclude that a flowering size corm will have taken at least three or four years to produce. It seemed a good time to divide and

replant some of my more unusual snowdrops. I have not yet become a snowdrop fanatic. As with hostas, I think the craze to collect hundreds of named varieties, many of which look the same even when the differences have been pointed out to you, can be overdone. Although not a dedicated collector I do take pleasure in possessing distinctively different forms. I have several different double snowdrops. For general purposes I think the commonly seen form *Galanthus nivalis* 'Flore Pleno' is hard to beat. It increases well and makes a good display. My special ones have much more tightly double flowers. When you tip them up you see closely packed petals rimmed with green and white, looking like ballet skirts hidden inside the outer sepals. One called 'Lady Elphinstone', hides buttery-yellow petticoats. She was very small-flowered and weakly when I first obtained her, but now she produces strong-looking

Cyclamens and snowdrops beneath the great oak

69

flowers. I think this applies to a number of bulbs, as well as plants; they need time to establish themselves before you can judge their quality.

I have several other named snowdrops but one which appeared here mysteriously, many years ago, is a really splendid snowdrop, very large and scented, producing two flowers to a bulb, appearing late and lasting longest of all in my garden. It may have arrived here as a seedling tucked into another plant or it may be a hybrid that has evolved here. I do not know. I have been told it is an extra fine form of *Galanthus byzantinus*. Each year I tell myself I will move and plant a lot more snowdrops, especially a fine single form called *Galanthus caucasicus*. I have managed a few this spring, scattering them along banks and beneath the young oaks in my little 'woodland garden', but there never seems time to plant as many as I should like. The job is best done immediately after flowering and as the years speed by I am surprised and delighted to see how soon bulbs planted in ones and twos have made fine clumps – a most satisfying retort to those members of the family who cry out when they see me despoiling flowering clumps.

All the Dog's Tooth Violets I moved a few weeks ago appear quite recovered, so today I dug and divided a large clump with extra large, but much paler flowers. There must have been at least thirty large, creamy-white corms, hidden in the leaf-mould soil where originally I had planted one.

The waves of yellow daffodils are receding, but daintier, white forms are taking their place, nodding over pale carpets of our native wood anemones. Largest and loveliest are two special forms of *Anemone nemorosa*. One, *Anemone nemorosa* 'Robinsoniana', is pure ice-blue. The other, 'Allenii', is of a heart-stopping blueness, warmed slightly by the plum-stained back of the petals. Both need a warm, still day to open their flowers wide, for you to be stunned by the effect. I love to plant the dark, purple leaved *Viola labradorica* among them, and to catch, out of the corner of my eye, the brilliant lime-green flower heads of *Euphorbia robbiae* nearby.

While I was busy moving snowdrops I made the effort to sort out mixed varieties of *Narcissus*. For me, the effect is spoilt if odd bulbs of a different variety are growing in the same clump, so while I can see the muddle, I try to extricate them and replant them elsewhere.

Although the severe weather in February and March damaged the blooms and stems of some Lenten Roses, *Helleborus orientalis*, the established groups in the garden have eventually given much pleasure. By April it is possible to go through the stock beds of young plants and pick out any which seem especially good. (I find them all lovely and find it hard to throw any away.)

The selected ones are planted in a reserve part of the nursery to be grown on and divided when they have made sufficiently large clumps. This may well take at least two or three years and then you might make four or five pieces. This is the time, with the plants in flower, when we split those which have already been grown on. It is an amazing sight to go into the shed where the stock plants are being divided. There stands a barrow, full of cut blooms, all dark purple and plum shades, some speckled and some shadowed, having almost a fruity lushness, reminding me of the insides of ripe figs. On a bench, a bucket overflows with greenish-white blooms, some rounded, like lampshades of the thirties, others with long, pointed, slightly twisted petals shaded green.

With all the flowers removed, the clumps are carefully divided into smallish pieces, each with a new shoot on a starchy base, just sprouting new roots. We find these pieces grow away well, provided they are well-watered after planting and not allowed to dry out if we have a long dry spell. Many years ago, I learnt not to lift and replant whole, heavy clumps of *Helleborus orientalis*. Not wishing to lose a large display, I moved some large plants with plenty of root, but they deeply resented my interference and took years to recover.

On Easter Saturday afternoon, I decided to plant a little bed which has been waiting two years for my attention. On the back of an east-facing wall Harry had made a low raised bed, supported by railway sleepers which had originally been part of my first frames. About 3.5 feet (1 m) across and 1 foot (30 cm) high, the bed was intended to show-off small plants requiring cool conditions since it only has morning sunshine. A rich mixture of well-rotted manure, peat, grit and good soil was packed into the bed and then left, rather longer than I had intended, to settle.

During the winter we have soaked in a ditch peat blocks that were bought last summer. They had been like wood, almost impossible to penetrate with water, but the strong-flowing stream in the bottom of the ditch has at last made them heavy and saturated. I needed just a few to create little outcrops or shelves here and there along the flat surface. I laid the design roughly, then collected Sallyann to come and help. While I went off to pick up little plants which had been tucked away for safety in my special reserved corners, Sallyann made a much better job than I had done of bedding in the peat blocks. By the end of the afternoon we had planted several different trilliums, small ferns, some single pink hepaticas and one rose-coloured double form. There were several *Corydalis* which were new to me and *Dodecatheon dentatum* 'Album'. This white-flowered Shooting Star was given to me by Elizabeth Strangman, of Hawkhurst in Kent, who specialises in really choice plants.

It would be foolish of me to think of making a proper peat bed, or to try to collect many of the exciting plants described in Alfred Evans' good book, *The Peat Garden and its Plants*. You need the climate to go with it, not only to keep the peat moist, but to provide the mist-laden atmosphere which many of these plants need. But I shall enjoy finding out what will look well and grow successfully on my cool raised bed. It will, I am sure, provide a setting for small, choice plants which need more care and attention that I can give them in the main garden and perhaps it will provide ideas for visitors who have a cool dim site in their gardens, which could be transformed.

Several years ago, against the opposite side of this wall, we made a raised bed facing west. It has been a pleasure every month of the year and easy to maintain; much easier than the traditional rock garden. The effect is infinitely more attractive if you can build against old brick or weathered limestone. But I went ahead with my wall of concrete blocks, deciding the width of the bed by the distance I could comfortably stretch to weed. Then Harry built the new retaining wall, forming a bed about 3 feet (1 m) across, and 1 foot (30 cm) from the ground.

I grow few rare or difficult alpines; generally speaking these need to be cared for in an alpine house. Outside in Essex, it is not easy to achieve both snow-melt at the root of the plants and a sun-scorched, wind-raked atmosphere above to maintain their true mountain characteristics. But there are, fortunately, many small-growing bulbs and plants which like our sun-scorched, often dry, situation. Presented on this long, narrow bed, as on a stage, they delight us with a continuous performance. Scarcely a day goes by that I do not walk along it.

I am much relieved to see *Tecophilaea cyanocrocus* has not been affected by the severe winter. This is a choice bulb, usually grown in pans in a frame or in a cool greenhouse. It originated in the high alpine meadows of Chile, but I am told it has been so heavily collected that it has almost been wiped out in its natural habitat. On short stems, about 3 inches (7 cm) tall, it holds crocus-shaped flowers which open wide in the sun – broad petals of electrifying blue. Some have a white-striped eye, others are entirely deep gentian-blue.

There are several unusual grape hyacinths (*Muscari*) on this bed. The most exciting is sufficiently different from the rest of its relatives to have been put into a separate genus and called *Muscarimia macrocarpum*. It used to be called *Muscari moschatum* var. *flavum* which describes the colour of the flowers. From dull purplish buds open fine stems of large, clear yellow flowers with little brown stains around their open mouths. They are heavily scented, rich and sweet as hyacinths. *Muscari armeniacum* 'Cantab', although much smaller is seldom passed by. Its densely clustered heads open from pale greenish buds to skimmed-milk-blue flowers, scented like lilac.

Seeding all along the wall bed are lovely forms of *Anemone pavonina*; in fact, some have to be treated like weeds (plants in the wrong place) and firmly removed. But for weeks, throughout April and May, their jewel-like colours highlight the planting. So much daintier than the St. Bridget Anemones (and easier to grow), their pointed, silk-textured petals are painted in sunset colours. There are white flowers whose buds

72

Sempervivum pilatus, Cotula potentilla and *Raoulia hookeri*
on the raised bed

are stained coral at the base, while silvered-pink buds open startling ruby petals. Apricot buds open to deep coral, and all have hearts filled with navy-blue stamens. Their foliage is finely divided, as refined as the flowers. They make fascinating seed-heads. Large, egg-shaped green clusters explode into creamy masses of wool which has to be gently teased out by the wind to carry away the seeds tucked safely among it.

Not nearly so showy, but nonetheless fascinating, are several fritillaries in bloom nearby. They are all relatives of the Crown Imperial Fritillary, *Fritillaria imperialis*, with its pineapple-like cluster of leaves above down-turned burnt orange or yellow bells, and the much smaller Snakeshead Fritillary, *Fritillaria meleagris*, still growing wild in a few protected damp meadows.

From warm slopes in countries bordering the Mediterranean, come the following drought-tolerating fritillaries. *Fritillaria tuntasia* stands less than 12 inches (30 cm) high; bloom-coated like sloes, its rounded bells of darkest mahogany appear almost black. Their thin, grey stems are surrounded by spiralling, narrow, grey leaves. They are exquisite. Further along *Fritillaria messanensis* stands taller, with larger, faintly chequered, chestnut-brown bells which are yellowish-green inside. Next month *Fritillaria pyrenaica* will be in bloom. We have a very fine form given us by our good friend and great plantsman, the late Sir Cedric Morris, which hangs matt-textured bells from each grey-leafed stem. The edges of the petals roll back like pixie-hats to show the enamelled, lemon-splashed linings. They have a strange, rather foetid, smell. I like

73

to underplant these fritillaries with bronze-tinted houseleeks and aluminium-grey mats of tiny raoulias. The primrose-scented, iris-like plant, *Hermodactylus tuberosus* is just past its best, but I still have a few on my writing table. I like to see the light through every part of the flower, through the sharply pointed standards and outer petals pressed stiffly against them, every part satinised silvery-green, except the broad, velvet-textured tips which fall back in startling contrast, soot-black. I should warn that this beguiling flower has invasive tuberous roots and the flowers are followed by very long, skewer-shaped leaves which can be bothersome in the wrong place.

Rosettes of silver-edged saxifrages, interesting but not obstreperous sedums, houseleeks (*Sempervivum*) in many shapes and sizes – these are a few of the plants which furnish the bed all the year round, in frost or drought.

Softening the hard-edged supporting wall are several kinds of mat-forming *Phlox*, and the pretty *Hypericum reptans* with its surprisingly large, saucer-shaped, yellow flowers cascading down prostrate stems covered with tiny, copper-tinted leaves. There are two or three kinds of *Gypsophila* which are related to the froth of starry-white flowers you put with sweet peas; these make tumbling mats covered with little pink or white flowers. *Gypsophila dubia* has attractive leaves, grey with purple backs, while *Gypsophila* 'Rosy Veil' makes a large plant, a cumulus-cloud of palest-pink double flowers caught in a mesh of wiry stems, about 12 inches (30 cm) high.

I should not bore you with an exhausting list of plants which grow on this bed, but situated near the house, sheltered any day of the year, it has become a favourite part of the garden. I cannot leave it just yet.

Small plants need a few bolder plants among them to create good design. Raised beds should not become museums of teeny-weenies, smothered with scores of white labels, looking like a war cemetery.

It has taken both time and search to find the right shrub or plant to form bold features or backgrounds for these mostly small-leafed plants. Small-leafed hebes harmonise with them and some create the note of drama I am looking for, but unfortunately they are not, in my garden (swept by icy blasts out of Russia), always the hardiest of plants. One of my favourites, *Hebe* 'Hagley Park', has in the past surprised me by the kind of winters it has survived on this wall-sheltered bed, but it has finally succumbed this winter. I shall replace it because it created such a fine feature. Now, having just walked out to measure the scorched brown remains of my old shrub – 2 feet (61 cm) high and 3 feet (91 cm) across – I have found a few live shoots tucked close against the wall, green with small leathery leaves and topped with clusters of deep-rose buds which will slowly elongate into handsome racemes of small pink flowers. (Well-done 'Hagley Park'! I am so pleased you pulled through.)

Quite different, almost architectural, is *Hebe* 'Boughton Dome', given me by Valerie Finnis, whose fascinating raised beds at Boughton House first inspired me to make my own. 'Boughton Dome' has, over several years, made a large, round, cottage-loaf-shaped bush, 18 inches (46 cm) high and more across, of a marvellously refined yet dense texture, not unlike a dwarfed *Cupressus*. It is a lovely colour, with bright green tips over bluish-green mature shoots, and makes a fine piece of scenery, a kind of bulwark among the little plants around it.

An unusual *Verbascum* performs a similar service in quite a different way. On a woody framework, *Verbascum dumulosum* carries flower-like clusters, about 6 inches (15 cm) across, of greyish-white velvety leaves, a surprising contrast in scale, contributing much to the general design. During May and June, each leaf cluster will erupt with 16 inch (41 cm) spires of bright yellow flowers. *Daphne retusa* appeared uninvited, the seed possibly dropped by a thrush sitting on the wall above. I thought it an unwise offering, that the site would be too hot and dry, but I neglected to move it. 'Time's winged chariot' has sped by – and there it thrives; a low, squat bush of thick, silvery-brown stems covered with defiantly healthy, leathery green leaves that are almost buried with clusters of sweetly-scented flowers. Each flower has a long, narrow tube stained dark plum which flares into four white petals backed with plum; so crisp they make you think of porcelain.

When we made this bed it was filled with a rich mixture of compost, gritty soil, and rather less peat than the new bed on the shady side. A few large pieces of ragstone or ironstone were carefully positioned and partly sunk to break up the flat surface. This conglomerate stone is formed in badly drained soil by the oxidisation of iron. Large lumps of stony soil are welded together into a rock-like layer and this is sometimes pulled to the surface in broken pieces when subsoiling is being done to help the drainage. Because they are made of our soil they look much more appropriate than imported limestone.

Finally when planting, the bed is topped with a thick layer of grit, about three-eighths of an inch, which we buy from local gravel pits. This not only makes an attractive finish to the bed, it helps to check seedling weeds and also helps prevent evaporation of moisture from the soil. Perhaps I should warn you, this style of gardening can become addictive. There are so many collectors' items which can be arranged along these outdoor shelves and there is never enough room left for half of those you would love to possess.

It is the middle of April, I have just dug the variegated hostas from the stock beds for Chelsea; their fat, pointed buds not yet showing through the cold soil. With scarcely a month to look their best, if they are prepared too soon their bright colour will fade by the end of May.

I dug several clumps of each variety that I wish to show. The lovely *Hosta fortunei* 'Albo Picta' has large leaves which look as though they had been hand-painted with large brush strokes of yellow and primrose inside the pale green edges. *Hosta f.* 'Aurea' has delicately textured leaves – almost transparently yellow. This lovely foliage plant needs light to keep its leaves yellow in spring, but direct sunlight scorches them. As summer comes, they turn to pale green.

Hosta lancifolia has already unfolded its long, narrow, green leaves. This *Hosta* is not so popular as it deserves to be (the variegated ones are the most popular), but I think it is a loss not to have it in the garden. It makes such attractive plants, the fresh dark green leaves lying back in ruff-like layers from the centre of the clump. Planted singly, or in groups, they make either a feature or good ground cover, and their tall, slender spires of trumpet-shaped, lilac flowers, produced over a long period, are among the best of all the hostas.

I also dug the variegated Masterwort, *Astrantia major* 'Sunningdale Variegated', whose strawberry-shaped leaves are vividly variegated in cream and green, lasting for several weeks before slowly fading as the flower stems arise. From midsummer until the autumn frosts an endless succession of little daisy-shaped flowers with pointed greenish-white petals is produced. For a few days, the weather has been kind. Our coats are off, the temperature has shot up to 73°F outside (this means over 80°F in the tunnels). The Chelsea plants need constant watching. Like batches of buns in the oven, I move some into open shelter to improve their colour, others into the cold house to hold them back. Some large tubs of ornamental rhubarb, *Rheum palmatum* 'Atrosanguineum', have been stood in the plastic tunnel to encourage 6 foot (2 m) flower stems. As I water, prune and generally coax and cosset my plants, I try to disturb every pot occasionally to break any roots which by now, may be attempting to root into the sand bed on which they stand. If they are making too much root, I repot them. By regularly disturbing the plants they will not suddenly be shocked and wilt when we box them up to make the journey to London.

Keith and Harry have been to a local woodyard to collect strips of bark and sawn wooden 'stepping-stones' to make the little path which crosses our show garden. The curved strips of bark look like logs, but without the weight of wood, and they help to create a woodland effect.

A list of plant names we have not shown before must be painted on new labels. Old labels must be checked, some to be replaced with new name changes we discovered during the winter when we were revising the catalogue. When they are all prepared they are put into a tray box in alphabetical order. Each label is simply fixed to the top of a cane which is painted matt black and almost vanishes, leaving the black label with its white lettering distinct but not obtrusive.

There is a postal strike! We are busy collecting the last file of orders, determined to get them away by the end of April. The packhouse floor is

Writing labels

full of assembled orders neatly set out in trays. Now they will have to stay there till we can be certain the parcels will arrive safely at their destinations. It is frustrating to have this sudden check, but it is a treat for everyone to have a free day at last to be outside. By the end of several months packing it feels good to be caring for plants again. There is much to be done, repotting, filling up blank spaces, tipping out dead plants lost in bad weather, making space for new stock coming out of the tunnels. We have had another incredibly warm day and with lots of visitors in the garden; it feels like summer. But what has happened this year to the 'Blackthorn Winter'? We rarely escape shrivelling cold weather when the blackthorn is in flower. Will this year be an exception?

We have caught the soil at the point when it is just right to sow a few vegetables. I prefer onions sown from seed; they seem much less coarse, have firm crispy layers and are not too large. I find they keep much better than onions from sets if they are hung up in long strings in the garage, from where I can collect them without going outside in bad weather. Last year's crop has only now begun to deteriorate, sprouting new shoots. We sow parsnips together with a few radish to mark the rows because parsnips are so slow to germinate. Next winter's vegetables – leeks, brussels sprouts and sprouting broccoli – are all sown to be planted out later. We lost our broad beans in February and forgot to sow

Home-grown onions

them again outside so we have put some in pots and they are just pushing through.

We lost all but four plants of sprouting broccoli, but it's amazing how many meals come from four plants. As vegetable gardeners we all tend to grow too much of a few things instead of a little of many different things. Why grow long rows of lettuce which go to seed, or cauliflowers, which all heart at once? Especially if you are a small family, try short rows and sow more frequently.

Basil needs heat to germinate successfully, so it has been sown in a tray and stood in the small greenhouse. This most aromatic of herbs transforms tomatoes, whether raw or cooked, with its rich, warm flavour, but it does need a good summer to do well out of doors. We prick the seedlings into pots, keep a few in the greenhouse and put the rest outside. In well-drained soil they make fine plants in most summers. While leaves are picked from them almost every day throughout the summer, some plants, before they run to flower, are hung up to dry for winter use. They are especially good in soups, or sprinkled over a pizza before it is cooked.

Various small-fruited tomatoes have been pricked out into pots, waiting for summer to come. 'Gardeners Delight' is still one of my favourites, but does better, I think, in the shelter of a tunnel. I am trying a small, bushy, outdoor tomato called 'Whipper-Snapper' which came from Suffolk Seeds near Sudbury. It has fruit the size of grapes, just right for grandchildren to pop into their mouths.

Peppers and aubergines will also stay in a tunnel, but the rest of the tender vegetable plants will be planted out about the end of May or beginning of June provided it is not still cold. These will include courgettes and ornamental gourds which look so attractive on the floor in winter, in big round, shallow baskets.

After a bad winter, April can be an empty month in the vegetable garden, so I am always grateful for my over-wintered salad crops. Several varieties of chicory are attractive to look at and good to eat.

There are several kinds of red-leafed chicory. Among them I have a speckled kind which makes plenty of soft young leaves. 'Grumolo' chicory makes small, green, open rosettes like opening rosebuds. I pick a few leaves individually, leaving the plants to carry on producing new leaves. To palates accustomed to limp, greenhouse, winter lettuce, these leaves may seem a little bitter, but mixed with milder leaves and herbs they are very appetising. The tender young leaves of spinach beet, shooting fast now from over-wintered plants, are surprisingly sweet and crisp at this time of the year. I add a few sprigs of feathery chervil, which tastes like aniseed, and some bright green leaves of chives. We have a specially fine form of chive with better foliage and handsome round heads of mauve flowers, also good to eat.

As I walk through the spring garden I often pick a few primroses and violet flowers to sprinkle over the dressed salad just before we eat it. They look most attractive when fresh but quickly become bruised and messy-looking if stirred into the salad.

I was in Rutland recently, helping to make a television programme; when on my way home, instead of hurrying South on the great motorway, I turned off at the sign which says Stamford. Too often in the past we have driven by, in a hurry to be somewhere else. The sun was warm through the car windows and I felt urged to step off the merry-go-round, to stop and stare for a while, to enter another age. Although I have not studied them seriously, I enjoy fine architecture and paintings. To look at them is inspiring. So I drove through the fine old streets of Stamford and around part of the three-mile wall enclosing the ancient estate. Driving through the entrace you suddenly see Burghley House above you like a picture from a fairytale. Although massive in bulk and structure, it is beautifully balanced; the classical, limestone facade fretted with well-proportioned windows, while the skyline is a delight. Cupolas, balustrades and chimney-pots, (which are themselves designed like little turreted castles) all soar, on varying levels, into the blue sky. From every angle the building forms elegant and most satisfying compositions; the whole, simply set, like a fine jewel, in a setting of smooth green lawns which swell gently into the rolling landscaped park, designed and created by 'Capability' Brown. Huge bundles of mistletoe hang high on ancient trees.

I shall not attempt to describe the inside of this historic house, but my mind having been with salads, I thought I would tell you of something which amused and interested me. On one of several exuberantly painted ceilings is a scene depicting a great outdoor feast, with guests disporting themselves and servants bearing immense platters of food. (We were told the models for the lightly clad and buxom lady guests were servants working in the house at the time.) Leading the procession is a young girl, proudly carrying her bowl of salad which she has just decorated all over with deep blue violets!

After ten weeks of waiting we have at last obtained permission for Kazu, our Japanese student, to work with us. During these weeks he has been living with us and travelling daily to the English language school, but I cannot report that his ability to communicate has noticeably improved. Fortunately, his understanding of English is much better than his ability to speak it, but when I look at his books and dictionaries, I have sympathy. It is difficult enough to learn another language, but to have to learn a totally different method of writing, compounds the difficulties. Because of this there has been little opportunity for exchange as the weeks have gone by. We have not learnt as much about Japan, either its culture or horticulture, as we had hoped, but maybe we have given this young man one aspect of life in England, living with two idiosyncratic hosts – my husband Andrew and myself. As light evenings tempted me to linger out of doors and the pulse of the garden and nursery started to race, I felt it was time to give Kazu the opportunity of seeing family life elsewhere. He is quietly well-mannered and his English allows him to understand much of the conversation although his responses are limited very largely to yes and no. How much of this I wonder is due to the language problem and how much to the differences between Eastern and Western culture?

A few postcards in appropriate windows soon found pleasant accommodation for him with a young family. So all is well; Kazu seems

A visit to Burghley House, Stamford

happy in his new home and works well on the nursery where he is learning our plants and methods of propagation.

There is a special feeling in the garden on Sundays. All the week I enjoy sharing it with visitors and staff; without them it would not be possible to have such a garden. Nor would the pleasure of it be so great. But to be alone, on a still dewy morning, is heaven. I went out to enjoy the epimediums in flower, opening just ahead of the new leaves. You can see them if you have remembered to cut off all the old over-wintered foliage; it often conceals these little flowers so successfully that some people imagine their plants never flower! They are not the kind of flower which shouts for attention from yards away. They float beneath the trees, a ground mist of pastel colour, fragile, fairy blooms which draw you down on one knee to look at them closely. There, on hundreds of thin, wiry stems, are poised flights of tiny columbine-like flowers. *Epimedium grandiflorum* has the largest flowers, in several different shades. I particularly like 'Violaceum' whose dark plum-purple sepals appear to have a silky-white lining which extends into long, curving spurs. But then I turn to 'White Queen' whose exquisite flowers let the light shine through gauzy whiteness, faintly stained with purple. 'Rose Queen' has dark rose flowers with white tips to the spurs. None of the other epimediums have spurs on their flowers. One of the most vigorous,

making splendid ground cover, is *Epimedium × versicolor* 'Sulphureum' which produces the best display of soft, pale-yellow flowers. There are several other varieties, including a number of sturdy evergreen types such as *E. perralderianum* which have long sprays of bright yellow flowers centred with dark dots. Although the flowers have fleeting charm, all these plants are grown primarily for their leaves which add to the garden scene for most months of the year. Dainty and heart-shaped, they are held on stiff wiry stems, arranging themselves in attractive over-lapping patterns like the fish-scale pattern of slate tiles seen in Germany. As they unfold, the young leaves show a variety of spring colour, soft beige-brown, warm maroon, or a marbling of bright coral-red over pale green. This colour reaches a climax and then fades as the leaves mature, when they all become green until autumn. Then, once again, they assume soft, pinky-brown and copper tints which last throughout the winter. These plants will grow and slowly increase in almost any soil, in sun or shade, but are best in cool part-shade.

Near to them I found lush colonies of the American erythroniums. These lovely flowers grow wild and abundant in western North America, under pines and oaks, as bluebells do here in the British Isles. Most of them have yellow or creamy-white, Turk's-Cap, lily-shaped flowers and are larger and taller than the Dog's Tooth Violet which I have described elsewhere. They have attractive local names, Adder's Tongue, Trout Lily or Glacier Lily. These names refer to the leaf shape or colour, or to the habitat where they are found. The leaves are much longer than those of the Dog's Tooth Violet, *Erythronium dens canis*, more tongue-shaped, wavy-edged and often handsomely mottled with chocolate-brown. The leaf texture is cool and crisp, most satisfying to touch, suited only to cool spring days. When summer comes all will have disappeared except tall, straw-coloured seed-pods, about 12 inches (30 cm) tall.

With so many lovely things in flower now in the garden, I have suddenly become weary of the large rose-pink cyclamen which has decorated my sitting-room for so long. Poor thing, it is tired of itself, having been full of flower for over three months. With leaves still buried and overlaid with heavy blossoms, I have removed the plant to the greenhouse to convalesce, taking off almost all the flowers. I gave it a little feed and hope it will have sufficient energy to restore the corm for next year.

During these past weeks I have made no time to do the flowers. The yellow daffodils have almost come and gone but not one has been picked. I like best to see them growing, but some years I pick big bowlfuls, just one kind together, and let them fall into a shape. Although I have enjoyed flower arranging, it is not something I practise according to the rules anymore. I like to let flowers and leaves decide the style of the arrangement, usually something small and simple, often a bunch of oddments collected as I walk round, to remind me to propagate them, or hold in my hand when I need to write about them.

Now with most of the long-suffering house-plants back in the greenhouse, I feel compelled to freshen my rooms with the cool, clean colours of spring. A tall Wattisfield jug seemed just right to support heavy branches of the Great White Cherry, *Prunus* 'Tai-Haku', which is now at its loveliest, full of promise, with more buds than flowers. Large clusters hang on the ends of curving knobbly branches. Young transparent leaves, just opening, are tinted soft chestnut and green, colours reflected in the dark glaze of the jug. In the shelter of the house, protected from the wind or frost, the large, saucer-shaped, single white flowers open to perfection from faintly pink-washed buds.

Flower arrangement with snowdrops and *Arum italicum* 'Pictum'

On low tables, in simple white bowls, I have posies of white, yellow and green flowers, strengthened by a few dark and marbled leaves of *Arum italicum* 'Pictum' and little clusters of *Skimmia japonica* 'Rubella' which scent the drizzly evening with a sweet fresh smell, almost as good as *Daphne odora*, now past its best. I picked white flowers, including the tall Summer Snowflake, *Leucojum aestivum* 'Gravetye' which in the garden is now making little fountains of tall stems, each curved with the weight of several green-tipped white bells. They grow in quite wet soil by the pond-sides, but seem to do just as well in heavy, but much drier soil elsewhere. I added *Narcissus* 'Tresamble' which carries two short cupped creamy-white flowers on each stem, while *Dicentra spectabilis* 'Alba' hangs low, over the edge of the bowls, white, heart-shaped lockets. Because white can look cold and severe, I added a few sprays of the pale lemon-yellow *Epimedium* 'Sulphureum', while the yellow lily-flowered erythroniums just arranged themselves round these other shade-loving plants. But the flowers which give style to these simple arrangements are a few stems of *Fritillaria verticillata*, adding height and elegance. Each stem stands a good 2 feet (61 cm) tall in the garden, and carries several open bell-shaped flowers. They are green, faintly chequered with brown. Between the flowers, at the top of each stem, are fine curling tendrils which are modified leaves. These, together with the curiously coloured bells, give a very distinctive air to a few spring flowers.

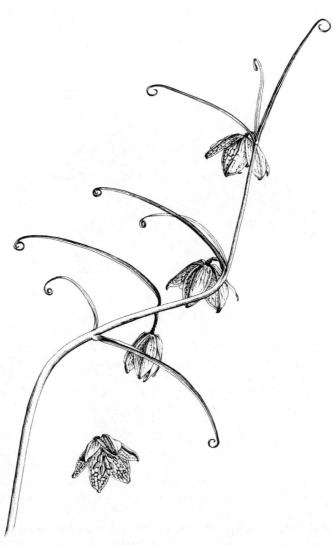

Fritillaria verticillata adds elegance to spring flower arrangements

This fritillary has the reputation of being very shy flowering, tending to split up into many non-flowering bulbs. Perhaps I have a slightly different form since, in parts of the garden, it is flowering like poppies in a cornfield, a carillon of pale green bells pealing above dark-navy and royal-blue heads of *Muscari latifolia* surrounded by thickets of pink smothered *Prunus tenella*, sometimes called the dwarf Russian Almond. Inside my flower bowls I use a pinholder and a piece of crumpled wire netting. For me, this produces a more natural effect than using plastic foam, and I find many soft-stemmed garden flowers will not allow themselves to be pushed into oasis. Occasionally, I use containers with narrow necks to support just a few flowers. The colour of the container matters. By repeating, or harmonising with, the colour of the flowers, the finished effect is more of a piece. But again, it can be exciting to flout this principle and use a dramatically contrasting container which might be black, or a metal, like pewter. I have a small, black, ornate urn on a stand which needs only a few hop vines to fall from it, or perhaps a tangling spray of the small dark purple flowered *Clematis viticella*.

These 'arrangements' take almost no time to do, falling into simple graceful shapes as if they were growing. If they last only a few days you have wasted little time on them, they can easily be replaced. Other plants suggest new ideas. Spontaneity, I think, needs to be the keynote for flowers in the home.

Everywhere, along the country roadsides, black tangled masses of sloe or blackthorn, armed with wickedly sharp thorns, are a froth of tiny, white-as-snow flowers. Despite high temperatures for a few days earlier in the month we feared the return of cold weather when the blackthorn would be in bloom, and sure enough, the temperature has dropped thirty degrees. 'Blackthorn Winter' has arrived. No wonder there is seldom a good crop of sloes. It was with difficulty last autumn that I searched yards of hedge to find enough ripe sloes to make a bottle of sloe gin.

During this last week of April there has been a sharp frost every morning. I go quickly to the Chelsea tunnels, to see if any damage has been done. In the plastic-covered tunnel all seems to be well. The round dinner-plate sized leaves of *Rodgersia tabularis* are still untouched, but young plants being grown for sale in a netting covered tunnel are scorched. These leaves will wither and collapse; new ones will be produced but will take several weeks to develop. Plants of *Euphorbia griffithii* 'Fireglow', put into the cooler house to hold them back, have already been touched by frost, the tomato-red flowers drooping, damaged beyond recovery. New ones will not be produced in time for Chelsea from these plants. Fortunately I have reserved plants, still in bud, which I shall bring on.

Every night while this capricious weather lasts, we have to prepare extra protection against frost damage. Light pieces of netting are dropped over hostas to shelter their pale delicate leaves. Outside, on the stock beds, I have seen rows of hostas burnt brown as though a flame gun had passed over them. They recover and make new leaves, but the early show is spoilt.

The Chelsea houses begin to look more hopeful. Containers are disappearing beneath mounds of fresh foliage. Looking down the length of the long tunnels there is almost a tapestry effect of subtle colours and varied textures. Several different grasses, some variegated, some plain, rise in columns or fountains above the round soft domes of plants like *Santolina* or *Ballota*. The large colourful leaves of ornamental rhubarb, (*Rheum palmatum* 'Atrosanguineum') begin to suggest a lush environment. The great *Gunnera manicata* cosseted in the warmest place I have, the propagating house, still has a long way to go. I should like to see its great umbrella-like leaves reach at least three feet across; they will be a good 5 feet (1.5 m) across on the established plants in the garden, later in midsummer. The hard winter killed some of the huge, feathery, folded buds which stood beneath the pile of old upturned leaves, but smaller, more protected, buds are slowly emerging, still needing protection from recent frost.

Brilliant patches of gold and silver plants add sharpness, but so far there is little sparkle as very few flowers are showing. Those that do may well be over by the third week of May. In some ways, I welcome this cold spell, to hold back lovely plants like *Paeonia mlokosewitschii* with its pale lemon-yellow bowls of crimson stamens. But I also hope for enough warmth to bring other plants into flower. (Not a heat-wave – we gardeners are hard to please.)

My Chelsea exhibit relies on contrasting forms, colours, and textures of foliage, put together like a jigsaw puzzle, with each plant contributing something to its neighbour. Some of them, seen individually, might not appear to have much to commend them at the time, but quieter more modest individuals provide a background for something flamboyant, whether it be a flower or another type of leaf. Too many star performers lumped together can be indigestible.

As the hours of daylight increase, there is a feeling of urgency everywhere. New growth has been slowly pushing ahead despite the cold, so my propagators have been kept busy. Many plants can be split and divided at this time of year. They are dug, lifted into trays and pulled on trolleys back to the propagating benches. There they are divided, or cut, into pot-sized pieces. Some are stout enough to be put directly outside onto a reserved area until they have made new roots and are sufficiently established to be sold. Others, needing more care, are stood in the plastic tunnels where the temperatures are often much higher, especially early in the year, where they will root more quickly.

Each member of the propagating team has a particular area of responsibility, but they also learn each other's skills, helping when needed, so that if anyone leaves, or is absent on holiday or through illness, then the work can be carried on.

When I began the nursery I could find enough cuttings or divisions from the garden, but now we have large areas of stock plants which must be kept clean and healthy to provide cuttings or divisions for new plants. We also propagate by means of root cuttings taken during the late autumn and winter months. Just now we are potting sea hollies, different forms of *Eryngium*, and the handsome leafed *Acanthus* too. Among other plants we grow from root cuttings are the oriental poppies and several kinds of *Crambe*, including *Crambe maritima*, the Seakale. All these plants have to be lifted very carefully out of the propagating boxes so that the delicate new roots will not drop off.

My chief propagator, David Ward, fills our propagating benches with cuttings. This programme keeps him occupied for much of the time almost all the year round. I enjoyed his flush of delight when he saw his first box of rooted cuttings; he was so pleased that he insisted on potting them himself. Now he is thankful for our team of potting ladies to take charge of them, but no matter how many thousands of cuttings we have rooted it is always a thrill to see new roots appearing from vulnerable cut stems. David is also very interested in bulbs, so he is responsible for developing our stocks of these plants. Lilies are increased by separating scales, while some of the more unusual daffodils are cut into small pieces and grown on for several weeks in bags of a moist, sterile medium until they have formed tiny seed-pearl sized bulbs, taking perhaps three or four years to flower. The most fiddly cuttings, where only tiny pieces can be used, or where tiny leaves have to be carefully nipped off without damaging the tender stems, are made by neat-fingered girls with strong nails. Problem plants, or plants in short supply, need to be watched over carefully and sometimes done again and again until stocks have increased sufficiently to be taken into the mainstream of propagation. Because they are so involved with plants as cuttings and seedlings, and with the garden, where mature plants often provide the original source of much of their raw material, my propagating team know the plants intimately and are able to give helpful advice to our visitors when they serve them with the plants they have raised.

Madge Rowell, who came to help me soon after I began the nursery more than twenty years ago, is busy sorting plants which are sufficiently established to be put out for sale. She also takes care to see that enough are put aside for orders by post. It is very hard sometimes to refuse to sell plants when they can been seen in the reserved section of the nursery, but plants which have been paid for throughout the summer by postal customers must be kept to fulfil those orders. Some plants, no matter how hard we try, are always behind the demand, usually because they are slow or difficult to propagate. My twin brother restored my calm one day when I was agitated by a particularly disappointed customer; he sugggested that I think of my more rare plants as signed copies of limited editions.

Each day I walk through the propagating house to see how everything is behaving. We have under-bench warming cables to encourage root formation, and overhead misting nozzles which spray automatically; these are of considerable help but they are only tools to assist us. They are not magic; they cannot produce plants without constant observation. It took several years of experience in using a small mist unit for me to learn how much management is needed to use it efficiently. Growing such a wide range of plants as we do, we never cease to learn new techniques. The two main benches are misted by a central control which automatically switches on according to the rate of evaporation, more frequently on hot days, less frequently on cool days. On either side of these benches is a weaning bench. These two side-benches have no soil warming cables and the mist can be regulated, so the plants being weaned receive bursts of spray at less frequent intervals until they are well rooted and can be taken away to be potted.

As the long season of propagation continues through to late autumn and into winter, until the weather turns very cold, we find some cuttings are better with considerably less mist and these go straight to the weaning bench. Even on the main benches there are heavier and lighter areas of mist since it tends to spray in an umbrella burst, leaving drier patches between. Here, where the mist is less dense, one may see a tray of soft-leafed cuttings starting to wilt. By moving them under the denser areas of mist, and by putting a pan of cuttings which resent too much moisture into that same spot, everything will be satisfied. Some cuttings which rot all too easily are better outside, in covered frames which must also be watched every day.

It is a lovely sight and smell in the propagating house. Everywhere is packed with living things struggling to survive. Almost every inch is covered; benches are full, the floor too. The space under the benches and even the paths are covered with trays and boxes, leaving just enough room to step through. Among the plants beneath the benches are boxes of ferns. During the winter we collected fronds of *Polystichum setiferum* 'Acutilobum', a very dainty, lacy-looking fern, one of the few which manage to survive in our dry East Anglian climate, in a favoured spot. It makes velvety brown knobs along the top side of the central vein on mature fronds. These knobs develop into baby ferns if the frond falls into a suitably damp and empty space. We take them in October and November and break each frond partly through in several places so that it will lie flat on a bed of peaty, sandy compost. We cut most of the old leaf close to the central rib and can lay them fairly close together on top of the compost, pinned down here and there with a 'hairpin' of bent wire. No soil is put over the fronds. Then the trays are put on a warm bench and covered with sheets of glass. Each day the glass is wiped to prevent heavy droplets rotting the small buds. Once the tiny fern fronds begin to unroll the trays are put on the floor beneath the bench. The trays could be stood in a cold frame where the little ferns would develop more slowly, but they must be prevented from either drying out or becoming too wet.

By the end of April, the trays are filled with rows of tiny ferns, while long thin roots will be delving down into the soft compost. Now they can be divided and potted individually to spend the summer outside under the shelter of a shade tunnel.

Some cuttings which take a long while to root make a heavy callus over the cut base of stem. Then they tend to sit, sulking. We watch for these, take them out, and with a razor blade or sharp knife, wound the callus in several places and put the cuttings back. They usually root fairly well after that.

Something guaranteed to make me cross is the sight of a pan of cuttings bearing flower buds. I may even explode if I see them in flower. While the cutting carries a flower bud it will direct most of its attention to maintain that flower, hoping ultimately to reproduce itself with seed. That is the whole object of its being. When the flower is removed hormonal changes take place and everything is directed to keeping the cutting alive. Only then will it turn its full attention to making roots and developing growth shoots. There are exceptions: some lusty cuttings manage both flowers and roots. But many flower-bearing shoots never make roots. Periwinkles, *Vinca*, are examples of this. In general, when taking cuttings of herbaceous plants, it is best to select new growth shoots without flower buds if possible.

For weeks we have peered under the frame-lights to look at blank, grit-covered pans and trays of seed. Then, suddenly, as if they could no longer wait for kind spring weather, they are bursting through in all shapes and sizes. It is always a thrill to see the germinating seedlings at last.

I was surprised to see two trays of *Aconitum* 'Ivorine'. (This elegant plant is rather like a small *Delphinium*, growing about 2 feet (61 cm) high, with narrow spires of creamy-white hooded flowers in early May or June.) In each tray was a single, large plant which had germinated last spring. This, and the label, showed that these pans had been saved from last year's sowing, when only one or two seeds had germinated. Now both pans are full of newly germinated seedlings. In another frame I found the same thing had happened with *Cimicifuga ramosa*. (This is a superb autumn flowering plant standing over 6 feet (2 m) tall, carrying slender bottle-brushes of tiny, fluffy white flowers.) I have sown seed of this plant many times but it has not germinated. Do both these plants need a period of double dormancy, or have the strange winter conditions, alternating mild and freezing weather, affected their germination? *Rosa glauca (R. rubrifolia)*, grown primarily for its rose-stained pewter-grey foliage and clusters of luscious hips, has also germinated like mustard and cress. This is another plant which sometimes takes two years to germinate, but I think the right weather conditions may have some effect in breaking dormancy.

The seed frames must also be watched regularly, to see that the pans do not dry out. The young seedlings grow slowly in this unseasonable wintry weather. Few seem to be affected by the early morning frosts. Any which looked slightly damaged, showing browned or transparent leaf-edges, are put into a plastic covered tunnel which, at this time of the year, is warmer during the day and usually a degree or so warmer at night. The length of time a young plant is subjected to frost is relative to the amount of damage done; in the tunnels this is considerably less than outside.

As soon as any of the more vigorous seedlings grow away well enough to be handled, they are taken to the potting benches, potted individually and again put under shelter until they have formed new roots and are strong enough to go outside. Once the weather warms up there will be a rush to pot the young seedlings before they become spindly. If that happens, some can be cut down and allowed to grow again, but not all plants can be treated that way.

A label is put into each pan to tell the potter how many plants to pot, whether to keep the pan or throw the rest away. It is very tempting to go on potting healthy seedlings, but we have to remember that space for other plants is more valuable than too much of the same thing.

This is the last Saturday in April. After a cold drizzly day, Andrew and I were sitting having tea, looking onto the tree of *Magnolia × soulangiana* which now fills the large south-facing picture window. We planted it twenty-five years ago, a young slip of a tree dug from our previous garden, bearing seven blooms. Today it shades the terrace and bears many hundreds of white blossoms, but we were commenting how much smaller the flowers seem to be this year. The tall shrub of semi-double bright pink *Camellia* 'Donation', is also looking poor. There is scarcely an open flower below my head when I stand beside it – all were frozen in tight bud, while among the open flowers there is not a single perfect bloom. I think the buds on both these spectacular trees were damaged during the severe frosts of February. The blooms must have been malformed or deformed then.

As we sat pondering the half-opened flowers on the Magnolia and enjoying showers of white blossom on the Great White Cherry, *Prunus* 'Tai-Haku', in the distance, it suddenly began to snow; large, wet, fleecy flakes mingling with white petals. Persistently it fell, for about an hour, and then suddenly stopped. A thrush sang thankfully outside the window. The garden is full of nests. Silly young thrushes with yellow gaping bills stand around, hunched and tailless, waiting to be fed, saved for another day only because Emma, our part-Siamese cat, prefers a warm chair by the office stove. I wonder how many heaving, naked little bodies have perished in the cold this past week.

April has been a most capricious month, with smiles, tears and frowns; warm temperatures for the time of year have alternated with dreary days of cold sleety rain, bitterly cold winds and over-night frosts.

MAY

WHETHER awake or asleep, my thoughts and dreams are dominated by the prospect of Chelsea. Yet now the day-to-day routine of running the nursery and garden smoothly must take precedence.

When you see the spectacular displays at this famous show, you might think that exhibitors have nothing else to do but plot and plan to make them so. Far from it. Although it may be chosen as the loveliest time of the year, the Chelsea Flower Show could not come at a more inconvenient time. Everything – just everything – inside and out, is screaming for attention at this most hectic time in the plantsman's calendar. Pans of seedlings appear to be more uncomfortable with each day that passes. New shoots needed for cuttings put on an inch a day if we take our eyes off them, and quickly grow too long and leggy if we miss collecting them at the ideal stage. Stock beds of parent plants needed to supply enough cuttings must be overhauled, pruned and top-dressed, or entirely replaced if lost in a bad winter, or again, if they have lost vigour, because they have become elderly.

Many groups of plants are propagated by division or splitting. Ideally, this should be done before the top growth is too advanced. The plants are dug and divided into suitable-sized pieces. Enough are containerised for selling later in the season, and as many or more pieces than were originally dug are replaced to make stock for another year. One must always look several years ahead. Today we harvest the stock of past years' planting. Now we must put back plants which need time to become established before they are divided again. When I began my nursery I learned this lesson, particularly with hostas, when I had only small quantities of a few varieties. I split them every year, hoping to achieve greater numbers quickly. But I soon noticed that the vigour of my plants deteriorated. For example, *Hosta fortunei* 'Albo Picta' normally has quite large, broadly ovate and beautifully variegated leaves when well established in semi-shade, but hard splitting produced very small, narrow leaves, looking quite uncharacteristic when potted and ready for sale. Subsequently the plant took at least two years to reproduce its best form. Now we have a system of three-year rotation. We dig one third of our stock, divide it, pot some for sale, and replace the rest. Next year we take another third. In this way each section has enough time to recover and increase, while the plants we sell show their true character.

At present there is something which could be called hosta-fever stalking the land. Collectors proudly boast of literally hundreds of named forms. In Europe and America hybridisers are busy creating varieties which are 'new' and 'different'. Some are certainly distinctive and worth recording, but to my mind far too many look too alike.

Like tulip-mania, the first few are snapped-up at any price by those who love to have the latest curiosity. To be fair, certain hostas are worth more than the average price of more easily produced plants because of the time, literally years, that it takes to build up stocks of a new variety in sufficiently large quantities. Micropropagation is certainly shortening this time, but it is still not totally reliable for some of the best variegated forms. (It may well be that any difficulties will have been overcome by the time this book is published.)

The biggest tree in my forest of worries, casting shade over all the good things which might make me feel complacent, is the unsolved problem of what will be the best formulae for our potting composts and which will be the most reliable machine to mix it.

When I heard that a well-known nursery in East Anglia had recently installed a machine recommended to me by both suppliers and the Agricultural Advisory Service (ADAS) I telephoned them to ask if I might see it in operation since that is the only way to find out about the problems and benefits involved.

Thus, on the second day of May, Keith and I set off to drive through the lovely Suffolk countryside on a perishing cold morning. We were met and welcomed by an enthusiastic young man in charge of the large and very efficient tree and shrub unit. We soon saw the problems we had envisaged. The machine we had in mind was only the tail-end of an elaborate (dare I say Heath-Robinson) construction of hoppers and chutes and pulleys required to feed-in all the various ingredients of the final mix. As I am the most un-mechanically minded person, it seemed altogether too complicated. Too much, for my nervous temperament, could undoubtedly go wrong. However, at any nursery I find many other helpful things to see and reflect upon. We discussed windbreaks, evaluated thermal blankets used as frost protection, looked at different types of shelter construction – information which was stored away in my notebook for use at a later date. By the end of a chilling morning we were thankful to thaw-out over a welcome pub-lunch. Then we visited the nursery's large production unit with all the latest facilities for propagation of trees, shrubs and plants. A huge glass-covered area luxuriously maintained a temperate atmosphere all the year round. No frozen fingers potted here. The whole area was subdivided by floor-to-ceiling plastic curtains which pull open and shut at the lightest touch. Under-floor heating gave the boxes of cuttings no excuse for not rooting. A section called a fogging room was filled with an almost still white mist rather than the heavier droplets of mist propagation which we saw in another section, together with a small area of micropropagation. We were shown all these very efficient aids and we duly admired them, but I was also impressed by the overall personal care and attention which resulted in floor after floor of evenly produced young plants, from seed or cuttings growing on and waiting to be transported to the containerising plant.

Most important, perhaps, was a compost mixer which might be the one we are looking for. This machine seemed much less complicated than the one we had seen during this morning and had the practical advantage that it had been in continual use for six years – and another had just been ordered.

We came away finally, feeling exhilarated and encouraged, largely perhaps because of the friendliness and keen desire to help which these fellow plantsmen had shown. My notebook contained useful addresses, various formulae and other helpful information which had been given most generously.

However, next morning I woke feeling inadequate and insecure, knowing I still had to make some vital decisions.

It is a treat to have Andrew bring my breakfast tray to me in bed with a large pot of Mate tea and a bowl of home-made muesli. For some reason, the feeling of simple luxury which this gives to the start of my day encourages me to think through my problems before I set foot to the ground. And so, suddenly, I made an unexpected decision. For some weeks we had been planning to make a new potting bench, based on a design given us by ADAS. Although the principle was right for us, I suddenly realised that the design was too specialised; we needed a more flexible working surface. It would be best to make a long continuous run of straight-edged bench where two, or several, girls could pot, and which could also be used as a packing bench in the posting season. On either side of the potters we would make removable work surfaces; one would hold trays of seedlings or cuttings, while the other would have room for filled trays of potted plants out of the way of the heaped potting soil. As in the kitchen, I like enough room within hand's reach for all the equipment needed, to prevent unnecessary movement.

Hurrying outside I found Keith about to carve large sheets of hardboard into the original design. Not for the first time in my career I explained my change of mind and called in the propagating staff to discuss the new proposal; then we made a mock-up of a section of bench to see how it felt. When the details of the simplified design were settled it went ahead quickly and by evening the new bench almost filled one side of the building. To make a smooth, long-lasting and hygenic surface I ordered thick ship's linoleum in matt-black. It arrived next day to make a very smart and practical finish to the job.

As my energy rebounded, having despatched one problem to everyone's satisfaction, I was met in the garden by my solemn-faced builder wondering if I had a moment to spare to look at the house roof. Engaged to repaint the house, he had removed a rotting facia board on the south side and discovered a squirrel's nest full of sprouting acorns. Would I climb the ladder and see for myself the rotted ends of rafters? This felt like the last straw, a matter of days before Chelsea. Climbing down, I felt only tight determination not to be panicked by the unimaginable problems which lay beneath the long, low sloping expanse of heavy tiles. Whatever was there would have to wait.

Sometimes, when agitated by domestic worries, I have found relief plunging my hands into the mindless routine of washing up! Now it was comforting to escape to watering the Chelsea plants.

The day ends with good news of Thomas. Soon he must start proper school, for he will shortly be five years old. There has been much discussion concerning the kind of school best suited for him. Finally, the family, the medical team and the teachers are all certain that he cannot do better than start in the local school, where he will make friends with children who live nearby and who can run to his house or help him to visit them. The local education authorities are also making provision for him and are even considering taking on an extra assistant to help. His mother telephones to tell me that the psychologist, who has put Thomas through some ability tests, has warned her that she may eventually have other problems to tackle because Thomas is unusually bright. He has passed tests normally given to eight-year-old children. Good for Thomas.

The bone-chilling cold won't go away. This is our first Saturday in May and three coach parties have booked to see the garden, but it is such a miserable day for visitors who have travelled far to visit us. Yet, in spite of the cold and wet, there is plenty to see. Although there are flowers in abundance, it is the tender and brilliant tones of green which create the atmosphere. The back-cloth of the garden, with deep base tones of wintry evergreens, has become illuminated as the bare bones of deciduous trees and shrubs are lightly veiled with half-opened buds and tiny leaves.

Slopes of sharp-green grass set off vivid patches of brilliant greenish-yellow hues which dominate the borders for weeks in spring and early summer. Among the first leaves to show this lively colour are the young emerging leaves of *Hemerocallis*. *Valeriana phu* 'Aurea' quickly joins them, forming clusters of rich yellow leaves which I can see from my kitchen window, rivalling the yellow of daffodils beneath the willow trees but lasting much longer. By the end of May they will have become light green, and in June they will produce tall slim stems topped with clusters of tiny white flowers, not very remarkable but creating a dainty effect above ferns or leaves of *Hosta*. Several different hostas have yellow leaves. They create pools of colour which appear sunlit beneath ragged curtains of clouds draped beneath the grey and violet skies of our chill spring.

If only there were a gleam of sun or a touch of warmth to encourage my poor visitors to linger. From my writing table I admire them, bent heads sheltering beneath clustered umbrellas, sensibly shod (most of them) as they plod round the squelchy grass, determined to make the best of it.

Unknown to me, Frances Perry was among my dripping visitors. One of my staff, hurrying in, came to tell me that she was in the nursery. I quickly invited her to thaw out by the office stove where we sat, while she kindly made light of the weather and we enjoyed the unexpected pleasure of a quiet chat in a more relaxed atmosphere than at Chelsea where we usually meet. But I was sad to miss the pleasure of taking her around, to share with her some of my more unusual plants tucked away in hidden corners.

I have just received a parcel of plants from Paul Aden who lives in Long Island, New York. His name is familiar to collectors of hostas, and known to me because he was a good friend and collaborator with the late Eric Smith of 'The Plantsmen' (a nursery for rare plants, well-known at one time in the West Country). They have both done much interesting work with hostas. Gardeners owe Eric much gratitude for his patience with the propagation of unusual plants and for his awareness of a good plant. About twenty-five years ago I visited him at his nursery and he gave me a *Hosta* which looks similar to the plant now sold as *Hosta* 'Frances Williams'. The original *Hosta* 'Frances Williams' was produced, noted and named in America, but the hybridisation which originally produced it has, I feel sure, been made several times with slightly different results. Eric Smith also worked on the same hybridisation and produced several worthwhile plants, all differing slightly. He gave me a piece of one he considered the best, and now after at least twenty years I have a small stock of *Hosta* 'Frances Williams' (Eric's form) which is quite superb, having – I think – larger leaves than the form usually offered for sale, with beautifully quilted blue centres and widely slashed yellow margins.

One day last summer I was delighted when Paul Aden came to see the garden. He came with Harold Epstein, another well-known American plant-collector, over eighty years old, who skipped about the nursery and gardens so full of *joie de vivre* you could not guess his age nor the number of engagements he would be packing into his typically crowded itinerary. We spent the morning looking at practically every plant in the

Hosta sieboldiana 'Frances Williams' growing with
Corydalis cheilanthifolia

garden, but in particular at the hostas. Paul admired Eric's form of H. 'Frances Williams' and agreed it was different, and finer. Now he has kindly sent me three new hostas and a tiny *Hemerocallis*. They are alive, but bleached almost white by the time spent on their journey. We have carefully potted them and stored them under the staging in the propagating house to recover slowly and to be watched and nursed as convalescents.

Sometimes, despite all this outdoor activity, I cannot sleep. It would be nice to use the time to write – when all is quiet and I would not be disturbed. But I do not have the energy or will-power to rouse myself and get up. So I read. Often it is a recipe book.

I have been reading Elizabeth David's latest book, *An Omelette and a Glass of Wine*. It is a delightful selection of her articles written in the fifties and sixties and linked together with observations of today. I enjoy no other cookery writer as I do Elizabeth. She recreates the warm and scented atmosphere of the south, the smells and textures of fresh ingredients. I can almost hear the clatter of tools in the kitchen, the regular swoosh-swoosh of a besom broom over the gravel, a cock crowing in a sunlit yard. Then – a hush except for the buzz of insects when it is siesta and everyone sleeps in the midday heat.

One article refers to Sir Harvey Luke's search through Europe for the strawberry-scented grape. Two or three years ago I was offered a small paper-bag full of white grapes by visiting friends and asked if I would like a cutting. Less than enthusiastic (it was at the end of a long and exasperating morning) I took the untasted bagful, fearing I would not find another inch of space for yet another plant needing a tall, warm wall. Half an hour later, slightly rested, I tasted the grapes. Electrified by the astonishingly rich, strawberry-like flavour, I rushed to find my friends picnicking in the garden, waiting for the reaction they knew would come. Determined to build a wall specially, if needed, I begged a cutting. Later in the autumn, Anstice Shaw brought me several pieces of vine from which grew a number of young plants. Anstice has since died but her vines live. Prompted by the sad and unexpected loss of my friend, I wrote to Elizabeth David to thank her for her books, and to tell her the story of the vine.

A book by Gertrude Jekyll is usually to hand by my bed. Over and over I can read her writing and share the same thoughts and emotions about plants and gardens. And other things too: old houses, houses built of natural, local materials, making homes with roots. It delighted me, when to outward appearances she must have seemed an elderly lady, to read of her pleasure each morning as she hurried along the upper wood-scented gallery of her house, feeling hungry for breakfast and for the life she made all around her.

From her I learned to cook the flower buds of Seakale. We already cooked the blanched stems from under the pots but now we steam the unopened flower buds (rather like purple Calabrese) from unbleached plants, all served with a little melted butter.

One evening I spent an hour or so thinning onions and a small patch of Rocket, *Eruca sativa*. This is an unusual tasting salad plant, with spicy flavoured leaves followed by handsome spires of cream and brown flowers, not unlike a wallflower. Giving some to a friend, she immediately said it tasted like beef (perhaps it does). The flowers are hot. I washed some and added them to onion thinnings, moistened with a little mayonnaise, to make a sandwich filling.

I do not enjoy the waiting days before Chelsea. Most of the plants look as I would wish them to be, but a few are still reluctant, even though I have moved them back and forth from the warmer plastic house to the cool shade house as the weather has changed. A heat-wave would be a disaster, but just a few degrees more of warmth would be gratefully acknowledged by plants and people.

Fortunately, there are other diversions, among them a young woman who has arrived from London to collect flowers for a photographic session. My immediate reaction on hearing about the project was an irritable desire to have nothing to do with it. The plan was to make several flower and foliage arrangements for a calendar, representing the four seasons and all to be made now in late spring. I confess, I thought the idea absurd. Looking at the crestfallen young girl, who had driven down from London to put herself in my hands, I relented and we began to walk round the garden. The large and impressive clumps of orange and yellow Crown Imperials, *Fritillaria imperialis* immediately took her eye, but she was too late; none were fit for the harsh eye of the camera. It may well be that none of the flowers we picked were of use but at the end of our journey round the garden we had found an uncommon mixture of colours and forms. We had tall, straight spires topped with the greyish-purple, grape-like bells of *Fritillaria persica* 'Adiyaman' while nearby the more floppy stems of *F. persica* produced similar flowers but with entrancing curving shapes. The Lenten Roses, which were at their best weeks before, still provided handsome heads of metallic purple flowers even though their centres were filled with handsome fat seed pods. A very late flowering form of Christmas Rose, *Helleborus niger*, gave us several large and well-formed white and pink flushed flowers which repeated the colour of *Viburnum* × *carlcephalum*, whose sweet bunches of rosy buds opening white waxy flowers were filling the garden with scent. Three large flowers (which I have never picked before) of *Trillium chloropetalum*, bright reddish-plum, at least 3 inches (8 cm) across, seemed the perfect focus to draw all these strange tones together and we enjoyed them – but I wonder if they were of the slightest use.

It is the weekend before Chelsea. I am longing to start selecting the best plants and to pack them into boxes and trays ready for the journey to London. Now that everything is so nearly ready I find it hard to concentrate on other matters. The two long tunnels of plants look to me like a scattered jigsaw puzzle that is waiting to be put together to make a picture I could not possibly put down on paper, but which will form, I hope, in my head.

At last it is Monday morning, 13th of May, just four days before we take our first load of plants to Chelsea. It is raining but not cold. Suddenly it is growing weather and the birds sing without stopping. An extra-large trestle table has been brought into the office for Lesley and Winnie Dearsley who are preparing 5,000 catalogues. Each must have a separate price list and order form put inside. Then they are made into bundles of fifty the bundles packed into plastic fertiliser sacks (obtained from our neighbouring farm) because they will (we hope) be stored underneath a rose exhibitor's stand, near to us. When the roses are watered we cannot risk water running into cardboard boxes. Rosie is checking our tickets and passes to enable us to get into Chelsea, while Georgina Cherry is taking care of the daily postal routines.

At such times I remember with amusement my brief career as a school-teacher, when the classroom buzzed like a beehive with everyone engaged in a variety of projects.

Our trolleys and watering cans are painted clearly with 'CHATTO'. We are pleased to let people borrow them but we like to see them returned. Thin, split bamboo canes are used to hold the plant names and these are being painted matt-black. They will scarcely show among the foliage.

At last, Sue and I could start to box the plants. We removed dead or damaged leaves, carefully tied those which needed support, and kept plants which needed similar conditions in the same boxes. (It is exasperating when I am staging to have both dry and damp-loving plants in the same box.) Most of the plants look well, with healthy fresh foliage, and many are in flower, some in bud or just opening. In a week's time all the anxiety and pleasure of doing it will be over. On the practical side, Keith is checking last year's list of all the odds and ends: the materials needed to make our little pool, large sheets of plastic to cover the site, rakes to clear the grass around our stand when we have finished, a dustpan and brush, small brushes to dust off the leaves, scissors, string, many pieces of dark material to hide our large containers, and so on. Large plastic fertiliser bags are filled with crushed bark to finally dress the stand. If a new idea to improve our methods comes up during the show we write it down and put it into our Show-box to remind us. Once Chelsea is over we turn to a thousand other problems which have been waiting for our attention.

It took two of us almost three days to select and prepare our plants. The beautiful large rosettes of *Verbascum* and *Onopordum* were carefully folded and tied upright so that the perfect shape and texture of the leaves would not be damaged. Other growers will be wrapping delicate heads of flowers such as *Iris, Delphinium* and orchids in cotton wool. Many plants have been rejected, but there still seems to be a great number to be packed into the vans.

The first day of staging arrives at last. It is a lovely warm, sunny morning. Two large hired covered vans arrive early, driven by the owner and his son who have always transported our plants to Chelsea with great care. Yet still I am anxious until I see the great pots of ornamental rhubarb, *Rheum palmatum*, unpacked and standing in London as perfect as when they were in my tunnels. Many hands are there to lift the heavy trays and boxes. I hover around making sure that all the right plants are packed. Then, Keith and I leave in our own van filled with all the practical accoutrements. As always, the journey is slow because of the volume of traffic into London. We pass one of our convoy halted in a lay-by with a puncture. 'They can manage,' says Keith. 'We will go on and prepare the site.' This was good judgement, since they did manage and we had laid the sheets of plastic sheeting to protect the grass site and emptied our van before the plants came in. As the men brought in the trolleys loaded with plants I directed where they should be put so that the drought-loving plants were stood along the 'dry' side of my stand and the damp and shade-loving plants in their appropriate positions. There seemed an awful lot of plants already, but the site, flat and empty, 30 ft × 20 ft (10m × 6m) looked very large. It would easily be dwarfed by a few large rhododendrons, but it takes many herbaceous plants to create a living garden-scene. Once we are on our way I always enjoy the first mornings' drive to Chelsea. The countryside looks fresh and leafy. This year the hedges are not so loaded with creamy masses of hawthorn blossom as on previous occasions but apple and lilac trees are in bloom, with laburnum still to come. As we cross Chelsea Bridge I see the

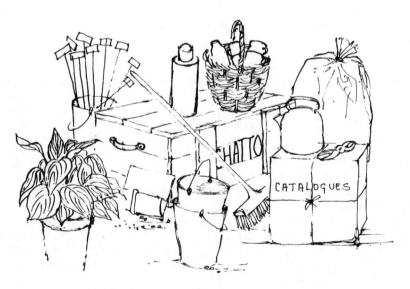

Packing the van for the Chelsea Flower Show

familiar blue and white striped canvas of some of the marquees and my
heart gives sudden jumps of apprehension and anticipation. So far,
despite the winter's worries, our plants look satisfactory, but the last
phase of this adventure, the staging is still, for me, the unknown
element. The principles behind my planning remain the same, but each
year the plants behave differently and I, too, have changed, so the
combinations are never the same.

The feeling between plant people

But always the same is the pleasure we have as we enter the great
marquee and find some of our old friends already there. The feeling
between plantspeople is genuine. You may not see someone for a year –
or several years – but the feeling of kindred spirit remains. It is very
heartwarming. On my return home that evening there are last-minute
things to be checked on the nursery, in the office and finally in the
house. Clothes and food sufficient for three days staging are packed.

Next morning I am in the garden early to find plants for my little pond
and to find a few extra-large hostas for another exhibitor who had
worries yesterday.

By midday, with two more vanloads of plants, we were back in
London. With everything unpacked there was scarcely room to move
around the stand because of the bewildering sea of plants; too many for
comfort I feel sure, and yet I can see at once that we lack really bulky

material for the central groups. The winter losses cannot be made up in one season.

I do not really enjoy the first day of staging, trying to find the main thread of my ideas which will lead me through the next three days; but first I stage the trees and shrubs which are needed to give height to the two main groups. Where and how they will be stood is vital because they set the proportion for the rest of the design. Almost invariably, most of them need to be stood on boxes, or on buckets, to achieve the overall height and bulk needed in relation to the length of the stand.

The 'pond' is put in place below a group of willow and bamboo which are lightened with the delicate pink, white and green tinted young leaves of *Acer negundo* 'Variegatum', and with spreading branches of gold and white forms of variegated dogwood. As each pot is placed it must be watered well and the name attached so it will be seen from a distance and the pot and boxes concealed. By evening I was less than happy, but knowing from experience that a night's rest often produces the solution next morning I was glad to be driven away to our hotel by David Ward who had been my calm and helpful assistant all day. Next morning he resited the pond, giving us more space to build up a design of ligularias, Solomon's Seal and the beautiful white *Dicentra spectabilis* 'Alba', which brought the white tints of the variegated dogwood down to the edge of the back of the little pool. Yet still there was a link missing because the dramatic green and white foliage of a fine Japanese grass *Miscanthus sinensis* 'Variegatus' was not, this year, sufficiently bold to make the feature I needed. Suddenly I picked up a very tall clump of *Arundo donax* 'Variegata' whose long ribbon-like leaves cascaded from strong stems over 6 feet tall. I had intended to use it properly among my Mediterranean plants because it comes from the warm south and can only be used in British gardens if bedded out in summer. Why not use it as we might use a *Canna* or *Phormium* bedded out in summer near the pool? My conscience salved, I put it into place and immediately knew that it was the piece I had been looking for. The rest of the day was spent with hostas, primulas, water iris and other moisture loving plants, fitting together interlocking groups of colour and texture to complement each other.

Around us the marquee was filling as more and more exhibitors were arriving and quietly unpacking; everyone was totally absorbed in the final stages of this most important gardening event of the year. Whether hauling fully-grown trees and shrubs or exotic orchids, there was the same degree of caring, concern, consultation and relief as the teams worked together and the designs took shape; everyone doing their damndest out of love for their plants.

By the end of the day, about 7 p.m., we were glad to relax in hot baths, change our dirty clothes and have a good meal. Before bed I telephoned Andrew, to give him love and good wishes for his birthday today.

It is Sunday morning and we are among the first to arrive, to find blackbirds and thrushes pulling fibrous strips from my pieces of bark and practically queueing up to help themselves from a sack of moss. All day they snatch pieces of wood fibre, sometimes from beneath my hands, then fly off to make nests in other exhibitors' shrubs. By the end of the show, eggs are laid.

Rosie and Madge have arrived to help with labelling and watering, and provide a hundred and one little services throughout the day which ease the strain of staging.

The Mediterranean side of my stand has worried me most. While I have a few fine large shrubs remaining from the winter's losses, I still have to create the effect of established plants by grouping several together and lifting them to appropriate heights. I can scarcely eat, or sit down, fearing to be distracted from putting together the groups which are in my head and which I have yet to find among the sea of boxes. Then, suddenly, the current seems to be switched off; the design looks penny-plain. I have to walk away, to rest my mind and eye, just long enough to refocus.

By 7.30 on Sunday evening almost the last piece of the puzzle had been found. But not quite: two pieces were missing, and suddenly I could not see them among all the bits and pieces remaining, nor had I the energy to kneel and get up once more.

The Damp Garden at Chelsea

Back in my room it was bliss to peel off soaking wet trousers and shoes, to lie as though weighted with lead in a long hot bath, and afterwards to go out and eat together with my young staff who have shared all the emotional ups and downs of creating our exhibit. But that night in bed my feet and legs throbbed from kneeling day after day, and my left hand was sore and swollen from placing and planting.

Our Chelsea lunch table

On Monday all exhibits must be finished, completed before 4 p.m. and all rubbish removed. As I walked towards my stand early after breakfast two plants suddenly appeared before me, tall blue polemoniums, Jacob's Ladder had opened overnight, just what I needed with purple-leafed *Viola labradorica* to make a carpet beneath them. Finally we finished planting either side of the wood-block path of circular wooden 'pennies' which winds through the centre of our exhibit, with ferns and hostas, completely screening the two wooden 'caves' hidden in the centre of the stand where we can store extra catalogues and our personal belongings. Some exhibitors have room for a summerhouse for these necessities. For us, it is a problem we must solve in a different way. Primarily, we depend on the generosity of a neighbouring rose stand whose bowls are lifted on tabling, leaving hiding-places between canvas covered trestles beneath. By 11 a.m. our large hired van had arrived with Keith and Kazu ready to clear away the debris. Anxious to the last, I am found brushing away the last crumbs of crushed bark clinging to any leaves which, if left, would spoil the fresh untouched look I have been striving these past months to achieve. At the same time I am trying to talk politely to an endless stream of visitors, mostly journalists, photographers, radio interviewers, and occasionally visitors from abroad. In the mêlée David is putting the final touch, tacking long pieces of rugged bark to hide the edging board which surrounds the stand. This very simple finish seems just right, partly concealed by foliage creeping over its edges. Last of all, a light mist of water applied with the thumb held over the end of the hosepipe removes the slightest film of dust and restores a true country garden freshness. Overall, the colours of flowers and leaves are soft and gentle, accented or shadowed here and there with darker tones. Thankfully, I can leave the clearing up and return to my room for a short rest. I lie on my bed, adrenalin still throbbing through my veins, yet there is also a deep feeling of relief. Whatever the outcome may be, we have managed to stage another Chelsea and I feel relatively content, to emerge in the late afternoon as clean as bath and nailbrush can make me.

It is a great moment at last, to be dressed for the occasion; to be calmed by a walk through the beautiful buildings and courtyards of the Chelsea Hospital and then into the swept and sprinkled show ground. Not a dead leaf or speck of rubbish remains; every exhibit is complete, with the traditional white ropes set in position, in an attempt to prevent the public falling over the exhibits and exhibitors in their enthusiasm to see everything. Naturally, I go straight to our exhibit to see it properly for the first time, without the piles of empty boxes, damaged or unwanted plants, and all the rest of the paraphernalia which collects around us.

I am always impressed by the layout of exhibits in the main marquee which covers nearly four acres and is, I think, the biggest in Europe. Usually the Chelsea schedule, rules, regulations and application form drop through the letter box before Christmas and we are asked to send the measurements of the exhibit we would like to make. Then, sometime in January, in the depths of winter, the plan of all the allocated exhibition sites appears and already Chelsea fever is incubating. But much care is taken to see that exhibits are sensitively grouped. We do not always have the same neighbours. This is good, because we meet new people, and by the end of the show we have made new friends.

Many people imagine that there must be great rivalry, both for awards and for customers, but this is not so. There are several judging committees consisting of about twelve people each, all experienced and knowledgeable in horticulture. Dark-suited and inscrutable they enter the marquee with papers and pens poised. There are no 1st, 2nd and 3rd class awards as we see them in country shows. If two exhibitors in the same section produce a stand which the judges consider to be worthy of a gold medal then two medals will be awarded. This means that we are not competing against each other, but strive to do as well or better than our previous exhibit. The standard of excellence can be, and is, raised each year. This may not be so in the case of every exhibitor but for many

The Dry Garden at Chelsea

it is, and this makes the Chelsea show a perpetual challenge for us all.

I wander around the widely varied exhibits with time and space to admire them and talk to old friends, also transformed for this special evening. Suddenly there are little flurries of movement; photographers dash around like children playing hide and seek between the banks of flowers and you realise that the royal parties have begun to arrive. Conducted by important members of the Royal Horticultural Society Committee, several little groups make stately progress, often hidden from view until they suddenly appear beside you, while blackbirds and thrushes continue to trill never ceasing fanfares ahead of them. Hearts beat when we are presented to each of the Royal parties, but above all to the Queen. Hands are touched, I make a curtsey (I hope I remembered), some words are exchanged, and the moment has passed. I am left light-headed by the great sense of occasion, but when I feel the ground beneath my feet once more I am conscious of admiration and concern for our Queen, who finds something kind and encouraging to say almost every day of her life to people she meets, concerning their many and varied activities.

Finally, the last party leaves and we may go home. I suddenly feel cold and very hungry. Finding my way back to where we are all staying, I hurry into the dark warmth of our favourite little eating place. My friends have eaten, but are waiting expectantly to ask: 'Who did you meet, tell us about it'. We all share the fun and excitement, while I savour the relaxed atmosphere and a comforting meal. For the first time in a week, I fall into bed ready to sleep, exhaustion blotting out the ceaseless hum of the north-bound traffic nearby.

With the pressure off, I slept heavily, dreaming wild dreams till 6.30 a.m., when a tap at my door had me down to breakfast by 7 a.m. David drove us to the main entrance to let the girls hurry to our stand, while we had to drive round the hospital grounds to the car park. Already, at 8 a.m., the pavements are three deep with crowds, more people hurrying from the Underground station to join the queue on this first day – Members' Day – which is perhaps more crowded than any other during the week. Our usual route to the car park was cut off by road works so it took more time than usual to park and find our way, again, round the stately hospital building and the already crowded avenues to reach our stand by 8.30 a.m. We arrived to find a wall of people around it, hastened to pick up our order books and catalogues and turned to face our audience. Suddenly as though the light had gone out, it became so dark we could hardly see the colour of the flowers. Lightning and thunder followed almost simultaneously and torrential rain hammered on the billowing canvas above our heads. (I suddenly remembered a story told me by Joe Elliott, about his father, Clarence Elliott, who never entered the Chelsea Flower Show tent without a small, very sharp knife. I also thought of all the luckless exhibitors outside who have been

111

rained on throughout the preparations and must suffer yet more soaking.) Visitors suddenly crowded into the big marquee and the congestion was almost unbearable. But soon the rain stopped, followed by sunshine for the rest of the day.

We all need the enthusiasm expressed for our stand; it affects us like champagne when we have been talking, taking orders, giving advice, selling catalogues, answering the occasional silly question and greeting friends from past years for hours, it seems, on end. Just when we think that we are totally drained, a particularly sympathetic visitor not only gives us a great lift, but kindles enthusiasm; sometimes even coerces those around him (usually her) to buy a catalogue, or to visit the garden. We all have a great laugh and everyone feels revived.

The day passed quickly in this euphoric atmosphere – and we did eventually discover that we had been awarded a Gold Medal, our tenth in eleven years; such a feeling of relief now, but not of excitement; only the public can produce that: the pressing crowds stationary around us, the comments which convince us that what we have done is giving pleasure.

Strangely, perhaps, I do not feel that rewarding little frisson of excitement when I see the Gold Medal Card propped against my plants. Relief I feel, yes, great relief. And of course there would be a tremendous emotional response to deal with if my exhibit were not up to standard. But the highs and lows have all been used up in the weeks and months which have led to this moment. There have been many moments of delight and anxiety as every piece was collected and eventually given its place – as every person on the nursery made a contribution at the right time whether directly, or indirectly.

Although the special atmosphere of Chelsea is very exciting, to be on duty from 8.30 a.m. to 8 p.m. is both physically and mentally exhausting. On the nursery we change our positions constantly, but to stand in a confined space for several hours together produces pains in unexpected places. We are confined to a small area about 1 foot (30 cm) wide all around the stand, between the rope and the edge of our stand. Often the press of people finds us with no space at all except to fall into our plants as they push forward to see what we have done. Each year it seems more and more people come to the Chelsea Show, but many go away without having seen the exhibits they most wanted to see. We advise our friends to stay in bed and not bother with the early morning trains. It is better to arrive at tea-time or a little later. By then it is possible for us to see our neighbours' stands, visitors can walk comfortably round the exhibits to see the whole design and find someone free to answer questions. Three hours in the evening of concentrated viewing is as much as most people can absorb without the frustration of peering over other peoples' shoulders and being physically jostled.

For the exhibitors it is disappointing to know that the very people one would like to have shown around the stand gave up in despair and did not even glimpse it. This problem must be giving the organisers much concern. The two-tier ticket scheme, encouraging visitors to see the show from 4-8 p.m., has helped. Members' Day is obviously crowded, but on the first public day costly tickets do not mean a quiet day. One of my staff and I were commenting on the price for the first day. Fourteen pounds each seemed a lot of money, especially when added to the cost of plants which might be ordered, Yet, we reasoned, how else, except in one's own garden, could one have a day's relaxation or pleasure for less? And so it proved; by mid-morning the main gangways in the great marquee were so full of people they were virtually stationary from end to end.

On the third evening I drove myself home, leaving my assistants to complete the show. Leaving London I felt fine for an hour or so, but within half an hour's drive from home my eyelids refused to stay open, weariness suddenly overcame me and I knew I must stop. I pulled the car into a lay-by and slept immediately. I do not know for how long, but the radio was on low and the programme had changed. Feeling refreshed, but also suddenly aware that I might have been apprehended by a police patrol (or a less objective traveller) I finished my journey easily and drove thankfully into my own drive. It was good to be home.

Although I have been away only a week it is exciting to be up and out on a fine sunny day, although there is still a fresh wind out of the East. The garden looks lovely, filling fast with soft fresh foliage and with new flowers opening every day. I try to make sure old friends are not being smothered and that new ones have settled in comfortably. The top-most branches of the Chinese tree *Paulownia tomentosa* are full of blossom and large, pale lilac-blue, foxglove-like flowers are scattered on the mown grass beneath, reminding me to look up. But the lower branches at eye level are bare. The flower buds were killed in winter when the freezing air lay like a lake in the hollow. The few azaleas in shades of soft yellow and apricot give an almost Chelsea-like look, tucked among the many shades of green, while my one *Rhododendron* 'Sappho', now a fine large bush rising high against a dark background of the Serbian Spruce, *Picea omorika*, looks positively opulent with clusters of white funnel-shaped flowers, handsomely marked inside with dark blotches of purplish-black. There seem to be a lot of blue flowers; sky-blue saucers of polemoniums, carpets of ajugas and dwarf phlox stand out along the border edges in soft shades of blue. The ajugas and *Phlox stolonifera* 'Blue Ridge' are to be found along cool, sometimes shady borders, but many forms of *Phlox douglasii* and *Phlox subulata* are making close dense cushions or sprawling carpets in open sunny places.

What should I do now that I was free to attend to the many jobs that had been piling up while Chelsea consumed me? I walked past them all and did the flowers. How lovely to have enough to pick an armful of

113

delicate colour, much of it sweetly scented. As I walked about it was as though perfume was being sprayed throughout the garden but with scents impossible to capture in a bottle. Fluffy heads of *Smilacina racemosa*, *Viburnum* × *juddii* and *V.* × *carlcephalum*, with pink and white buds, *Elaeagnus angustifolia*, with clusters of thin tubular flowers among long, narrow, silvered leaves, all wafted intoxicating perfumes across my path, stirring nostalgia for springs gone by, as perfume does. When I put my face into wallflowers, peonies or border phlox, the sudden response is almost a pain; my senses are kindled once more as they were when I was a young girl in my father's garden.

The weekend after Chelsea is a Bank Holiday so Monday was to be a free day. I was up early to make the most of it. What should I do? Still too bewitched by the week at Chelsea and the thrill of being home, I wandered idly among my plants, marvelling, like every gardener who is away for a few days, at the change in them.

Soon after 9 a.m. a large blue mini-bus appeared on the broad stretch of gravel outside the office window and out tumbled the short burly figure of Heinz Klose, a nurseryman who has entertained me in Germany, and five other sturdy Germans. I hurried to greet them. A huge bear hug from Heinz left me breathless and everyone else in fits of laughter. Heinz speaks no English but his passion for plants is intense, while his frustrated inability to communicate is sometimes rendered comic. Fortunately there were English-speaking members in the party, especially as I have no German to speak of. I was particularly pleased to meet Ewald Hugen, who introduced himself to me as the head gardener from the nursery of Countess Helen von Stein Zeppelin, at Laufen in southern Germany. It so happens that I have been invited by Helen to celebrate her eightieth birthday during the last week of June. We first met many years ago after I had been given an introduction by Alan Bloom who thought we might get on together.

It was with a little trepidation that I made my first visit, in 1974, to her lovely old house and fascinating nursery, but Alan had been perceptive in this as in so many other matters. I am grateful to him for my introduction to the plant nurseries of Germany where there is much for us to learn.

It was a morning of sunshine and showers, but tunnels, shade houses, sale beds, stock beds and garden were all scrutinised by my continental visitors with great thoroughness and enthusiasm. All these men are connoisseurs, travelling world-wide in their search for good plants. But it was not the sin of acquisitiveness which made our morning sparkle, rather it was the joy of talking together about plants and of sharing the common love of growing things. However, a fork and a barrow are always useful on these occasions, as little pieces are pried off here and there from some secret stock tucked well away. Two years ago Graham

Stuart Thomas sent me a generous piece of a double flowered form of *Helleborus orientalis*. Like the skirts of a ballet dancer, flowers hung lightly double in a dusky plum shade. On receiving it I had divided it into two and tucked each piece into a secret reserve bed. Herr Klose, visiting soon after, saw the one flower I had allowed to remain. It was too much, he could not bear to tear himself away and return to Germany without it. With much gesticulation, wide smiles and a torrent of German, he said he had plants at home which had double, pale-pink flowers; would I part with the smaller piece of mine in exchange for the promise of his pink one when available? Amid general laughter I dug the precious piece and handed it to him.

'Do you really need to show again at Chelsea?' I am sometimes asked. I answer by referring to the famous firms who have been showing since I was a child. Undoubtedly the time will come when I will be unable to summon the enormous mental and physical energy which Chelsea demands, but it is the one show we attend, and the very best possible way of making personal contact with old and new gardeners. Although we love to see old friends, both at Chelsea and in the garden, there comes a limit to the plants they can find room for. We need to see new faces and have new addresses in our order-books to bring fresh impetus into the nursery where young people entering horticulture seek a future. It is always uplifting to hear the comments of visitors who walk into our world as though through a magic doorway, discovering beauty in plants they never dreamt existed. It is a magical world for me too, as plants newly introduced come into flower, or a difficult seed germinates; as we discover new methods of propagation, or find new ways to delight our visitors, whether highly-informed specialists or beginners.

For several weeks after Chelsea, everywhere is a buzzing hive of activity; there are many more visitors, propagation is in full swing, garden and stock beds need maintenance. However much I may intend to organise my own day, I often feel like a piece of waste paper, blown from place to place. Dashing around, I hear: 'Can you spare a minute? Someone would like to see you'. 'Could you have a look at . . .?' 'Will you sign this?' 'Can I have a word with you?'

It is vitally important to keep track of stock plants. The main stock beds are generally planted by the propagating staff, but when there are only a few plants, usually in short supply, or newly introduced, I look after these myself, making sure that they are properly labelled and watching their subsequent progress. Some of the plants I have planted this month on the nursery have included *Uniola latifolia*, a handsome, broad-bladed grass with curious seed-heads which look as though they have been pressed with a flat iron. I saw it in seed in a garden in New York and was given some to bring home; now we have a small stock. (Since writing this I have discovered it needs really warm summers to flower well.) *Iris innominata* 'Clotted Cream' was one of my seedlings several years ago, while the pale pink *Primula pulverulenta* 'Bartley Strain' needs to be split to be certain of the true form and so does the lovely cream-coloured *Trollius* 'Alabaster', although when we tried it from seed we found a fair proportion came true. The seedlings must be flowered, however, to be sure you are selling the named variety.

In the garden I am seeking space for newcomers. I try not to need tender plants which must be dug before winter and stored in a frost-free house. But needing is one thing, temptation quite another. My small heated greenhouse is almost entirely given over to the protection of exotica. The dark, purple-leafed cannas and the beautiful variegated form of the tall Mediterranean grass *Arundo donax* are among some of those now planted out to make dramatic points of interest. I need to check plants tucked into 'Pets Corner' (reserved spaces at the ends of tunnels) to make time to plant them in suitable places. Usually it is not just a matter of finding the right place, but of collecting a barrow, filling it with compost, preparing the holes, then carting cans from the pools or taps to water them well in. Once established they are not watered again, but must fend with whatever the clouds deign to offer.

One of my favourite ways to unwind is to spend an evening in the vegetable garden. I love to crouch among the neat orderly rows, thinning onions, parsnips, beetroot and spinach thinking of many delicious meals to come. Provided the rows are short and the hoe is kept moving regularly between them, and one is not searching desperately about in a forest of weeds, it really is a pleasant mind-resting task. The season is late this year, the cold nights make too great contrast with the warmth of the sun during the day, resulting in tardy growth. Dwarf beans have germinated, but their leaves are yellow. They appear not to move, they just sit, looking peaky.

JUNE

Every year I intend to plant my pot gardens much earlier, but my good intentions never materialise. There are always too many other jobs which seem more urgent. The half-hardy plants spend the coldest months in my small greenhouse where a fan heater keeps the temperature around 40°F (5°C). By March, the ivy-leafed geraniums need more room so they are put into a plastic-covered tunnel, and·the weather forecast is watched so that another layer of protection can be put over them if frost is threatened.

On holiday in France, many years ago, I was fascinated by the use of plants in all kinds of containers and situations. The unexpected sight of great leafy hostas among fountains of fuchsias, planted in old petrol cans (or piled-up spent tyres) to decorate filling stations, remained with me. Even more inspiring were tantalising glimpses through old doorways into little courtyards where multitudes of pots, all shapes and sizes, overflowed with anything which flowered, all lovingly tended.

Now I make my own pot gardens, for the summer months, in the little yards near the house and nursery buildings where they are within easy reach of a hosepipe; in hot weather they need watering every day. First I collect together all the pots and containers. I find the groups look best if some pots are raised, so I use light building blocks stood one on top of another to make a plinth. Next a large barrowload of potting compost is prepared. For this I use our general peat/sand mix which contains slow-release nutrients, but I also add a small proportion of prepared compost based on farmyard manure. You can use garden soil with added peat, well-wetted beforehand, but be sure it is sufficiently drained. Heavy clay soils need additional grit and humus – they are not ideal in pots.

Where the pots stand in sun for most of the day I use bold succulents which have overwintered on the greenhouse shelves. There are large, fleshy, blue-grey rosettes of *Kalanchoe*, *Crassula* and *Echeveria* with *Aeonium arboreum* 'Atropurpureum' making a small tree, its tall thick branches topped with large chocolate-brown rosettes. Strong sunlight and heat intensifies this dark colour. These dramatic plants add style and contrast grouped around large tubs which overflow with pink and red pelargoniums peeping through felted greyish-white trails of *Helichrysum petiolare*, formerly known as *H. petiolatum*. This is an invaluable foliage plant. It grows very quickly, weaving around pots and tubs, creating an established look by July, long before the pelargoniums have begun to make a show. Giant tubs of *Agave americana* 'Variegata', crimson *Amaryllis belladonna*, and sky-blue saucers of Morning Glory, *Ipomaea rubro-caerulea* (which should now be called *Pharbitis tricolor*) add to the profusion of colour and form which grows more luscious and colourful as summer progresses.

Against the cooler east wall of the house, beside the back door, stand tall shrubs of *Datura*. Throughout late summer and autumn they flaunt huge trumpet-shaped flowers, peeping into the utility-room window, inviting me to put my face into them and breathe deeply their exotic perfume. I have two kinds. *Datura suaveolens* has long, white, double flowered trumpets, one trumpet inside another, making a whirl of frills like a ballet skirt. The other, whose correct name I do not know, was given to me by a nurseryman, Ed Carmen, with whom I have stayed near San Francisco. The flowers open greenish-cream, but as they mature the wide, fluted mouths flush rose pink, an exquisite sight – and scent. Unfortunately, daturas can be badly infested with Red Spider mite.

Another sweet, hard-to-place perfume, with undertones of almond, comes from the deep violet Cherry Pie Verbena, *Heliotropium peruvianum*. Cherry stones when cooked give off that rich, faintly almond scent. On the cool north side of the house large tubs are almost smothered with the free-growing, peppermint-scented pelargonium

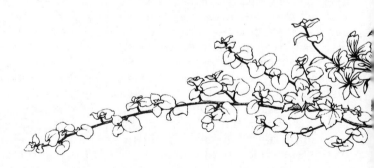

Part of the pot garden

Datura candida

while heavy heads of Regal Lilies provide height as well as an invasive perfume. The curious feathered rhizomes of a little fern, *Davallia mariesii*, creep over the edge of a low earthenware bowl, while the soft, yellow-leafed form of *Helichrysum petiolare* also grows much better where it is not scorched by direct sunlight. Surrounded by white-painted brick walls with a cobbled-and-paved floor, this group makes an inviting entrance to our front door. I feed my pot plants about every month or six weeks with a compound fertiliser, applied dry and watered in. The important thing to remember is to apply it, but not to be too generous. A small teaspoonful to each pot is plenty, unless it is a very large pot. The result is very good, healthy growth with plenty of flowers, so that by August the pots themselves have almost vanished. From time to time it is necessary to trim and prune the most exuberant plants to prevent the whole effect becoming a confused jumble.

It takes time to prepare the pots anew each season, to plant and place them, and keep them fed and watered, but they add tremendously to the atmosphere of my dry 'Mediterranean' garden, providing colour and interest when most plants have finished flowering in the dry borders.

Gradually the greenhouse is almost emptied leaving only the winter house plants which are now resting, or have been hard pruned to encourage strong new growth. Pots of cyclamen lie on the floor beneath the staging in an attempt to dry them off, but I see the persistent creatures are still trying to make new leaves.

So far, this month of June has tried us with teasing weather. Unseasonably cold winds and sombre skies releasing floods of soaking rain have been followed by the odd beautiful day when you cannot take your eyes off the sky, washed clean, a deep, dark blue afloat with dazzling white clouds bowling along, or frozen sunlit mountainous scapes extending the garden into infinity. One such beautiful and innocent day followed an horrendous thunderstorm which swept across the flat, fat farmlands of the Rodings in west Essex, spitefully hurling down 'hailstones as big as golf balls' they said. (Surely an exaggeration I thought.) A day or two later I visited an old friend in the affected area whose porch had been shattered; glasshouses, plastic tunnels and crops in the region had been flattened. My friend was able to produce a newspaper picture of a farmer who had scooped up the hailstones and put them in his freezer before the press arrived. Over the whole area a million pounds' worth of damage had been caused in a few minutes. How thankful I was that our corner of Essex had missed such devastation.

Suddenly the cold winds of the past few weeks have ceased and we all soak up the sun with relish. Everything has grown well in the cool, damp weather, but now, the flower colours are heightened by sunlight, faces have become more cheerful, while the sudden warmth has cast off winter coats and replaced them with pink arms and reddened noses.

The nursery looks well, empty spaces left by winter losses have mostly been refilled. The cycle of propagation – taking new cuttings, potting-on seedlings and rooted cuttings, sheltering them all until they have become established, then putting them outside to harden-off and grow on – is going on every day throughout the growing season. Visitors walk in the gardens where they can see established plants in the kind of situation and association which suits them best, and can then visit the selling area where they can choose their own plants, putting them into the baskets or little trolleys provided. Sue is responsible for the maintenance of this area, with her small team of helpers. She decides when plants are ready to go outside and keeps the sales area well stocked. At the same time she must watch the reserve area where enough plants have to be kept for postal customers. Sometimes it is hard to refuse a customer plants which they can see but may not have because these have already been ordered and paid for by customers who live far away, and who cannot possibly visit us. Postal customers have only the catalogue to choose from, but our personal visitors have a much wider choice of plants which are produced in quantities too small to be listed. Some plants are not listed because they are too fragile to withstand the hazards of the postal system. A charming little plant

121

which comes to mind as an example is *Antirrhinum hispanicum* subsp. *glutinosum*. Low mounds of lax stems with small, slightly sticky, grey-green leaves are practically smothered with chubby white flowers that are stained faintly purple with a bright patch of yellow on the lower lip. They flower for weeks on the edge of a border or nestling among stones on the rock garden. But pot-grown plants, however carefully packed, arrive with brittle stems smashed. Another desirable plant, not well known, is *Silene lempergii* 'Max Frei'. Lolling brittle stems carry a wealth of rich rosy-pink campion flowers for weeks in late summer and autumn among the ash-grey foliage of the dry garden. Plants which survive midsummer drought in light soils sufficiently well to flower enthusiastically in the autumn are to be treasured.

Some plants may be in short supply because they are slow or difficult to propagate. Occasionally I feel tempted to remind visitors that most of our plants cannot be taken down from a wholesaler's shelves like factory-produced cans of beans. They have taken us months, sometimes years, to produce. Every day they must be considered and cared for. Because they cannot complain noisily like a herd of cows, or a flock of hens, it is important that signs of distress are noticed.

When we see plant pots pulled about and left lying on their sides while the customer searches for a larger or 'better' specimen, we know these plants will deteriorate or die if we do not make time to stand them upright so that the evening watering will reach them. We sympathise that the plant in the middle of the group may look the best, but in fact, all are much the same quality. It is the base of the plant where new

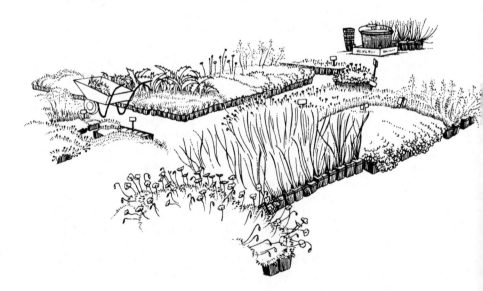

The nursery sales area

122

shoots will emerge, and the good root system in the pot, which will perform well for you when the plant is put into properly prepared soil.

The nursery stock beds

I had spent the morning planting small stock beds of special plants: *Meconopsis* × *sarsonsii* with its delicious tissue-paper petals of soft creamy yellow, and the old *Chrysanthemum* 'Emperor of China', whose closed-fist buds of incurved crimson petals open slowly from the outside edge, each quill splitting open to become the palest-pink petal, while the tight red centre remains to the last as a contrast. *Chrysanthemum* 'Emperor of China' was given to me by Graham Stuart Thomas, who had it for many years, unaware of its true name until he discovered it by chance in one of Gertrude Jekyll's books. The plant was raised prior to 1889. As it was a rare, hot day, a bowl of home-made yoghurt and fruit seemed ideal for lunch. I had just prepared it when my friend Janet Allan, the potter, arrived. We shared the bowl and were sitting chatting when Andrew appeared from his little hide-away study to tell us there was a swarm of bees just outside. Through the open window he had heard the air outside full of agitation. Looking up, we could see immediately, outside the glass doors, the air crowded with frantic bees. Quite quickly they developed a sense of purpose, concentrating towards the end of the bedroom wing. We stepped outside to watch. A vigorous vine, the claret-leafed *Vitis vinifera* 'Purpurea' has been trained over the far side of the white-painted, boarded wall. Soon a small, quivering bunch of bees could be seen clinging to the stout trunk of the vine. Quickly it became a dark, dense cluster of shining, brown bodies which hung like a long dark beard almost to the ground.

The queen must have been safe inside, guard bees, and traffic wardens perhaps, still whizzed about our heads, but we were concerned by the distress calls of blue tit parents who, despite bombarding bees, tried desperately to fly into a small hole (one of several originally made to keep the boarded wall dry) where they had been raising a nestful of babies in the warm cavity. Suddenly a fully-fledged youngster appeared, fluttered out and flopped into the flower bed beneath, cheeping pitifully. By this time I had fled to the telephone to find someone who could come to take the swarm since pioneer bees were investigating other holes in my wall and could well lead the swarm into the cavity behind before nightfall. In the first years of my marriage I kept bees, so I realised we were unlikely to be stung by bees in swarm (unless they are provoked) since they have loaded themselves with honey and are maintaining all their strength and energy to keep the queen safe until they find a new home. But now I had no equipment and did not feel brave enough to shake the swarm into a box. Eventually my call brought a young neighbouring farmer who obligingly climbed off his tractor and came along complete with hat, veil and gloves. He asked for

Collecting the swarm of bees

a small handbrush and soon had both shaken and swept the hypnotic bees into a large cardboard box. He left it almost closed and upturned on the warm, paved terrace, so that disorientated bees would be drawn to it, and all could be collected and rehived in the evening. I hoped the swarm would reward him for his trouble. 'A swarm in June is worth a silver spoon', although 'A swarm in May, is worth a load of hay'.

By now, a second baby blue tit had emerged; it clung to a tall stem of *Campanula latifolia*. Poor little fellow, it was dazed and suffering no doubt from bee stings. Janet lifted it off the plant but it clung to her finger and would not let go. The first little blue tit had ceased its pathetic cheeping and quietly died.

Cooler, damp weather has returned, kinder to our complexions. Motionless clouds cling to the earth, soothing our brief sunburn, making outdoor, mist-propagating conditions for plants. Twice in a few hours I have put on a dry jacket and trousers, but the wet atmosphere is pleasant. I am at last paying proper attention to the show plants which came home from Chelsea. It is one of the few jobs I dislike. Such a confused jumble of pots and boxes to be sorted and decisions to be made at a time when countless other jobs seem more pressing. But this cannot be neglected. Almost all of the smaller plants were sold on the last evening of the show. The few which come back are usually too tired and damaged to be worth the cost of repotting. They are easily despatched to the compost heap. The rest, which are the mainstay of my exhibit, have to be repotted, pruned, fed and watered, to make them better specimens for next year. Surrounded by mud, puddles and plants I have spent a couple of interrupted days, deciding to keep this or throw that, or replant something else in the garden. At the same time, an area of sheltered space, where show plants spend the summer, had to be cleared out and a new, clean sand base prepared. This year I need a larger reserve of well-grown plants in containers since we have been invited to put up a small exhibit at the Sandringham Flower Show. Some of the plants needed for this show were prepared during the winter, but now they too need attention. Like most jobs, when the muddles have been sorted out the work becomes less of a chore. When the travel-weary plants are trimmed and fed it is a pleasure to set them in their prepared site, in orderly fashion, leaving enough room for the tops to grow without touching and room to move around them with a hose. Although we have an overhead watering system, I find the larger pots especially, need the attention of a hand-held hose. During the summer months a young assistant is responsible for this task. Early one morning, however, poking around my newly-sorted treasures, I bent quickly to pick up the hose and felt a sharp pain in the middle of my back. Bent double, I could not move! I called for help but no one could hear; fortunately, neither could anyone see as I gradually unknotted myself and crept on all fours to the door of the propagating house where I could haul myself semi-upright, then creep round the building until I was seen and rescued. Eventually I was helped to the office and finally laid flat on my bed with a hot water bottle. How exasperating, on a lovely morning, to be suddenly so helpless by doing such a simple everyday thing. I lay for an hour, took another hour in a chair, and then managed to walk gingerly outside to a bench where I sat and potted celery plants ready for the vegetable garden. The pain was tolerable, although I still stood like a capital C.

My letter to Elizabeth David brought a friendly response and now, we were going to meet her. She was coming to lunch. 'What on earth will you give her?' my family and friends asked, somewhat in awe. Well, I wondered as I went about the nursery – 'what would I?' I remembered a lesson I learned long ago which applies to most things, and certainly to entertaining. Don't overdo it. Much as we love to offer our best, the important thing is for the effort not to be visible. Of course I would hope to please Elizabeth David, but I wanted to enjoy her too, to have time to talk and show her the garden. What is more, I thought, she would already have sampled the best, and possibly some of the worst, of cuisines, so I decided, 'I shall give her a country lunch, the kind of things we enjoy ourselves'.

The day arrived, the sun shone but the air was cool; snow was forecast in Scotland.

This is what we ate:

Sorrel and spinach soup with warm cornmeal and cheese scones.
Green salad, including rocket.
Potato salad with green mayonnaise, slightly minted.
A cheese plate with wheat-and-oatmeal biscuits and warm
    wholemeal bread – served with wine.

At the end of the table stood a large glass jug of chilled strawberry purée, flavoured with elderflower and frothed with thin yoghurt. Most of the meal, the soup, bread, biscuits and strawberry pulp are basic ingredients of my storecupboard and freezer. The scones and potato salad were quickly made the night before. As I had hoped, Elizabeth was delighted to taste rocket again; it is not often to be found in London shops.

It was a happy, relaxed meal, dipping into little bits and pieces. The nicest compliment is when guests help themselves.

A walk in the garden, full of midsummer riches, ended in the vegetable garden where I was able to fill a trug basket with fresh salads and to include a few plants of rocket for a window box. Garden viewing is tiring so we were glad of a reviving cup of tea and, believe it or not, the comfort of a wood fire. I have never before seen firelight and great bowls of flame-coloured poppies together in mid-June.

Because of the cool weather, the poppies (varieties of *Papaver orientalis*) have lasted in water for days. We have been enjoying them for several weeks. I pick the flowers in the evening, drop them into a deep flower bucket and bring them into the room to arrange them *in situ*. I use fairly narrow-necked pots which hold about a dozen or fifteen large blooms and buds. I cut afresh each stem the length I need and then stand several together for a few seconds in a jug of hot water poured straight from a boiling kettle. This dissolves the sticky sap which would seal the cut ends if they were placed in cold water. You could achieve the same effect by holding the cut end in a gas flame. (Crumpled wire netting was a nuisance in the pots, so it was rejected.) I like these flowers to arrange themselves naturally, as though a handful had been dropped into the pots, with hardly any foliage, except perhaps their own, or a little of the handsome greyish-white leaves of *Centaurea pulchra* 'Major', near the neck of the jars. Standing on the floor against a long low window, they give a simple and dramatic effect.

Curving stems present buds, open flower faces, and shadowed-purple backs, the light filtering through scarlet, crimson, rose-pink and white crinkled petals.

Sorrel and Spinach Soup

This is how to make the soup which we had. Take two or three good handfuls of both Spinach and Sorrel – I use either Spinach Beet or Chard – wash well, remove stalks and central veins. Chop two medium-sized onions in small pieces, cook gently in vegetable oil till transparent, not burnt, then add all the drained leaves. Stir them around and add enough boiling water or vegetable stock to barely cover. Chicken or turkey stock gives a delicious and richer flavour. Simmer till barely cooked, with still a good colour. Put through a mouli sieve, blender, or liquidiser. Add salt to taste. Thin with a little milk, or more stock if necessary. If you have no stock use an egg beaten into thin cream or milk and add when the soup is hot (but not boiling or it will curdle) – this gives a pleasant richness. The colour of the soup should be bright emerald green. It is good, on a hot day, served chilled, with a spoonful of yoghurt.

Here also are the recipes for the muffins and biscuits.

Corn and Cheese Muffins
Sarah Brown's *Vegetarian Kitchen*

4 oz maize meal
4 oz wholemeal or 85% plain flour
1.5 teaspoons baking powder
1 medium-sized onion, finely chopped
4 oz Cheddar cheese, grated

1 tablespoon yoghurt or milk
1 or 2 eggs
1 dessertspoonful honey

Cook the onion in 2 tablespoonfuls of vegetable oil and let it cool. Mix all the ingredients together, adding liquid carefully. Do not make mixture too wet. Spoon into greased bun tins and bake at Mark 6 400°F (200°C). Delicious, served warm and buttered with any soup.

Wheat and Oatmeal Biscuits
(The Cranks Recipe Book)

6 oz 100% wholemeal flour (plain)
2 oz medium oatmeal
1 teaspoon baking powder
0.5 teaspoon salt
3 oz butter or margarine
2 oz dark brown sugar
milk to mix

Mix all dry ingredients except sugar. Rub in fat until mixture is crumbly. Add sugar, mixing well. Add milk (just sufficient to make a soft dough). Put into the refrigerator in a polythene bag to firm and rest (about one hour or the next day when you have time). Roll out thinly and stamp into rounds. Place on greased trays and bake at Mark 4 350°F (180°C) for 20-25 minutes until turning colour. Cool and store in air-tight containers. I usually make double quantities, putting one box in the freezer, while the other provides quick handy lunches with soft cheese and salad.

Strawberry purée with yoghurt

In this dish, the rich grape-like perfume of elderflower greatly enhances the flavour of crushed strawberries. To make the Elderflower Syrup make a strong sugar solution (2 lb white sugar, 0.5 pint water). When this is boiling, I hold a handful of fresh elderflowers by the stalk and swirl them around in the syrup with a wooden spoon, pressing to the side of the pan to extract syrup and flavour; I then put the sticky flower stem into a sieve to drain. The process is repeated with fresh flowers until the syrup is well flavoured. It will become pale green. It is strained, cooled and put into plastic bags and kept in the freezer till required. As ripe strawberries are picked, hulled, and mashed for the freezer I add enough syrup to sweeten lightly and add the flavour of hedgerows. Add home-made yoghurt, ideally made from goat's milk, to the unfrozen purée, beat well or put in a liquidiser with ice to make a delicious summer drink.

Another job which is often not started until after Chelsea (although ideally, it should be done earlier) is dividing the hostas to increase stocks. We have good quantities of some varieties which have been built up during the past twenty years. But others, introduced more recently, are still in comparatively small numbers. The most choice varieties, including the dwarf-blue forms, various yellow-leafed and variegated forms, are all given the most favourable situation I can find to encourage them to increase as freely as possible. The best site is in my little Wood Nursery, where the soil has been double trenched. Well-rotted vegetation, peat and grit have been added to improve the texture and shelter from strong sunlight is found in the dappled shade of a few fine oaks. Most yellow-leafed and variegated hostas produce much finer foliage in partly-shaded conditions.

Some hostas are rare because they have only recently been introduced, usually from America, where breeders are doing their best to invent new forms. 'Hosta-mania' tends to encourage too many new named varieties, not all of which differ greatly from those we already have. But from time to time an outstanding break does occur. Other hostas are scarce because they increase very slowly and cannot easily be divided. This problem is being alleviated by the practice of micro-propagation. Minute sections of virus-free plant are grown on in test tubes under laboratory conditions, making hundreds – even thousands of plants from one small section. This is not always too successful with variegated hostas. Young plantlets do not always appear identical to the parent plant, as a normally divided plant would be. So, for the first few years especially, patience is required to increase a small stock into sufficient numbers to advertise and sell.

When our choice, but scarce, varieties had been divided and replanted, we turned our attention to the main task this year, which was to dig the entire stock of our remaining hostas, prepare enough for sale, and then replant fresh stock beds on our new Damp Nursery where we have spent so much time and effort.

Despite the unusually wet summer, the drainage and soil preparation appears to be successful. The low-lying land is in good heart for planting, while the soil in the untouched wilderness beyond lies black and saturated with water. While trolley loads of divided hostas are being replanted, the next task is being prepared. Our many different kinds of ornamental grass must also be divided. Some containerised for sale, the rest replanted. Although they could have been done sooner, they will suffer no harm now, whereas many grasses that are divided and replanted in autumn almost invariably die. Although we have had a brief warm spell during all this period of division and planting, the persistent cool, damp weather has favoured us. The plants have shown no distress; all are growing away well. Since the hosta leaves were well advanced when they were lifted, many had to be removed and those that remained were cut in half, but this apparent butchery does no lasting harm. It reduces transpiration until moisture-seeking roots are in action again. Within a very few weeks new young leaves are appearing from the crowns. Most of these plants will not be subjected to such drastic treatment next year. They need time to re-establish and regain their strength, to produce good foliage, and increase in stock. Normally about a third of each variety is dug each season, compost is dug in or rotavated into the old site and divided pieces put back to grow on. These will be left undisturbed for two or three seasons to re-establish and develop good crowns.

Ever since the invitation came, in the depths of last cold, long winter, to celebrate the eightieth birthday of the Countess Helen von Stein Zeppelin, I have looked forward to my holiday on her nursery in Laufen among the vineyards and forests of southern Germany. However, the last few days before I go away are full to bursting. There are many visitors, among them old acquaintances who have watched the garden change over many years; people whom I love to meet, to stop and chat with or show them something special. There is so much to see and to do.

I am torn between longing to go and regret that I shall miss something here.

For several days I tried to ignore the pain in my back, but the thought of feeling so ancient on holiday drove me to make an appointment to see an osteopath. His firm hands travelling up and down my spine soon found the cause of pain. What a relief to have one's architecture put back into place. But Mr P. does more than that. He reads the tale the body tells of stress and strain like a book. The shocks and blows of everyday life are absorbed by our nervous system as we try most of the time to cope with problems quietly, in a civilised manner. We cannot scream and yell (as I would sometimes like to do) to let out the occasional rage or frustration. Troubles would only be made a thousand times worse if we reacted with a two-year-old's tantrums. But over a period of time, stress does knot up the body's telegraph system, causing pain, lack of energy, loss of *joi de vivre*. Many people are aware of this and have their own ways of dealing with it. Badminton perhaps, or gardening, or sleeping in front of the television. But sometimes it helps to be shown yourself through another's eyes; teaching you how to help yourself.

It is almost the end of June and we are all wearing much the same clothes that we wore in the winter; long trousers, woollies and often an anorak against the everlasting cold wind. Looking at the weather maps shows that southern Germany is faring no better. So I have packed half and half – hoping a summer dress or two will be needed, but putting in another winter shirt in case the cool spell lasts. (It did.)

The plane was scheduled for 4 p.m. so there was time to take a last look round my domain, and say goodbye to everyone, including Emma, the cat. It is hardest to say goodbye to Andrew, who has long since refused to give up the peace of home for gallivanting abroad.

Keith drove me to the airport. Because I am not often away, every new scene and event is a novelty I can immediately enjoy, since I am not responsible for anything except myself.

The flight was scarcely more than an hour. As we crossed the south coast I could see France through thin cloud, and then it seemed no time at all before the plane was losing height to come down in Basel, Switzerland. As the map-like pictures below me became clearer I could pick out villages, farms, towns and rivers. I remembered Alan Bloom telling me of his visits to German nurseries before the Second World War, of the friendships he made and the concern they all felt at the impending war, not knowing if they would meet again. Somehow, despite having to make way for food crops, plantsmen held on to their treasures, and to their friends. When the war was over, they travelled again and welcomed each other in their houses, speaking a common language: the language of plants. So it came about that I am indebted to Alan for my friendship with Helen. When, as a young girl of twenty years old, she inherited the lovely old Meierhof in Laufen, she was determined to be a plantswoman even though it was not conventional, those many years ago, for a young lady to contemplate such a career. But the determined character, which shows today in the proud tilt of her head and remarkably upright carriage, has taken her through more than fifty years of ups and downs running her nursery. Without belittling our own gardens and nurseries, I am inclined to think the Germans are even more enthusiastic about herbaceous perennials than we are. Many good plant introductions, especially named cultivars, have come to us from them. I always see new plants and learn new ways when I visit nurseries in Germany. But it is not all serious and businesslike. There is a sympathetic understanding, although we cannot always communicate directly (I have almost no German and rely on interpreter friends).

There is much delight in recognising together good plants, and warmth, expressed by plant exchange, perhaps a hug or much laughter.

At the Basel air terminal I waited alone in the milling crowd until with sudden pleasure I saw a member of the family coming to meet me. Then followed a drive of about fifteeen miles into the beautiful countryside of the Schwarzwald, the Black Forest. Soon I was recognising the old cherry trees along the road sides, grassy verges full of flowers, narrow winding roads between the vineyards and little fruit orchards. We passed through pretty old villages where almost every house is a farmhouse, or wine cellar, with great piles of wood already stacked to dry for winter, where chickens run about freely.

Suddenly the car has turned alongside a high wall and passed under tall lime trees into a broad, gravelled courtyard that is surrounded on three sides by a beautiful old house. In the centre stands a wrought iron ornamental well-head, bearing a lamp and covered with a cascade of old roses, with water dripping into a large hexagonal tank. Assembled nearby stands the family: son, daughters, grandchildren, who have come to celebrate the birthday. Most of them are unknown to me, but as I get out of the car (a little apprehensive to see so many strangers) two children come forward to shake my hand and greet me. They speak no English but the style of their welcome is touching. Suddenly, the dear familiar face of Susan Weber, Helen's companion and assistant for forty years, appears by my side and I am hurriedly taken to my room to refresh myself so that I may join the party below. As I descend the wooden stairs Helen comes to welcome me. She leads us all into the library where we sit to listen to a flute and piano recital; the first event to celebrate her birthday. It is as if I have dropped off a magic carpet. To have suddenly arrived out of the sky, scarcely three and a half hours away from the bustle and pressures of my own life, into this special family occasion – to gradually feel calmed by the music, dropping like cold water into the high shaded room – is an unforgettable experience.

Next morning the house was a-bustle with preparations for family lunch so I made my way to the nursery where Helen and her dog were already involved in day-to-day affairs. The nursery lies a few yards beyond the entrance to the house. Passing through a little latched gate one finds a narrow path bordered with many familiar plants. Frothing heads of *Alchemilla mollis* almost smother the path, making a soft setting for hostas, oriental poppies and peonies. Tall creamy plumes of *Aruncus dioicus* tangling with pillar roses on either side – it all looks very familiar, reminding me very much of Cedric Morris's garden.

Soon we drop into plant talk, passing slowly among borders and frames, the air full of the scent of old roses and Orange Blossom, *Philadelphus*. An unfamiliar plant caught my eye, 4-5 feet (1-1.5 m) tall, narrowly columnar, it stood isolated on the edge of a path. Leafy stems were topped with tall spires consisting of whorls of tiny, tubular lilac-mauve flowers. By the end of ten days, when I had looked at many plants, I remembered it still for its colour and form, but it had not, as yet, been propagated. The day I left, Ewald Hugin, the young head of the nursery, dug down and cut off a small section of the tuberous rootstock and brought it to me with only a vestige of root and a few large floppy leaves which had to be removed.

Could it possibly survive? On my return home I dusted the cut surface with Captan (a fungicide which helps to prevent rotting), potted it carefully in a well-drained compost, and put it on a sheltered bench. I watched it daily, willing it to live. Before too long new leaf shoots emerged, and by the end of summer I had a fine healthy plant. It is called *Phlomis tuberosa*. I don't think it is often seen in English gardens, but it is listed in Graham S. Thomas's book *Perennial Garden Plants*, where I see it was introduced in 1759 and is found wild from Eastern Europe to Siberia. Graham tells me he saw it in the botanical beds at Kew Gardens. I hope it will look as effective in my garden as I thought it did in Laufen. Then, if it is admired by visitors, we will propagate it, by a less drastic method no doubt, hopefully from seed. (Since writing this, I have visited the nursery in North Germany of Herr Ernst Pagels, who selected this superior form which does not set seed, so must be propagated vegetatively.)

This first morning on the nursery was the actual birthday of my friend, but you would not have guessed it as she wore her normal gardening clothes and led me enthusiastically around. Not, that is, until we reached the office, where she showed me her desk. All papers had been removed and replaced with an intricate design of flower-heads and leaves, made for her by some of the young staff. Around the room on the floor and tables stood great bowls of garden flowers. Throughout the morning neighbours, old friends and young women in aprons came walking through the gardens to find her and present their gifts: flowers, home-made cakes, a bottle of wine – simple things, given with warm hearts. Everyone shared the happiness of this lovely day; the sun had banished the great piles of cloud which had earlier hung low over the mountains, and the air was warm and still. Soon it was time for the ceremonies. The Mayor and important people from the village were due to arrive at any minute. There was time for me, before I must change for lunch, to steal into the vineyards and look at the view. I walked slowly up through the nursery and, turning round, stood waist-deep in a small field of paeonies where I could see the village below and the country stretching for miles around. It is a comforting landscape, making me think of an illustration in a child's story book of the old-fashioned, happy-ever-after kind. Warm russet tones of tiled roofs, cream-washed walls and timbered buildings peep from among sheltering masses of fine old trees – lime, sycamore and walnut – all providing mixed shades of green. Drawing the whole scene together is the church, which stands just below the nursery. Its narrow spire rises high above the village, while four clock-faces set in the cream-washed tower chime the quarter-hours away into infinity in this little enchanted valley. Behind and beyond the village lie well-tended vineyards, stretching far up into the valley along shallow slopes. Here and there are planted tiny orchards of cherry, apple or pear, while often along the roadsides are the remains of very old cherries and walnuts.

There are small orchards of black cherries used in making the famous Black Forest Gateau, a rich chocolate cake, split and filled with large, juicy fruit – a little Kirsch perhaps, made from the stones, and finally coated with whipped cream. I prefer to eat the cherries fresh from the trees but it is sad to hear the familiar tale: that it is getting too

133

Laufen, a village in the Black Forest

expensive to grow them. The costs of production, of picking and marketing are often not covered by the price fetched in the market for a commodity which has no shelf-life.

The vines stop where the land becomes steeper, rockier, and less fertile. Above them, dark shades of spruce forests clothe the mountain tops, relieved here and there by bright emerald slopes which provide pasture for cattle and sheep. The far-away mountains form a bluish backcloth, heavily forested, the skyline broken here and there by a low pass. Sometimes fine, white, wispy clouds accentuate the dark blue sky when the whole scene is sunlit. Now and then, massive clouds of purple and grey enhance and magnify the mountains, trailing veils of rain as they slowly drift across the scene, drenching the rich forests and farmland. A small, winding road twists and turns between the vines which lie like a great patchwork quilt around the village, and disappears between the contours of the land.

Just in time, I remembered to hurry down to the house to make myself presentable for the family lunch. It was the one day of the holiday when it was warm enough to wear a summer dress.

By mid-afternoon everyone retired for a siesta. It was not difficult to sleep. But about 5.30 p.m. I awoke and lay listening to the sounds outside: chickens, blackbirds and a donkey braying in a farmyard nearby. Suddenly, I heard the sound of two tractors and trailers crunching onto the gravel below. I looked out and saw that they were prepared with boxes and trestles for a trip round the vineyards. (Apple growers sometimes do this at home, taking family or friends around the orchards on Sunday afternoons.)

The eldest son, who runs the family vineyards, led a large party, mostly of young people, children – and myself – through the village and into the narrow lanes full of the smells of summer. We dodged the wild rose briars and let the tall, feathery grasses brush our hands. There were beautiful views at every turn as the trailers circled the low hills contoured with vineyards and we could look down on the village below, gilded in evening sunlight. But it was not all light-hearted. We stopped to inspect the severe winter damage where many vines and young fruit trees had been killed. Later, sitting in the garden, the German language rumbling around me with the occasional translation, I felt at home knowing they were discussing much the same kind of family or business problems as we would be doing in England.

Each day I enjoyed the freedom to do as I wished – to walk, take a drive, or write in my room, something that I rarely have the peace to do at home in summer. Often I spent the morning on the nursery, free to enjoy it without the responsibility. Always there is much to learn about new plants and new methods. Not all their ways would be suitable to us, but every new aspect gives me something to think about, to consider, in relation to our own methods and practices.

After lunch I retreated to a little world of my own in my room. A large table stood across the tall, shuttered windows where I sat most afternoons, looking down onto the other two sides of the courtyard. Immediately to my left was the central portion of the house, while the wing opposite showed a façade of archways curtained with *Vitis quinquefolia* which hung from the eaves, almost to the ground, practically screening the cars parked on the cobbled floor where carriages stood in years gone by. In the centre of the gravelled courtyard lies a large octagonal stone tank filled from a well beneath. The pump is attached to a handsome pillar surmounted by decorative wrought-iron from which is suspended a fine old lamp. Although the effect is most

The courtyard of the Manor House, Laufen

decorative, the purpose of the water tank was originally practical. Here, Helen told me, great piles of straw were brought to be soaked and trodden to form tough strands. Then they were used to tie up the young shoots of the vines.

From my window I looked onto the vast sloping roofs which sheltered the central block and the opposite wing of the house. Here and there the level of tiles was broken by small ventilating windows, each wearing its own scale-covered roof like a cape. In the attics above me lived several students who worked on the nursery, absorbing much more than a training in horticulture from this lovely old house. I too felt the past and present seep into my veins and feed my imagination. The monotonous call of ring-doves, and the liquid notes of blackbirds rising and falling above the steady splash of rain falling on the gravel below, made my heart ache. Beyond the village I could just catch a glimpse of vine-clad hills rising in gentle mounds to melt into the dark forest mountains beyond. There was a feeling of timelessness. I walked across the polished floor boards, smooth as silk beneath bare feet, to the high-sided, elaborately-carved bed, in the depths of which I slept immediately, like a child.

The big event of the week was to take place on Saturday evening. More than a hundred nurserymen from all over Germany were coming to an evening party to celebrate the special birthday of a much-loved colleague and friend. The evening before, Susan and I picked armfuls of flowers from the nursery stock beds. It took almost till dark, searching the paeonies (almost finished) to find enough good blooms, but there were plenty of delphiniums, campanulas, old roses, iris, great plumes of Goat's Beard, *Aruncus dioicus* and heavily scented branches of Orange Blossom, *Philadelphus*. Then we picked many little flowers for the supper tables. All were placed in buckets and bowls standing on the stone floor in the service entrance, where rows of gardening boots and shoes stood on one side, two chuntering washing-machines on the other. By Saturday morning a dozen long trestle tables and benches had been set up in the carriage lodge (now the garage) behind the curtain of vine leaves. We carted the bowls and buckets of flowers across the yard, collected containers and dozens of saucers, plus invaluable plastic foam, to make the decorations.

Two electricians climbed up and down ladders and trailed leads between our feet as they put up extra lighting. The sound of a flute floated out of the house. The young cook-housekeeper, who arrived in her little car every morning just below my bedroom window, was busy before 7 a.m. and soon a party of young helpers were dashing about the kitchen, or seated at the long scrubbed table chopping, mixing, beating and rolling. All kinds of delights were being prepared. By mid-afternoon there were flowers everywhere and all the mess was swept away. The kitchens and pantries were filled to overflowing with dishes, platters and bowls of food which were as decorative as the aroma was tormenting.

The guests from far and near were expected for 7 p.m. when a group of young folk dancers were also due. All afternoon the skies had looked ominous. Suddenly, at 6 p.m. as I was sitting at my window, I watched torrential rain pouring into the gutters and across the yard below, washing rivulets through the gravel to form shallow spits and sand banks. But by 7 p.m. it ceased, everyone arrived, and the evening began. A group of a dozen young couples from the village, wearing costumes that had been handed down to them, danced to nostalgic old tunes, regardless of the wet ground. The men wore red waistcoats, full sleeved white shirts and broad-brimmed black hats. They looked very dashing. Like hen-birds, the girls wore more muted colours, with soft embroidered bodices and long, full skirts with white petticoats and aprons. When it was finished, we parted the curtains of trailing vine to sit in the shelter of the old coach bay where the side tables were loaded with supper. Such a feast: cold meats of every kind, a score of different colourful salads, cheeses, great baskets of unusual breads, dishes of paté and many other unnameable confections. I had thought I might feel a little lonely in this great gathering of friends who all greeted each other with great shouts and much laughter, but suddenly I was approached by a tall stranger who put out his hand, called me by name, and introduced himself. He was joined by others and soon I was being invited to other nurseries and botanic gardens – invitations which I could not accept at that moment, but which I hope to follow up one day.

Then I was twirled round to see several familiar faces: people who have visited my home and garden. There was much laughter and rumbling conversation as we collected plates and sat all together at one of the long tables. The wine flowed. We refilled our plates, or piled fresh ones, with home-made gateau, fresh strawberry ice, or the nicest-ever-I've-tasted chocolate mousse.

Then Anka, the top student on the nursery, appeared with her flute (it was she who had been practising) and with her she brought a little group, all members of the nursery staff, whom she had trained to blow into empty bottles, each producing different notes. Together they played an enchanting piece. It was an amazing performance which received tumultuous applause and had to be repeated.

While our attention was being diverted by the musicians, other young people had placed night-lights, protected in fruit jars, all around the courtyard, outlining the curving steps to the main entrance and along every window-sill, even the attic windows. The effect was magical.

Then came gifts and flowers for Countess Helen. She responded with a speech which paid tribute to her staff and expressed her warm regard for everyone gathered there. This was a party for plantsmen and their wives, most of whom had come a long distance. All were sensibly dressed. Ample German hips were encased in decent warm skirts. Shawls and cardigans were much in evidence. I was foolish enough to wear a rather thin jersey suit (having decided to look relatively smart for a change) but as the evening wore on I shivered in the chill damp air that rolled down from the hills above and was grateful for the rug wrapped round my shoulders by a more experienced guest.

I was interested to meet the grand-daughter of George Arends. Between the wars the Arends nursery had been famous for its introduction of new cultivars of asters, astilbes and other herbaceous plants. One evening, Helen had shown me an old catalogue in which I found listed many of the plants we grow and sell, making me realise how much we owe to the past. Comparatively few of our plants are new. They may be new to us, but many were grown and enjoyed by several generations of civilised gardeners before us. George Arends' grand-daughter still runs the nursery, and she told me that her daughter was in England visiting Alan Bloom and Beth Chatto's nursery. It is good to know that his famous name, Arends Nursery, is being carried on by the descendants of the original founder.

At midnight I went up to my room. Candles still flickered on the windowsill and many more lay like a sparkling necklace on the ground below. Through the tracery of vine leaves I could see the long tables covered with green cloths, the posies of mixed flowers, the orange-painted seats and the sparkling fairy lights. In the centre, still talking animatedly to a few old friends, sat the small, beautiful woman who had inspired the events of the whole day.

On the last day of my holiday I went down to breakfast to be greeted by Helen. I suddenly saw that my place at the table had been garlanded with flower heads and leaves, arranged by Anka who must have got up very early to pick them. This time it was for *my* birthday. On the nursery everyone joined in warm greetings and then I helped to wrap and pack the best of gifts: a collection of tiny plants which I could carry home. Just a seedling, or rooted cutting, is enough to make a start with an unknown plant. I also had to find room for a box of plants from Herr Klose who had brought me a double flowered form of *Helleborus orientalis*, a creamy-white flower speckled with pink which amazingly, still had a flower on it, giving me the chance to see how lovely is this great rarity. Such a treasure will take years to build into a saleable stock, but it is a joy to have even one plant. This was Herr Klose's gift to me in exchange for the double plum form I had given him about two years ago.

One of the nicest things about going away is the homecoming. After only a day or two away from familiar surroundings you see things differently, but after a holiday your mind is refreshed and all your senses sharpened. That is not all. You have absorbed a different landscape and begun to feel at home in rooms no longer strange. Even the unfamiliar smells, which struck you as you first entered, have meaning. Perhaps the most intimate part of every home is its own characteristic smell, created by the lifestyle of the people who live in it. I am not referring to the days when we burn the potatoes or when the cat has been sick. After returning from the Black Forest I was immediately struck by the smell of my house. Living in it every day we do not notice this compound perfume which reassures us we are back on our own territory, but as I stepped through the door it was there. It was partly the scent of last year's pot-pourri which I am rarely conscious of, except when I stir up the bowls and put my head low over them to breathe in the faded scents of last summer.

It is exciting to be back with Andrew, so much to tell and to share. I was shown the table full of cards and gifts to be opened, and flowers arranged for my homecoming. So heart-warming, so good to be back in my own home. Next morning I could hardly wait to be outside to see how everywhere looked. Usually, when we have returned home from trips away in midsummer, it has been to find the countryside parched, but it has been a dripping wet June in England as in Germany. Thunderstorms have travelled the country, and on several occasions the nursery has been deluged. Consequently everything has doubled and trebled while I have been away.

The nursery overflows with plants, the lawns look like bowling greens and the garden still has that fresh bloom we love to see in early June before flowers have had time to fade and nothing looks weary. It is a credit to everyone – and not least to the weather. The rain has been exceptional for June, but for us it has been welcome. It has not been so excessive that damage has been caused, or work held up for long. As is usually the case in East Anglia, we have had less rain than many other districts.

After a quick look round – too much to take in – my first job was to deal with the plants I had brought home. On my arrival I had unwrapped them and stood them in shallow bowls and trays to recover from the trip. Now I replanted them all into small pots to grow on a little before they could be safely planted in the garden or nursery. Then I made fresh labels with the long-lasting Rotring orange-label ink on stiff plastic labels and put them all into 'Pet's Corner' at the end of a shaded tunnel. Finally, they were all recorded in a stock record book.

Next, I went to see my twin brother at Wivenhoe and share with him my news and a day-late birthday tea. On arriving home with baskets of groceries, ready to drop them on the kitchen floor and fall into bed, I met Andrew who said: 'You have visitors; they are in the garden'. At 8 p.m. on Friday night! All prepared to hustle them out with indignation, I discovered that they were Friedolin Wagner, a German

journalist, and Pam Toler who takes exquisite garden pictures. Back to
the house I went, picked up the shopping, made beds, and quickly found
food from the freezer and vegetable garden. Soon we were tucking into
hot soup, warmed bread, new cheese, and salad from the garden. I felt
restored by the food and the enthusiasm of my friends, since they knew,
and could share with me, many of the people I had met in Germany.

On the last day of June I picked a large basket of elderflower heads (to
make Elderflower Syrup) from the Cut-leafed Elder, *Sambucus nigra*
'Laciniata'. This is a variety of our common hedgerow elderflower,
which has finely shredded dark green leaves, making it a handsome and
unusual foliage shrub.
   I find it strange that it has much larger heads of creamy blossom than
the native plants growing nearby. With such narrowly dissected leaves
you might have expected it to have poorer heads of flowers. Instead, it is
a wonderful sight, with lace-like doileys each almost as big as a dinner-
plate.

J U L Y

THE WEATHER is fine, sunny and warm. It is like a sauna in the tunnels, too hot and humid to work in them by midday. Suntops and skirts have appeared at last, and everyone looks healthy, rosy and tanned. The soil is just right for planting so I collect the plants I need on a trolley and try to remember the rest of the things that will require a long walk back if I forget them: watering cans, labels, secateurs, a notebook and pencil, and a few paper bags for ripe seed.

Dicentra spectabilis is already ripening. The superb white form of this lovely plant – sometimes called Lady's Locket or Bleeding Heart – continues to flower much longer than the pink form and it ripens seed over many weeks. Both are usually propagated by division or cuttings in early spring, but I like to collect seed as well, as an insurance. Some years there is quite a lot and the young seedlings make up quite well in the first year, being ready to sell by the end of the second. *Dicentra spectabilis* 'Alba' comes true from seed.

I have been planting new stocks of *Digitalis*. Although I like the common purple foxglove in natural places, I tend to keep it out of the garden, allowing only white forms to seed. (You can tell if a young plant will have purple or white flowers. The leaf bases are tinted purple on plants which will have purple flowers. The white flowered ones will have green stalks.) Sometimes a few primrose-yellow or cream forms appear; I also take care to preserve the salmon-pink variety, called Sutton's Apricot. These are all biennials, making large rosettes of soft, downy leaves the first year, flowering, seeding, and dying the next. As volunteers they often put themselves in places I would neither have thought of, nor had time to find. Almost always they are just what is

143

needed to create a breathtaking effect – emerging in a dark void, lifting the eye from a flat piece of planting, or repeating an accent of colour. So they are desirable, but unpredictable. I like perennial foxgloves because I know they will return next year, and the next, just where I have placed them. They may have seeded themselves around and the seedlings been allowed to stay where the seed fell if there was room for them, but the decision to have the original plants there, to repeat an effect in the design, remains.

Digitalis grandiflora (D. ambigua) is one of my favourites. Standing about 2.5 feet (76 cm), it produces branching stems which carry creamy-yellow flowers, netted inside with brown. *Digitalis ferruginea*, from woodland meadows of the Caucasus, is not a bit like our native foxglove. It has smooth, dark green leaves and tall slender spires of buds which open short, rounded, bronze-coloured flowers. Another, with similar coloured flowers, has such a curious form that many visitors find it hard to believe it is a foxglove. It is *Digitalis parviflora*, which grows wild in stony places in northern Spanish mountains. You might think it dingy from a distance, but its habit and colour make it very distinctive. The flowering stem, which does not branch, is short, about 2-2.5 feet (61-76 cm), and is crowded for the top half of its length with narrow, copper-coloured, tubular flowers, densely set all round the stem. Rigidly upright they form interesting verticals in flower, no less so when they become polished brown seedheads. *Digitalis lutea* has small, greenish-yellow flowers, not impressive, but if allowed to seed in generous groups it creates light vertical lines in the garden, and it is unusual enough to put in flower arrangements. If you grow this and the common foxglove, *Digitalis purpurea*, there may occur a marrige between them resulting in a strange offspring. It has the main characters of *Digitalis lutea*, that is, it makes branching heads which carry small, narrow flowers, but the pale yellow is strongly suffused with the rosy-purple tones of the wild foxglove and is very pretty. These plants are mules, that is, they do not set seed; but they make good perennials, flowering all the late summer and autumn, and can be divided when conditions are right, in spring and autumn. They can also be propagated by cutting the leafy flower-stem into pieces and putting them into a tray of compost. After a few weeks plants will grow from each node.

Another interesting plant which we propagate in this way is *Oenothera glaber*. This is a much-admired dwarf Evening Primrose. From mahogany-tinted rosettes of leaves arise reddish stems that hold clusters of brick-red buds opening to yellow-cupped flowers. The effect is startling and attractive, because the proportions and tones of colour are right. On the whole I do not greatly care for 'improved' delphiniums; with most plants I prefer them as they are found in the wild, although there are exceptions. I would not like to be without the old roses with their bewildering variety of buttoned, quilted, quartered and double

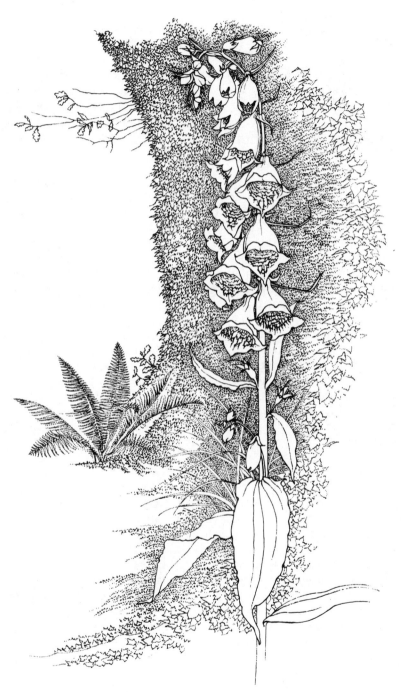

Digitalis grandiflora, a perennial
foxglove, with yellow flowers

145

flowers, nor the capricious double primroses, which have to be cosseted and cared for constantly to satisfy their delicate constitutions. Show delphiniums are a triumph for the breeders for whom bigger must mean better. Most are a bit too much for my taste in the garden, but like most people I crane my neck at Chelsea and gasp at them as exhibition pieces. Two much more modest specimens have found a place in my garden. One was sent to me by James Nuttall, so we call it after him. It produces tall, elegant spires of pearl-grey flowers with scarcely a hint of blue. The other I admired in a garden in Portland, Oregon, for its dark indigo-shaded stems which added character to the dark green leaves and enhanced the blue flowers. Both are hybrids, I think, but both have smallish, neat flowers, not too densely crowded on the stems – just right for the garden and for cutting. Unless they are used to decorate a church or banqueting hall, I find some of the modern hybrids too gross, with flowers as big as pansies. I have a very small stock of the old double-flowered *Delphinium* 'Alice Artindale'. Before I saw it I could not imagine what sort of an unholy mess might be made doubling the complicated, hood-shaped flower. But if you recall that delphiniums are related to buttercups, and also, if you gently push your finger into the face of a *Delphinium* flower you will see it open flat, showing a central boss of stamens and strangely cut, but simple, petals set around them. So 'Alice Artindale' turned out to be an enchantress who turns all heads. Tall stems, 5-6 feet (1.5-2 m) high, carrying tapering spires of buds which open to perfect rosettes like flat, double buttercups fastened tightly against the stem, the petals brilliant blue, edged with acid-green. We are doing our best to increase stock by removing shoots from the base in spring. On my trolley I had put a dozen young plants of 'Alice' to add to the stock bed, since we cannot take many shoots till we have a reasonably large stock.

Not nearly so exciting, but pounced upon by the observant plants-man, is *Asarum europaeum* of which I have only a small patch in the garden. By taking some of the surface running shoots I now have a few dozen plants in pots to start a small stock bed in the little 'Wood Nursery'. It makes attractive carpets of round shining leaves in woods throughout Central Europe, Russia, and West Siberia, taking the place of common ivy, *Hedera helix*, which is primarily found in maritime countries. There is an American form called *Asarum caudatum* which has slightly larger, matt-green leaves. Both have extraordinary, ugly flowers; few people notice them, but if you part the leaves you will see around the edges of the plant, pressed close to the dark earth, flesh-coloured, blotched petals surrounding a dark hole down which pollinating beetles will stumble gleefully in search of pollen.

In one of my shelter tunnels I have a few pots of Japanese forms of *Asarum*, which could be very exciting if I can eventually establish them outside. They look very similar to cyclamen leaves – more heart-shaped, but beautifully mottled and shadowed, pale and dark green, sometimes silvered. However, I am not certain how hardy they will prove to be. I think it will be a long time before I have a trolley load of these plants to set out as a stock bed. We have also been short of stock plants of *Lobelia cardinalis* hybrids. Some were killed by last winter's severe weather, although most winters they survive. The most dangerous time is in spring, when late frosts kill the emerging shoots. I have found that most years a good mulch of leaf mould protects the new rosettes of leaves, delaying their appearance until the frosts have passed. The wild form can be grown from seed. It has green leaves with tall spires of scarlet flowers, but it is not seen in gardens as often as it might be. The popular hybrids have been bred with the more tender *Lobelia fulgens* as second parent to produce dark beetroot-coloured leaves and various shades of red and pink flowers. These can only be reproduced from cuttings. On my trolley I had several trays of potted plants, including 'Queen Victoria' with the richest coloured leaves, and 'Dark Crusader' with slightly greener leaves and magnificent flowers the colour of newly spilt blood. When established plants are carrying strong flowering stems we cut them at ground level, remove the glowing flowers and then cut each stem into short pieces, each carrying a leaf. As the leaves are rather long we reduce the tip by about a third. They are then dipped into a rooting powder, or solution (which we prefer); this not only aids rooting, but prevents rotting of the wounded areas as it also contains fungicide. Then we bury the cut stems, placed upright, about 1.5 inches (3 cm) apart in trays half-filled with potting compost and topped with sharp sand so that the leaf axil rests just above the surface. They are then placed on a mist-propagating bench. A shaded cold frame would do provided you didn't forget all about them, and remembered to water them occasionally with a quick spray from a watering can, especially if the weather turned extra warm during the first week or two. By the end of a month, or six weeks, the embryonic bud at the base of most leaves will have developed into a living shoot and white roots will be seen emerging from the cut stems. Although I have made thousands of cuttings during the forty years of my gardening life, I never cease to be thrilled by the sight of newly emerging roots.

By late autumn the *Lobelia* cuttings will have made sturdy little plants. I used to be impatient to pot them on into individual pots at that stage, sheltering them in a plastic tunnel ready for the spring. But I was surprised and disappointed to find almost all had rotted away by the spring. They resented disturbance late in the season; it was too cold for them to re-establish themselves. Now we leave most of them in their rooting trays, even if they are a bit crowded, until the weather warms up in spring. We have experimented by potting a few in late autumn and leaving them on a bench in the propagating house which, although it has no space heating, is warmer because the polycarbonate walls are of double thickness and retain warmth quite efficiently. Although not on a heated bench, these plants have grown away and not been troubled by rotting. But they take up more room in pots in this valuable space, so we leave most over-wintered cuttings in trays.

Some visitors travel long distances to see the garden. Sometimes a long distance is the next county; other times it may be the southern hemisphere. It is always a pleasure to find other people enjoying the garden, wherever they have come from. I met an enthusiastic couple from New Zealand one heavenly, moist morning this summer, and was glad for them since they had come so far. It was early in the morning, before the sun was too high in the sky, when everything looks freshest and at its best – when colours, textures and shapes all stand out and the whole scene is brought alive by highlights and shadows. Some days, when the sun is lost behind a flat ceiling of dun-coloured cloud, the garden can look drab and lifeless, like the faded props and back-cloth of a theatre seen in daylight. Nor do I find the garden charming on a blazing, bright day in high summer, when it may be full of colour, but looks drained of detail from midday till late afternoon. It is too bright, too exposed. I prefer to go out after tea, when everything looks quite different. Tall, graceful plants, whether ten-foot tall grasses or aristocratic lilies, emerge like prima donnas as they are spot-lit by the sinking sun, while more modest characters remind us how much they contribute to the scene. Background plants become as fascinating as intricately tiled mosaic when the evening light sharpens every shade, shape and design of leaf.

I love rain in high summer. It rarely lasts more than a day here. It is much more likely that we will have a threadbare shower, a miserable quarter of an inch, while barren pavements in towns not so many miles away will have a generous inch, or two. But we thankfully receive the leftovers from clouds which have spilt most of their contents long before they reach us. Sometimes when driving a mere half-mile away from home the road will be awash with water, but as I approach our village it remains dust-dry; no drop has fallen on 'Unusual Plants'. Occasionally, as happened this year, we have, like the rest of the country, been caught up in great turbulence which has brought alternate periods of warm, drying sunshine and recurring thunderstorms, keeping everywhere fresh. To walk in the garden in summer, in light, warm rain, or immediately after, is an exquisite pleasure. The light must be right, with no wind. There will be a faint warm mist hanging in the air so nothing is too distinct. There are no hard edges, distance is seen through a silvery haze.

Walking in the woodland nursery I caught a breath of the sweet, grape-like scent of elderflower. On a steep bank above the boundary ditch were ancient bushes loaded with flat heads of blossom. On these still, warm

Climbing roses cascade from branches of trees

mornings, when everything is full of moisture, all kinds of perfumes hang in the air. *Philadelphus* 'Beauclerk' (one the finest of mock-oranges), with its large milk-white petals faintly stained purple around the yellow stamens, has most people stopping to see where the strong, sweet scent is coming from. The bright yellow-leafed mock-orange, *Philadelphus coronarius* 'Aureus' fills a dim corner with unsuspected fragrance. I have planted three bushes beneath the light shade of a cherry, *Prunus serrula*, which has beautiful polished mahogany bark.

This is backed by several Serbian Spruce, the narrow-formed *Picea ormorika*, so the thin-textured leaves of yellow mock-orange are not browned by sun scorch. Still following my nose, I stand at the foot of a medium-sized oak which is now almost covered with Paul's Himalayan Musk Rose. For several years the rose grew unnnoticed. Each summer it threw up from the base, long rambling shoots, 15-18 feet (5-6 m), which were tied to the supporting trunk. As the years have passed it has formed, over the head of the tree, a cobweb of thin, trailing stems and sprays which fall from the topmost branches to the ground. Now every summer it is a delight to see frothing clusters of tiny, pink and white blossoms cascading down to touch the grass beneath. I shut my eyes and breathe the spicy scent in deeply. It is indescribable, and unique. Long, rambling shoots no longer lie in wait for me across the grass walk, but instead are produced high up among the branches where the wind blows them towards another oak; there, in time, they will become entangled to form another flowery, perfumed arbour. Another strangely perfumed rose which I always make a point of visiting is *Rosa* 'Frühlingsgold'. The large, creamy-yellow, single flowers have a rich, fruity smell, not a bit like the clean apple-scent of the wild rose. We don't always remember to stop and smell the flowers or the plant itself. Not until I read in Graham Thomas's books that this or that plant had a perfume did I realise that I hadn't taken notice. Now I try to smell everything, although I still miss some things and only find out what I have missed in winter when I am trying to describe a plant and cannot – and it's too late to go out and see and smell for myself.

Sometimes, when I am discovered working in the garden, I am presumed to be one of the gardeners (which of course I am), and am asked if I can identify a plant, or help with a problem. Occasionally I am asked if Mrs Chatto is in the garden today; I have even been asked if she is still alive. I have also been informed by a visitor that now, of course, there is no need for her to work. In a sense this could be right: there is little distinction between work and play if one is fortunate enough to be doing what one loves best. I must be a disappointment to those romantics who expect to find a graceful figure deadheading the roses, but occasionally it is I who am disconcerted, as when I saw starry-eyed illusion drain from one small boy's eyes.

150

It had been a hot, tiring afternoon. The nursery was full of visitors. Everyone was busy. I noticed that some plants in one of the tunnels were wilting. Although there is an irrigation system which can be turned on, a good soak with a hose is sometimes needed for a particular block of plants, while the rest would be better without it. So I picked up the long length of hose and pulled it along the tunnel path. At the entrance stood a small boy of about eight or nine years old, hot and bored, gazing inwards and being lectured by his mother who obviously wanted some peace to look around. I do not usually encourage people into my tunnels. There are notices saying 'Staff Only' – but impulsively I said 'Would you like to help me with this hose?' His face lit up as he bounded into the forbidden jungle. We got chatting and after a time he asked, 'Are you one of the staff?' 'No,' I replied, 'but someone has to water these plants'. 'Does Mrs Chatto work here?' he persisted. I gave in 'I am Mrs Chatto,' I replied, and was taken aback to see disbelief darken his face. 'But you write books, don't you? My mother said ...' (how could an author be found wearing wet jeans, watering plants like anybody else). I laughed. 'Yes, I have written some books. But this is what I write about – growing plants, making a garden, and meeting people, like you.'

'Please see the hose doesn't tangle with the pots'

Part of the vegetable garden

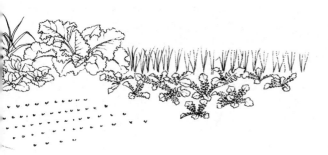

'But aren't you famous then?' he asked, struggling to get his values sorted out. He had been brought to see a 'personality', and could not square his imagination with reality. If I said 'No,' would it ruin his afternoon, when he might otherwise have gone down to the beach? I thought for a while, then said, 'Well, sometimes people tell me I am famous, but I am still myself, and whether I am famous or not we must rescue these plants, so please help me and see the hose doesn't tangle with the pots'.

The garden and my thoughts about it have evolved over the past twenty-six years. This has involved considerable change, learning to work on a larger scale than we had originally imagined. As new areas are developed the early plantings sometimes appear confused and con-gested. Some kind of simplification is needed; shapes of beds have to be altered, some are removed altogether. This summer we have grassed over most of a large bed of hostas and other shade-loving plants which lay beneath the canopy of *Paulownia tomentosa* (a Chinese tree with huge, heart-shaped leaves). Now a smooth, gentle slope balances and simplifies other borders nearby, while sunlight filtering through the branches creates a moving pattern of light and shadows on the grass which I had not noticed when the ground was covered with plants.

It is Sunday. The garden feels quite different – not because there is no one about, but because nobody needs me. I can sink into my own thoughts, indulge in little personal pleasures. Among my favourite indulgences is the vegetable garden. During the busy summer months there is scarcely a day in the week that I do not visit it to collect something for the kitchen, but on Sunday I can stay longer, perhaps spend all day, sowing, hoeing, harvesting, and just revelling in the abundance of delicious food which can be grown in a comparatively small space.

For much of the early part of the year I am too involved with Chelsea and everyday events on the nursery to prepare soil and sow early seeds, so I am thankful to have Keith taking care of this season for me. We discuss the programme of cropping and rotation, and then he fits this job in among many others.

One of the first things I did on returning from Chelsea was to visit the propagating houses; I was amazed to see how everything had doubled in size in the short time we were away, including the tomatoes and peppers which I had been raising in pots. These, and my ornamental gourds, pumpkins and zucchini were ready to be planted outside. But we have to be careful, even as late as the end of May, not to be caught by a devastating frost. So I keep a few spare plants inside, as a precaution. Now in mid-July, after exceptional wet weather, the vegetable garden is full of lush growth. As soon as the rows of small seedlings are large enough to handle I steal a little time to thin them out, treading the soil back firmly as I go.

The rows of carrots have abundant dark green foliage, no sign yet of the yellowing leaf which indicates that the roots are being riddled with the grub of the Carrot Fly. This year we sowed four rows, about 6 inches (15 cm) apart, and surrounded the narrow bed with polythene sheeting securely fixed to wooden posts. This is to deter the Carrot Fly as it flies along at ground level, guided by the smell of young seedlings. As it reaches the plastic wall it flies up and beyond the carrots. Another deterrent is to sow rows of onions and carrots alternately.

The golden and white rooted beetroot have grown vigorously enough to produce spare foliage for cooking, which is treated just like spinach. All the half-hardy subjects: the tomatoes, courgettes and squashes are far too rampant after the rain. I fear there will be little fruit setting if we do not have warmer weather than we have had up till now. Only the courgettes are setting well. Radishes love wet weather, they need very rich growing conditions (the soil laced with well-rotted vegetable waste) to encourage them to grow fast, so they can be picked and eaten before other creatures have discovered them. I especially like those which make long, crisp, white roots; but the round Cherry Belle type are the prettiest.

Surprisingly, the bush Basil has done well in this cool summer. Both green and purple leafed forms have grown well enough for me to cut off most of the top growth to dry for the winter. They will make new growth for fresh pickings during the rest of the summer.

Broad beans are a very satisfying crop. They're such easy vegetables to grow and can be eaten at several different stages. This year I lost my red-coated beans in the cold winter, but my daughter Mary had preserved her plants in Southwold, so I know I shall have the seed back again in the autumn. They do not taste very different from green-seeded beans, but look unusual when cooked – remaining dark. They make an attractive dish if a few green-coated beans are cooked among them. The variety which has succeeded with me this year is called 'Superfin'. It has produced smaller sized pods and beans than other varieties, but in great quantities – the beans hang on the pods like clusters of green bananas. Almost every part of the plant produces a delicious dish. We enjoy our first taste as soon as the flowers have set, when I pick out the tip shoots to make a tasty supper dish. Lightly cooked, they are dark green and succulent, like spinach, but with the distinctive broad-bean flavour. Picking out the tip shoots is supposed to discourage attacks of blackfly; usually it does, but this year I have also planted Summer Savory on either side of the rows. This herb is reputed to discourage blackfly and is also a delicious aromatic herb, good sprinkled over soups, or used to flavour cottage cheese. Before it has formed flowers I pull up most of the bushy little plants and hang them to dry, rubbing out the scented brittle leaves and storing them in a screw-topped jar. When the developing bean pods are no thicker than my little finger, with beans scarcely formed, I pick a handful or two, top and tail them, and cook them whole. They are not woolly as you might imagine, but simply delicious with butter or a sauce, or served cold with salad dressing. Finally, we enjoy the beans themselves, still finding more than enough despite our earlier nibblings, when there was a scarcity of green vegetable during that hungry spring gap as we waited for peas and French beans to be ready.

The cabbage tribe cannot be overlooked. I have given up growing summer cabbage since there is so much else to be eaten then, but I do reserve space for late summer, autumn and winter brassicas. Calabrese is number one favourite from late summer often through to December. By keeping a row continually picked as soon as the flowering shoots appear, it lasts us well into winter provided there are no severe frosts. It is not as thick-stemmed as those you can buy, but I suspect most commercially-grown fruit and vegetables have been dosed with stimulants to encourage shop-worthy specimens. The grower, after all, has to please the public and make a living – but I prefer my vegetables to live a less pressurised existence. They may be a little smaller, but they are tender and tasty and not full of suspect chemicals. Brussels Sprouts and Purple and White Sprouting Broccoli are all making sturdy plants – I do hope they will not have to face such a winter as last, when all my plants were totally destroyed.

The pole beans are at last running up their canes. I still prefer the purple-podded Runner Bean. It sets basketfuls of silky smooth beans, bright puple when raw, changing to dark green when cooked. I cut the canes that support them from a huge old stand of *Arundinaria nitida*, a very elegant, fine-leafed bamboo which produces surprisingly strong,

155

slender canes more than 10 feet tall. It is a satisfying job on a warm, still evening, to creep around the base of the clump selecting mature canes. I trim off the leafy tops and thrust them well into the soil on either side of the rows of beans, tying them firmly to horizontal canes laid across the top where two canes meet. Finally I collect a barrowload or two of rotting straw which has been placed near the vegetable garden and carpet the ground around and between the beans – and between anything else which would benefit from it. By midsummer most of the vegetable garden is covered with a mulch. The marrows, tomatoes, strawberries and spinach, all benefit and the soil is less damaged where you walk on it. The roots of Mange-Tout Peas or Sugar Peas hate being dried out, so they too are thickly blanketed alongside the rows.

I gave up growing ordinary peas long ago in favour of Sugar Peas. With these, you have something to eat almost as soon as the flowers have set, since you eat the whole pod, just topped and tailed, either raw or lightly cooked, before the peas have swollen to full size. By picking every few days the vines are encouraged to go on producing new flowers, so the length of cropping may be extended for weeks, with plentiful supplies of deliciously sweet and tender, pea-flavoured pods and none of the disappointments of maggoty or floury peas. There are, however, a few problems. Preferably cool temperatures with plenty of moisture and well-prepared soil are what they demand, and must have, for a maximum yield. Mildew can be a nuisance some years, especially late in the season when I have optimistically sown a second crop, rather too late, about the end of June. But this year I encountered a new problem which I have not seen before: we have had pea leaf-spot, a disease which spreads in wet weather. (For the most part this wet summer has been a blessing on our arid East Anglian acres, but in this case it is encouraging disease.) This fungal leaf-spot, *Asochyta pisi*, appears as minute brown spots on the fresh young leaves, gradually spreading onto the pods, distorting them and making them look distinctly unappetising. Inexorably, the plants become so debilitated they cease to produce the long succession of fresh flowers and pods which normally we might expect. Surprisingly, this disease starts from infected seed, and there is no satisfactory way of controlling it once it appears, so we shall have to wait for fresh seed and another season's crop to indulge our taste for this luxury.

It is not surprising that many people, men in particular, dislike eating vegetables. I had a Dutch friend who shuddered when I showed him a healthy crop of Mange-Tout Peas I had grown from French seed, the sweetest, most flavoursome I have ever grown. 'Ugh!' he protested, with childhood memories of 'poellen', as they are called in Holland. 'They are revolting, but I was made to eat them!' I am sure they were revolting, well boiled in plenty of salted water until they were yellow. One would imagine that, by now, everyone knows the golden rule of cooking vegetables, with so many food programmes on television and every magazine printing mouth-watering pictures. But I have stood (not silently, I will admit) in a kitchen watching a fine fresh cabbage being finely chopped, then well packed into a saucepan full of cold water, and left to simmer, until wanted. Who would want it? The least time possible is all that is required to cook vegetables – preferably in steam, and without salt, which can be added, if needed, at the table.

After the longest day has passed, I start to think about sowing winter salads. Joy Larkcom, author of *Vegetables from Small Gardens*, pressed a few packets of seed into my hand when she came to my exhibit at Chelsea this spring. Now they are sown. Among the Chinese vegetables that she gave me, 'Tat-Soi' makes a flat rosette of shining dark green leaves with wide, white stalks. It can be eaten raw, finely shredded and mixed with lighter leaves, such as lettuce. Or it can be quickly stir-fried. 'Pak Choy' quickly makes another small, green-leafed plant which adds variety to the leaf vegetables. Quite distinct is 'Mizuma' which produces fern-like leaves. It makes a crisp and attractive addition to salads, and lasts well until very cold weather spoils it. These all belong to the cabbage family and have a slight cabbage flavour, sometimes with a hot after-taste. I must not forget the large Chinese Cabbage to be found in most greengrocers' shops throughout the autumn and winter. These plants must not be sown too soon (the end of July is time enough in the southern half of the country), or they will grow too fast and run to seed. Initially, at the seedling stage, they are plagued by flea beetles. You may have noticed young plants riddled with tiny holes. If you bang the ground with your hand, you will see minute black beetles hop into the air, then drop down to continue their feast. If they become too persistent I use an insecticide called 'Picket'. It discourages most vegetable pests, and the vegetables can be eaten the same day, although I never do, leaving more time for the chemical to break down. (I have read that a mulch of any kind helps to discourage flea beetles.) After the Broad Bean site was cleared, I planted out leeks from the seed row. For this I used a heavy iron dibber which I watched my father use when I was a child. It may not be the best thing to use in a heavy clay soil, but in my gravelly soil it does no harm. I let the heavy dibber fall into the loose warm soil, drop in a leek and when the row is complete, fill all the holes with water. They grow about 12 inches (30 cm) long and 1.5 inches (4 cm) across – just right for the kitchen.

Another country pleasure is going to the fields to pick strawberries. I do not grow enough to freeze – there is a limit to the time I can spend pandering to my stomach – but an evening spent in the strawberry fields is pure delight. On the outskirts of the next village a friend of mine has a story-book farm with cows, calves, sheep, pigs, even honey-bees and guinea fowl. They also grow all kinds of soft fruit, everything in small quantities by today's farming standards, but all looking healthy, happy and well. I soon fill my baskets with strawberries and am home in time to prepare them for the freezer.

As I stood in the kitchen pressing the fruit through my mouli sieve and stirring elderflower-scented syrup into the thick pink purée, Andrew came into the kitchen with his binoculars and took me to watch a beautiful barred and mottled partridge with her babies. With only two of her original brood remaining, she preened on top of the garden wall, having climbed the compost heaps piled on the opposite side. Down she flew into the garden, chuk-chukking. What would the babies do? We watched and waited. Obeying the call, they followed, floating down into the stems of pink *Alstroemeria*. Mother perversely flew back. Could they follow? No – she returned and they all processed towards the house, the young ones running very fast on little stick legs. I hoped Emma, the cat, was nowhere near.

It was one of those days when I was expecting a special visitor. The weather was overcast, occasionally turning quite chilly. My hands were cold and I was glad to find a woolly jersey. The morning was spent planting in the garden, filling in gaps I had left in a new curving border leading down to a little bridge. I planted *Campanula turbinata* 'Alba', (such a pretty thing for a sunny edge in cool soil), three different forms of Sticky Campion, *Lychnis viscosa*, and the dark blue *Salvia ambigens* which looks well in the autumn, but is not too hardy. I watered everything in, dipping my can into the pool nearby. I was frequently interrupted by visitors, including an elderly Frenchman who sat sketching on the bridge. A Belgian talked for ages, very sympathetic I thought, until I later found him marching across one of my borders. (Such carelessness does not often happen, but surely, I reason to myself, he would be astounded if I were to be found stepping over his precious possessions.)

On my way in to lunch I picked a basket of old roses which bear romantic names like 'Madame Hardy', 'Charles de Mills', 'Camaieux' and 'Empress Josephine'. There are many beautiful modern roses, but I do not think I have seen any which have the quality of the old varieties. (It's a bit like comparing pure silk with man-made fibres.) Some of them have been handed down through many generations, together with fine old pieces of furniture which seem to have a matching quality. Their petals have a texture reminiscent of ancient tussore silk or faded velvet. Many are enchanting in bud, especially those with 'mossy' calyces, but most are beautiful when full blown – which cannot be said for most modern roses and certainly not for hybrid tea roses. The charm of old roses often lies in the arrangement of petals. 'Charles de Mills' looks as though each flower had been part of a ball, cut in half across the middle to reveal the intricate quartering of tightly packed petals inside. The shadows within add depth to a combination of dark purple and glowing crimson. Another purple rose, but quite different, is 'Cardinal de Richelieu'. Smaller flowers, fully double, of tussore texture on the top side, show rounded incurved petals of greyish-pink on the underside – fit lining for a cardinal's cloak. *Rosa mundi*, a sport of the oldest rose known in cultivation, *Rosa gallica*, forms a low suckering thicket of stems covered with light green leaves, exactly the right shade for the abundance of semi-double flowers which cover the bush to the ground. The wavy-edged petals are bright cherry-pink slashed with darker pink and white. It is one of my best-loved roses, both to pick and for effect in the garden, and impossible to do justice in a description. I admit, in certain circumstances, the suckering habit could be tiresome, but it is not rampant and each sucker comes true and can be used to establish a low hedge – or can be given away to friends.

There are, I admit, disadvantages to some of the old roses. Many flower only once, in early or midsummer; but then so do lilies and we do not reject them for that reason, rather we treasure the days when they bloom, adding their heavy perfume to the lighter, fresher fragrance of roses. In some conditions certain varieties make malformed blooms, and one of the drawbacks of frail antique petals is that they are spoilt by rain – especially the tissue-paper-white ones. But individually all have a unique character. All are carried on stems which seem right for the flower. Slender enough to allow one full bloom to droop gracefully, or strong enough to display a vast bouquet of tiny shell-like flowers. Just one stem of these lovely old roses can bring a room to life, while a basketful on the floor is a feast for all the senses to see, to touch, to smell – and to taste.

One midsummer day Julia, my eldest granddaughter, picked a mixture of rose petals and brought them into the kitchen. We whisked white of egg, dipped each petal into it, shook fine castor sugar over them, and put them on rice-paper-covered trays in the coolest possible oven until they were dry. When cold and crisp, but still showing shades of pink, we filled a large glass jar, and tried to keep it stoppered, but they did not last long; too many hands dipped in to sample them though they had been meant to make unusual and pretty decorations for desserts. In my garden, roses are not confined to a formal rose garden. In such a very informal garden, surrounded by farmland, there were no constraining boundaries or achitectural features which might have inspired such a design. But personally I do not greatly care for rose gardens. Heresy this may be, but I can walk through a great municipal rose garden, in full bloom and garish glory, and scarcely look to left and right. There are too many flowers *en masse*, just blobs of bright colour. I can enjoy none of them individually, while many of them I would not have anyway.

I mix my roses – some species, some old-fashioned, and a few modern shrub roses – in among other bushes with suitable conifers and evergreens for background, together with groups of herbaceous plants and other shrubs. So when they are not in flower, or hip (we should say hep), they fade into the background. Do you take a second glance at a proper rose garden, or even a small bed of roses, except when in flower? Can you afford to waste that space for most of the year? If roses mean all, then you will forgive or ignore the empty months, but for me the garden exists all year round, every square yard is valued (not by being packed – the spaces are important), but by being a satisfying basic design of lasting, living material. Some roses, like 'William Lobb', make a large, strong framework which can be used to support a clematis that will flower when the roses have faded. *Rosa* 'Complicata' makes a densely bushy shrub, radiant when covered with large, bright-pink, single roses, but ignored, in my garden, except as a bastion for the rest of the year, until I gave it for company *Clematis viticella* 'Purpurea Plena Elegans', which creeps unobserved, up and over, to dangle trails of small double flowers here and there. They remind me of certain of the old roses, being of similar shade, with slatey-purple petals pressed into a slightly flattened rosette, and are strangely attractive.

In theory, we should prune roses lightly after flowering, but there is so much else demanding attention at that time it is easy to overlook them. However, it does not take too long to trim back ungainly shoots and prevent the shrubs becoming a lax tangle. More precise pruning can be done in late winter, or early spring, when there is more time to think and you can see what you are doing. The principle I apply to shrub roses is: aim for a strong basic framework, about 3-4 feet (1-1.5 m) high, from which will spring the flowering shoots. Where there is space, and where I need much taller growth I allow a larger framework. Occasionally old or diseased stems are cut out at the base. Woody plants tend to break buds just below the point where you cut, so if you only chip about at the top end of a shrub all new growth will start at that height and little will be encouraged to break from the base. Weakly, crowded or crossing stems should be removed. This will also help the production of fine, strong replacement shoots by letting in more light and air to the base.

I confess to occasional envy of owners of ancient mansions, with courtyards, outbuildings, or even old walled kitchen gardens. There has been a sad lack of spare walls in my life. To overcome this I train certain rambling, scrambling roses into large and impressive bushes. Perhaps the loveliest and most amenable is 'Félicité Perpétue'. During flowering I watch for the current season's strong new shoots, which would easily make ten feet (3 m) if left to themselves, and nip out the tender tips, aiming to keep a large but controlled bush, perhaps five or six feet (1.5-2 m) high, and as much or more across. 'Félicité' makes large quantities of new shoots, so by the next flowering season she is a wondrous sight – a mound crowded with clusters of small perfectly formed rosette flowers, opening white from red-tinted buds, set against small, shining, dark green leaves.

160

Another vigorous rose I treat in this way is *Rosa* 'Venusta Pendula' which has rather larger flowers, more loosely put together than the prim rosettes of 'Félicité Perpétue'. The large, drooping clusters of blushing white petals unfolding from deeper, creamy-pink buds are everything you would wish for to frame an archway, or to train over a mullioned window. My plant over the east-facing wall of our low single storey house has to be restrained; it begs to be allowed to sprawl over the roof tiles and drop down to the bedroom windows on the other side. But what trouble I would get into with the roofing man, who is already upbraiding me for allowing fat cushions of moss to act like sponges and eat into the tiles. So this lovely, headstrong rose has elsewhere submitted to being treated as a large bower-like shrub, and as such she is none the less admirable.

Once started, I am tempted to go on and on about old roses and the not-so-old ones. If you have yet to become acquainted with them I would beg you to read anything you can find on the subject, but especially the writings of Graham Stuart Thomas, who produces the most enticing descriptions. He rescued many old roses from obscurity after the Second World War and has published three books about them: *The Old Shrub Roses, Climbing Roses Old and New* and *Shrub Roses of Today*. His paintings and drawings make exquisite illustrations in these treasurable books.

It was for Graham I had picked the roses, but I did not expect him until early evening. After lunch I found a trolley load of new plants waiting to be dealt with by me. First I catalogued them in my stock record book and then I stood them aside in a safe place at the end of one of the tunnels until I had time to make labels for them. Some were from the Royal Horticultural Society seed list, some from abroad which I had either collected myself or had been sent by friends. My staff have learnt to keep an eye on these odd collections as they emerge from the propagating house, to see they are not swept outside and sold before I have had time to assess their worth. By keeping them in a special area (Pet's Corner) less time is wasted looking for newcomers among thousands of others. The remainder of the afternoon was spent watering and trimming my show plants. As we have been invited to put up an exhibit for the Sandringham Flower Show at the end of the month there is another big collection of pots to be cared for.

I went in to tea, wet and muddy below the waist from watering, wet and bedraggled above from a sudden thunderstorm. Time for a quick cup of tea and then a bath I thought; but I was too late. I heard a familiar voice in the hall and there was my guest, Graham Stuart Thomas, earlier than either of us had planned, but it was a bonus since it gave us a nice long evening. I left him to relax with Andrew among the tea things and hastened off to repair my appearance.

Both of us restored and refreshed, Graham suggested a look at the garden. It had almost stopped raining so we started first with the nursery, where we could take shelter in the tunnels if need arose. Although I am in and out of the nursery much of the day, it is a pleasure still to dally among the neat and orderly rows of pots with a friend who does not wish to hurry. I imagine it must be like stamp collecting – searching through thousands of little squares of perforated paper which all look much alike to the uninitiated, but which may produce something unique to the knowing eye. On almost any plant nursery there is the chance of finding treasures you have loved and lost, or have never seen before. Although there was no sun, the light was good and colours were lovely, enhanced by dampness everywhere. We walked on and on. In the back of my mind nagged thoughts of supper. Suddenly I saw Graham shiver so we hurried back to the house; the fire blazed up in no time, sherry was poured, and the two men were left deep in conversation as I heated soup and sesame bread and set the table with salads, cheese and a big bowl of strawberries and cream. It was a lovely evening, spent with a great horticulturalist and artist who generously shares his wide knowledge and spices it with dry humour.

Strawberries and cream for supper

Next morning, after breakfast, we were outside in wellingtons and macs, with umbrellas pouring waterfalls down our backs.

On the far side of a large, dripping shrub we discovered Joy Larkcom with an American visitor, a lady who is an authority on 'Erbs', as they are called in the United States, and at the same time, from beneath a multi-coloured umbrella, Ashley Stephenson appeared. He is bailiff for the Royal parks in London. The American lady had only a short time to spare so the men and I left her and luckless Joy to splash around at top speed, and we repaired to the kitchen for hot cups of coffee. Ashley Stephenson was not going to be put off by a bit of wet weather, he said, so warmed inside, we put up our brollies and set off to look at the remains of my wasteland. This is an area of about two acres of low-lying soggy soil through which the spring-fed ditch runs. Below this piece of land lies my water and woodland garden, which was originally just as soggy and boggy. But now after twenty-eight years, and much effort making pools, digging drainage ditches, and endless carting and incorporating of many materials to aerate and improve the soil, it has become a congenial home for shade- and moisture-loving plants which would curl up and die in dry seasons on the remaining acres of gravel.

It is not often that one has the opportunity to see something of the origins of an established garden, so it was with mutual pleasure that we visited the scene – a long, low hollow bounded by a few oak trees, holly and blackthorn on the higher ground, and much of the rest waist high in rank weeds and grasses. Not all of it, though. For the past two years I have been preparing part of this land to make nursery stock-beds for plants which need damp soil. That is not the same as water-logged soil. Because the land lies in a hollow, water from the surrounding farmland drains into it constantly, taking months to travel down through the soil to reach the lowest point. To retain some of this water would be an advantage, to dispose of the surplus meant we had to make an efficient herring-bone system of drains leading into the main stream which feeds our pools.

Once we dug into the soil we found a deep black structureless substance, much like an Irish peat bog, totally saturated. Our ditches were spaced 10 feet (3 m) apart, dug to about 2 feet (61 cm) with a machine and then filled almost to the top with pebbles bought from the local gravel pit. This drainage material was then covered with polythene sheeting before the last spit of soil filled the top of the trench. This was to prevent the fine silt washing down into the stones and blocking the drainage. The surface of the drains, separating beds 10 feet (3 m) wide, became our paths 2 feet (61 cm) wide – just wide enough to take trolley loads of plants. But more had to be done to improve the structure of the soil itself. As the newly-made drains began to collect surplus underground water and drying winds firmed the surface, we were gradually able to use the sub-soiler to drag deep furrows through the soil, leave it a few days, then scattered tons of pea-sized gravel over the surface. This was rotavated in, together with bonfire waste, spare gravel soil from elsewhere on the nursery, and waste peat and sand from spent nursery pots. All this was done over several months, together with routine work, but it vastly improved the texture of the black, peat-like soil. It is now a pleasure to dig a hole in this soil and see the difference between it and the land a few yards away, which we have yet to tackle. Hostas, damp-loving *Iris*, *Trollius*, *Ranunculus* and astilbes are some of the plants now thriving on this restructured soil which we had come to see through curtains of rain. But now no water lay in sheets on the surface as it had done for years previously. Beyond the planted beds, where no drainage work has yet been done, we squelched in water over our boots and gloated over the difference. Then back we plunged through the midsummer garden, which still looked as if June had come and was staying for ever, with not a wilted blossom or tired leaf in sight. Nothing seemed to be past its best to remind you that August and harvest were close at hand.

Wet weather is bad weather to almost everyone, especially to weather reporters and cricket fans, but in this exceedingly dry corner of the country, I would love, most summers, to be able to 'pull a chain' on my garden at least once a week. So often in July, great grey clouds boil and coil just above the tree tops, but they don't spare a splash, the plants stand stoically in the dust and all that lovely promise can fade away. It is the thin sand and gravel soil which suffers first, trickling through one's fingers like sand in an egg-timer after only a few days of sun and wind in high summer. Covered now with a collection of drought-loving plants and shrubs it is still not easy to maintain the best effect after weeks without rain, despite liberal dressings of compost or mulch. But this summer the Mediterranean gardens around the house look as prosperous as the lower water-gardens. My visitors and I wandered among spicy scents of drought-resisting plants until damp and hunger drove us into the house for a bowl of hot soup. Maize-meal scones vanished, potato salad too. It was all very relaxing after an exhilarating morning. However, my visitors had long journeys home and I had shopping to do for the weekend. As we collected ourselves and set off, the clouds lifted, the late afternoon sun smiled radiantly over the gently steaming garden, and I would have wished it so all day.

I have been collecting plants from seed lists, gardening friends and occasional trips abroad for more than forty years. I spent the first twenty years of my marriage as any other housewife and mother, caring for my family and garden, and helping my husband run his fruit farm. Since his retirement twenty years ago due to ill-health, I have gradually established a plant nursery alongside the garden we began in 1960. As the nursery has grown I have also been able to train a team of local men and women who, in turn, have enabled me to expand the garden and my collection of plants. Without their enthusiastic co-operation it would be impossible to maintain such a garden. It is useless to plant new areas if you are powerless to care for them. Several labour-saving methods are employed freeing people to do productive work rather than endless repetitive weeding, but no garden or nursery, however well organised, remains totally weed-free so there must be a regular, but bearable programme of maintenance. On my light soils especially, seedling weeds germinate like hairs on a cat's back; too depressing and too expensive for anyone to be paid to remove them several times a year. A further cost to be considered is the continual loss of top soil if weeds are removed. By covering the soil with a layer of some sterile material such as peat, straw or pulverised bark – even slates or stones in suitable areas – tiny seedlings are stifled, so weeds occur much less frequently and those which do come out more easily. Deep-rooted perennial weeds such as dandelion or dock, or running grass along the edge of a border, are painted with systemic weedkiller, one of the few occasions when it is well justified.

Two girls, Lesley and Winnie, are responsible for keeping the garden clean from May to September. Their knowledge of plants and native weeds is very extensive. They know when to save seedlings and when to clear them to prevent too many plants becoming weeds in the wrong place. Winnie is one of our 'summer swallows', returning to the neighbouring fruit farm in autumn, but she has been with us for nineteen summers and has become an expert in the spot-treatment of deep-rooted or invasive weeds. When we began the garden the gravel areas were sheeted with bindweed; I have not seen a piece now for years.

My aim in the garden is to create attractive scenes and to provide suitable settings for plants. I also hope to please visitors, without whose support we could not survive. In the garden I hope they may find ideas, as well as plants, which could be useful – whether they live in a cottage, a town-house or a mansion.

'How do you know how to put plants together to create this effect?' I am asked. It would be stupid to say I do not know, but it is not easy to say exactly how I know, or why I do this and not that. Sometimes I use the analogy of writing, of taking words, putting them into phrases and then sentences, until finally I have made a statement – in living plants. (I use plants as an overall term, including trees and shrubs.) It helps to have a basic comprehension of form and construction, even if at times such knowledge appears to be ignored. But I think it is necessary to know the rules and to know when to break them to produce something unexpected, but not bizarre.

I am deeply indebted to Andrew, my husband, for teaching me to respect and understand something of the natural environment of plants; where they come from, what kind of conditions they prefer, whether they grow in shade or sun, on a dry hillside or a boggy meadow. He remains my first and primary source of information, understanding and criticism, and can usually answer my queries from a lifetime's research and writing about plants and their ecology.

In writing these notes I have been troubled that Andrew seldom appears in my crowded days. Being a very private person, he rarely comes into the garden, except on an occasional evening to share the latest excitement, or to walk partway with me on a Sunday morning until we fall out over a piece of planting I have done which does not suit his ecological viewpoint. At the time I am put out by the criticism, but deep down I know that I shall not be pleased myself if the design does not fit together harmoniously as in nature. I think again; sometimes I reconsider and change; sometimes not. There cannot be two painters daubing at the same canvas. When I was first married I followed Andrew's lead in the garden of our first home as goslings do the first moving object that imprints itself on their consciousness (except in the vegetable garden, where I was undisputed). In 1960, when we began this new garden, Andrew knew the kind of garden we would make when it was still an overgrown wilderness, and I was only feeling my way, much of the time lost on the edge of such a novel experience. Those first few years were crucial in establishing the three main ideas: the Dry Garden, the Shade Garden and eventually the Bog Garden. Over the past twenty years these original ideas have been developed and expanded into something we could never have imagined at the beginning.

It is a rare and beautiful morning in high-summer. The grass is green, the soil dark with recent rain, every plant sparkling and lush. (No one will believe me again when I speak of drought-stricken East Anglia.) But in many summers the wide sweep of grass alongside my entrance border is brown by the end of July. This summer it looks like a bowling pitch, unnaturally green. You may wonder why I put up with the poor effect of this area, since we appear to have plenty of stored water. That is true, (and the water is used extensively on the nursery), but many people who visit us come from areas of water shortage where the use of hosepipes is banned in times of drought. Although the grass may be patchy, the plants in the gravel-based entrance border are not. Trees, shrubs and herbaceous plants have been chosen because they are adapted to withstand drought conditions. If regularly watered, they lose characteristics which make them appeal to us: the white woolliness or the blue coat of wax which form protective covering for a green leaf. Heavy soil and wet climate are unsuitable for most grey plants.

A tall tailored hedge of × *Cupressocyparis leylandii* forms a background to drought-resisting shrubs, including *Cistus* and brooms with many grey and silver-leafed shrubs which become white and woollier as drought bites deeper and as the air becomes filled with spicy scents from all those aromatic plants. Because the soil is so stony and well-drained, these plants have not suffered in the wet summer; instead they have grown twice as vigorously – which is good to see, since they have plenty of room after last winter's losses. *Artemisia ludoviciana* can be a nuisance in small gardens, but it is lovely here where there is plenty of room. It stands outlined against the holly-dark leaves of *Cistus cyprius*. Running rootstocks have pushed up tall, silvery-leafed stems, topped with thin spires of little grey buds which open insignificant flowers. Whether it is picked or in the garden, the delicate, silvery-grey shape is what counts. *Alstroemeria ligtu* hybrids in several shades, from almost white to deep rose, push their large bouquets of small, lily-like flowers between the *Artemisia* stems. Several years ago I walked along this border dropping handfuls of seed. They like to be sown *in situ*; they also relish the well-drained soil. *Geranium* 'Russell Prichard' sprawls trails of pink flowers across the edge of the border, climbing into green and white bushes of variegated rue. In another group, in a bay, surrounded by the white-flowered *Cistus × corbariensis*, is a cloud of tall, bronze-leafed fennel making a background for lilac-blue *Salvia haematodes* and shorter, dark-blue spikes of the grey-leafed *Veronica incana*. Big sprawling masses of yellow variegated sage, *Salvia officinalis* 'Icterina', contrast with bold, edging clumps of *Bergenia cordifolia* which set off the small-leafed *Hebe buchananii*. These last three plants all make very effective ground cover. Planted in bold groups they cover several square yards, spared from monotony by the plants I have allowed to mingle among them. These include the Sea Holly 'Miss Willmott's Ghost', *Eryngium giganteum*, and lovely she looks. Her silvery, milky-blue thistle heads, so clean-cut and long-lasting, make a feature for weeks, even months, by which time they will have bleached to straw colour. Nowhere do they make such a contribution as mixed with the pale, creamy heads of a yarrow-like plant called *Achillea taygetea*. Their colour is repeated in the arching foliage of a handsome blue grass, *Helictotrichon sempervirens*, while a fountain of bronze, oat-like heads shimmering in the sunlight belongs to a very tall grass, over 6 feet (2 m) high, called *Stipa gigantea*. Weaving among this group is an apricot *Alstroemeria* which luckily appeared among my seedlings and seems just the right shade amidst these soft grey-blues and creamy yellows. To come upon a group like this tempts me back to the house to fetch my scissors and fill a big jugful for my sitting room; the soft colours look as lovely in lamplight as they do in the garden.

July is the month for daisies and related plants. We grow several different forms of *Anthemis*, yellow daisies making a great show with literally hundreds of thin stems rising from tight, woody rootstocks. *Anthemis tinctoria* 'Grallach Gold', a bright strong yellow, stands up well and is very effective seen waving above blue and mauve erigerons (more daisies, good for edging) or hardy geraniums or cranesbills. My favourite, *Anthemis tinctoria* 'E.C. Buxton', is a jewel of a plant, growing happily in any ordinary garden soil. It flowers from midsummer until the first November frost extinguishes those pale lemon faces. It is lower growing than *Anthemis t.* 'Wargrave', whose 2.5-3 foot (1 m) stems can certainly be described as lanky, but nonetheless its pale yellow flowers make a magnificent sight if lightly supported by surrounding plants. In better soil I have *A. t.* 'Wargrave' mingled with

Euphorbia griffithii 'Fireglow', and love the mixture of pale lemon and hot tomato-red. *Catananche caerulea*, another daisy-shaped flower and sometimes called Cupid's Dart on account of the peculiar shape of its grey leaves, is not all that often seen in gardens. In France many years ago, I was enchanted to come across it on the dry limestone 'pavement' of the Causses – the very poor stony uplands to the south of the Massif Central – where it stood, in thousands, in the dry grass as we might see dandelions on the sides of a British motorway. Transparent, papery and pointed buds are poised on dry, wiry stems, opening square-tipped, pale-violet petals whose darker centres are flecked with yellow anthers.

Achilleas are also daisies – although you might not think so – since many of them seem to have no apparent petals but rather appear as densely packed heads of colour. *Achillea* 'Moonshine' is deservedly popular. Its finely-cut, silvery foliage makes a perfect setting for graceful, branching stems of clear-yellow flowers. They are not so hard in colour, nor the stems so rigidly stiff as *Achillea filipendulina* 'Gold Plate', but this well-known old border-plant can still be a great sight in the right place: up to 5 feet (1.5 m) high and with perhaps a hundred stems, topped with wide, flat heads of yellow and never requiring a stake. This plant is at its best during July and August. *Achillea ptarmica* 'The Pearl' is sometimes thrown out because of its wandering habits, but my stock beds are a lovely sight for weeks in midsummer, packed with thousands of stems holding themselves upright to support branching heads of dazzling-white, double flowers. We pick armfuls to decorate the house and the sales table in the pack-house. Various members of staff try their hands at flower-arranging in the large earthenware jar which stands against a whitewashed wall.

Today the choice has been blue and white flowers. We have a strange pearl-grey *Delphinium* sent to us by James Nuttall, so we named it after him. It is more off-beat than the straight-forward bright blues, so does not 'kill' *Campanula lactiflora*. This spectacular bellflower displays a multitude of small, soft-blue bells clustered into large loose heads on 5 foot (1.5 m) stems. A few stems create a grand effect in an arrangement.

Many people are attracted by *Chrysanthemum maximum*: large chalk-white daisies in several different varieties, some plain, semi-double, double, or with finely shredded petals. The same may be said of *Chrysanthemum corymbosum*, a lovely plant, which I have only discovered recently. White daisies are held in clusters on top of 3 foot stems. I have placed it at the corner of a grass walk where the whole plant, including pretty feathery leaves, causes me to pause a moment and enjoy it. *Anthemis tinctoria* 'Wargrave', with lemon-yellow daisy flowers, adds sparkle to all the cool colours in this simple arrangement, while a froth of *Alchemilla mollis* trailing through the flowers softens the rigid stems.

Some hybrid lilies I find difficult to place. They are so extravagantly beautiful, demand so much attention, and are often unsympathetic to their neighbours. Perhaps I have the wrong varieties, ones which would be better grown in rows for picking, to decorate the foyers of impressive hotels. They have solid clustered, upturned heads of brassy yellow or screaming orange. I am not sad when these pass on, but I do value two red varieties which are more than a straight, bright red. 'Ralph' holds clusters of trumpet flowers facing upwards so that you can look into its scarlet-red petals stained with a hint of brown and softened with a sprinkling of brown freckles. 'Pirate' is similar in colour, but with darker shadowed centres and the flowers face downwards, their petals reflexed. These two lilies follow each other in flowering, extending the pleasure of an unusual colour. I pick one or two stems at a time and put them into a wine decanter standing on a low table where the evening sunlight catches them when I sit down. (Do remember not to pick lily stems too low down; they must have enough leaves left to make good bulbs for the next season's flowering.)

There is so much to see, not nearly enough time to stand and absorb it all. Each summer month I think I could fill a notebook with the details, although I doubt whether I could hold any reader's attention through the long lists of names and descriptions.

Stopping us in our tracks is *Macleaya microcarpa* 'Coral Plume'; this used to be called *Bocconia cordata*, the Plume Poppy. Towering above us are loose, drooping plumes of soft apricot buds, opening frail tassels of cream stamens. Handsome grey and green leaves, brushed with a patina of pewter, ascend strong stems. Both young stems and new leaves show touches of the warm colour seen in the flower buds. Beneath these tall plants is a ground covering of dark *Heuchera micrantha* 'Palace Purple', with wonderfully rich foliage. Rounded lobed leaves, puckered and veined, glisten in the sun. They vary in tone from warm orange-tan to dark copper-bronze, while the backs are a light beetroot-red. Tall, upright sprays of tiny white flowers are held in reddish-brown calyces which slowly swell to form seedheads, just as attractive as the succession of fresh flowers still among them.

Passing from the areas of well-drained soil, it is often noticeably cooler in the lower garden on the retentive silt soil. Here is growing a fine stand of *Veratrum viride*, the earliest *Veratrum* to flower. Above its stiffly pleated leaves stand tall branching flower spikes, closely set with small, cup-shaped, acid-green flowers. Cousins of this plant, with white or plum-purple flowers, growing wild in the Alps, were considered by Reginald Farrer, on one of his off-days, to be 'of unmitigated dinginess'. He would not, I think, have disputed the right of all veratrums to stand in the front rank of architectural plants. From head to toe *Veratrum viride* stands apart. Carved and clean in outline, it retains its pose many weeks later when only the fine seed head remains. Like many other wild plants, it relishes the peace and plenty of an English garden, asking only for time to rest undisturbed and to establish a big rootstock and throw up several fine flowering stems.

It was a thrill to see this plant growing wild in Oregon at the base of Mount Hood in black soil sodden with melting snow. We had come up from Portland through mixed coniferous forest and had arrived at the timberline where the trees become stunted and scarce. Dirty, melting snow lay around us in early July, while far above glittered the white cap of Mount Hood, where we could just see black figures practising ski-runs for the Olympic Games. Little more than an hour's drive away in Portland, on the Pacific, water skiers rose and dipped in sparkling spray behind powerful speedboats, while we stood halfway between winter and summer in the mountain's springtime, surrounded by newly emerging plants.

Scrambling up a steep bank I found vertical patches of *Phlox douglasii* in shades of pink, rose and white. Further on, the short grass was full of it, so you see that it can stand competition, but I was amazed to find how wet the soil was. As soon as the immediate snow had melted, however, this area would become pretty dry and much hotter than we experience in Britain. Dwarf *Polemonium pulcherrimum* caught my eye, and at the foot of a Giant Fir I saw delicate trails of *Mitella caulescens* whose tiny, tiarella-like leaves make carpets among my hostas at home. *Mimulus guttatus* hung over a sunny saturated bank and so did the famous *Castillera coccinea*, the scarlet Indian Paint Brush, which is semi-parasitic and so would be difficult to grow – even if we could supply it with melting snow in July.

I was being shown the sights and flora of the Columbia River Gorge by Faith Mackaness, an amazing lady who knows this beautiful natural area 'like her own back yard'. She writes, collects seed, and works incessantly to help preserve the rich flora of the Northwest States, and of Oregon in particular, from the destruction and scavenging that continually threaten to destroy all life in man's search for temporary material gain. Suddenly, turning off the track, Faith would rustle about beneath a tangle of stems to show me the home of some treasure she knew I would love to see. Many plants we think of as 'our' garden plants grow wild throughout the Northwest States. They include *Aquilegia*, many kinds of *Iris*, *Erythronium*, *Fritillaria*, *Smilacina*, *Heuchera*, *Tellima*, *Trillium* – and many more – I must not be tempted to dwell on all the treasures we grow which come from that rich area. (In Vancouver my hosts were amused at my incredulity seeing swamps choked with the great leaves of *Lysichitum americanum*. To them the sight was as ordinary as docks along the roadside would be to us. *Erythronium* seed-heads dotted over grassy banks showed me where these had bloomed, as bluebells do in our beech woods.)

I would have liked to spend a week – or better still a month – with Faith Mackaness and her English husband Frank. In spite of poor health he cooks like an angel, and made us the best picnic I have ever eaten. Out of sight of Mount Hood, but overlooking a tumbling brook full of rockslides and great boulders almost as large as a house, we found a large rough plank table surrounded by bench seats and shaded by great firs. Here were unpacked the baskets, bottles and jars of an amazing feast – Frank Mackaness' picnic. There was:

Raisin bread, made with home-ground wholemeal flour.

Boston Brown Bread – I had never seen this before, but I had read the recipe in my American mother-in-law's Boston School of Cooking Cook-Book. Frank served this moist dark bread, thinly sliced, sandwiched with cream cheese. I could hardly wait to try it out when I got home.

Hard-boiled eggs, chicken breasts and legs, fresh-fried in crumbs, cucumber in dill pickle, gooseberry jam, and a special plum jam from little wild plums called Klamath Plum.

A cheeseboard, including soft cheese rolled in split almonds, chilled butter.

There was coffee, tea and delicious iced-lemon made with purified water.

There were fresh peaches, Bing cherries and a great bowl of mixed fruit salad.

All of which had been prepared for ten people by a tall, frail-looking man, whose state of health one would have said merited him a chair in the sun and waiter-service. Such is the effect of mind and a warm heart over severe disabilities.

After lunch we scrambled among the boulders along the edge of the river bed and found *Mimulus lewisii* in flower. There were not many, most having been swept away by flooding, but I found a few mother-plants sheltered among tussocks of sedge and dwarf willow. *Anaphalis margaritacea* was common and there was plenty of small flowered *Philadelphus* in bloom.

I did not see *Phlox pilosa* on my travels as its home is on the prairies, in central United States and Canada, but I returned to find it running through one of my cool borders where it flowers most of the summer. It is far too pretty to be a nuisance. The stems, about 12-15 inches (30-38 cm) high, carry loose heads of soft, mauve-pink flowers, delicately scented. It is quite different from the large, hybrid border-phlox with their rigid stems and over-large flowers. I think we tend to overdo the so-called improvement of many garden plants. In some cases the original wild species can gain by selection, or even interbreeding, but coarse blooms with strident colours do not fit easily into groups of predominantly species plants. Again it is a matter of taste and situation.

large public borders are expected to provide a cheerful blaze of colour, supported on strong, wind-proof stems, and are usually to be observed from a distance, if not passed at a brisk trot. The very antithesis of such plants is *Nepeta govaniana*, which stands behind the tumbling stems of *Phlox pilosa*, the two very different shapes and colours creating an attractive partnership. This unusual catmint comes from Kashmir. It likes sun but prefers cool soil. From a base of light-green, lemon-scented leaves come open-branched spires about 2-2.5 feet (61-76 cm) tall, set with greenish-yellow buds which open to dangle soft, creamy-yellow tubular flowers. It is a fragile-looking plant, but persistent, producing a succession of blooms well into the autumn.

Behind this cool little group of soft mauve, pink and creamy-yellow, is a background of *Fuchsia magellanica*, *Skimmia rubella* and *Azalea occidentale*, all draped with yards of *Tropaeolum speciosum* aflame with small scarlet flowers, like garlands of long-tailed tiny nasturtiums. *Phlox paniculata* 'Alba' (one leggy parent of the aforementioned border phlox) has been toppled by these clambering ropes of flowers, while asters and foxgloves are bearing up more sturdily. Never before have I found myself stripping *Tropaeolum* off its neighbours like bindweed. This is the way I have seen it growing in Scotland, in cooler wetter conditions than we usually experience. How different our gardens would become with even a small, but regular change in climate. It is the unpredictability of our weather which makes every gardening season an adventure.

Pale, ghostly shapes swaying in the background are 4-5 foot (1.5 m) stems of the white-flowered Willow-Herb, *Epilobium angustifolium* 'Album'. Unbranched stems carry close-set white flowers, backed by green star-shaped sepals which show in gaps behind tissue-paper petals. From the centre of each flower tumbles a cluster of pale stamens, while beyond them extends a curly, four-pronged green pistil. A spire of unopened buds extends above the open flowers while sterile, pale grey-green seed pods below them maintain interesting form and colour. Narrow grey-green leaves stand upright along the length of stem.

'A restful plant', commented Ness Buckle, busy below them, touching up here and there the disturbed mulch of crushed bark. I had been adding *Campanula·turbinata* 'Alba'. Its low cushions of small leaves are covered with large white saucer-shaped flowers, stained faintly blue. The colour drains into the dark central spot. It is a plant hard to pass by.

I have just dug my crop of garlic, about a hundred and fifty bulbs. This sounds a lot but I use a good deal, and it is nice to have enough to give away. In normal summers they come out of desert-dry soil, clean and papery-skinned, but this year the soil is wet and the bulbs are very muddy. I laid them in open slatted trays to hose off all the mud, then propped the trays against a warm wall where the sun and wind is drying them quickly. Sometimes I spread them on a strip of wire netting supported above the ground. As soon as the stems are dry enough I shall hang bunches of bulbs beneath the roof of an open shed, where they will be protected from further downpours, but where the circulating air can nonetheless continue the harvesting process. When absolutely dry, the loose skins are rubbed off and the bulbs tied into fresh bunches, or ropes, and are kept in a cold but frost-free room. Garlic is easy to grow in this country, but can be lost through mould if it is not thoroughly dried in the open air. Once I put some to dry in one of my plastic tunnels thinking the warmth would dry them quickly, but the humidity encouraged blue mould and I lost most of the crop.

Home-grown garlic

Suddenly it has become very warm, too warm for work. The air is full of thunderflies, blown in from the corn which is being harvested in neighbouring fields. They drive us mad, getting caught in our hair, or drowned in the sweat of our arms and faces. We look down and see our T-shirts black with them. During the night I was woken by thunder, so close it sounded like heavy crates tumbling and crashing down a great wooden staircase. Flashes of lightning penetrated my closed eyelids, then a short shower of raindrops hit the *Magnolia* leaves outside my bedroom window.

Going downstairs to breakfast I found a round heat-mark on my teak work-top! Last night's muddles were still with me; I had burnt the potatoes and the hot, dry saucepan had scorched the wood. I found some sandpaper and began to scrub, finishing with fine wool. After an hour the mark had almost gone. A rub with linseed oil and it would be almost as good as new. I was winning, I thought. But the day had scarcely begun.

One of my young staff suddenly appeared. Could she speak to me on a serious matter? It sounded ominous. She handed me a letter and I read it. She was giving me her notice! During her year with us Sallyann had

173

impressed us with her enthusiasm and she had studied hard for the National Diploma of Horticulture. She had just heard that she had passed. This was wonderful news, a great achievement, since the course covers a wide range of horticultural subjects. Now she would like to move on, to fresh fields and pastures new. I felt sad. I too had nursed hopes for this lively young woman. But it was not to be; such is life. Young people need opportunities for experience and development, they need to move about to see what best will suit them; but the people left behind are hoping for a team-mate, someone who can stay for a few years at least. For those who become involved with the garden and nursery, each day is packed with a variety of jobs, and no two days are alike. As the pattern of flowers changes in the garden, so we are involved every day with dozens of different activities on the nursery. We are recording much of our daily work in carefully kept files, but it still needs experienced eyes on the spot to judge priorities. A sudden change in weather often means a change of jobs, for there will be tasks which have been waiting for just such conditions. Knowing how and when to propagate thousands of different plants takes many years – you could say a lifetime, since we are continually learning new things. In three weeks time our young friend will be gone. We are sad to see her go but we wish her well in whatever field she may put her capacity for enthusiasm and hard work.

Picking myself up, I walked out onto the nursery and came face to face with a German lady and her daughter who had pursued me by telephone when I was in Germany. They badly wanted me to offer a place to this girl so that she might learn about plants and study English. I had said 'No, I am sorry' on the telephone, and 'No' I meant. I could see no reason to change my mind. But I could understand the mother's concern. Feeling for them, I invited them into the office and made several telephone calls to other nurseries and schools of horticulture; I was lucky to make an appointment for them elsewhere. It was not the help they would have liked, but better than sending them away empty.

By afternoon I felt lifeless, so I drifted through mechanical jobs at my desk. Tea-time brought a welcome end to a trying day, or so I thought. Then the telephone rang. It was Kazu, my Japanese student who has been obliged to change his lodgings in the neighbouring village. He was very sorry to bother me, but his new landlord was ill; could I come? Imagining all kinds of dreadful scenes, I jumped into the car, cowardly wondering if I would have the stomach to cope; but on arrival my over-active imagination was put in its place. I found a sad man, addicted to the bottle, trying to escape himself and his worries. He could talk coherently and he was aware that he was destroying himself and his talents. I felt pity for the waste. There was nothing I could do to help him, but there was plenty I must do for Kazu. In three weeks' time the caravan on the nursery, occupied by Sally Ann, would be empty; I cannot search for another lodging which might prove unsatisfactory again, so Kazu must stay in my house until he moves into the caravan to complete his time here with me. Arrived back in my kitchen, Kazu picked up the tea-towel with a big smile. We all like him. He works well and understands much of what we say. If only he could express himself in words.

I have been collecting herbs to dry, for use in winter. It has been difficult to catch plants when they are dry enough, before the next downpour, but it is a waste of time to hang up bundles of damp leaves. In warm, humid conditions they become musty in no time. I wash some herbs, like parsley and marjoram, strip off the coarse stems and put them into little polythene bags to freeze. These are almost as good as freshly picked herbs for soups or salads in winter when the plants may be under snow or spoilt by frost. Tarragon, *Artemisia dracunculus*, I hang up to dry, then rub it out as soon as it is brittle, to store in a screw-topped jar. It is delicious in fish pâtés, in salads, with eggs, or with herb cheese.

There are several different kinds of mint. Horse-mint, *Mentha sylvestris*, is a strong-growing mint preferring damp soil. It has large woolly leaves which retain their flavour well when dried. *Mentha spicata*, spearmint, with smooth leaves, is more usually grown. Both have the kind of flavour one expects to find in mint sauce. I rarely make mint sauce, but use the strong tangy flavour of both these mints in mint tea served hot, either plain or sweetened with honey, or iced, with fruit juice. It is a vital ingredient for the brilliant green drink we make from liquidising green-leaf vegetables, with just a touch of lemon to add zest. Another refreshing way to use mint is finely chopped into chilled yoghurt, with just a touch of chopped shallot. Let the flavours blend, then use it to cool your mouth as a side dish with hot curry.

Next to the back door, tangled among the roots of a climbing rose, I can always find the dark-leafed purple-stemmed Peppermint. This also makes a pleasant tea, very soothing for disturbed stomachs. My teenage grandchildren and I, with undisturbed stomachs, enjoyed it after swimming with Janet Allan, the potter, and her husband Nigel Henderson, the painter. Their ancient red-brick and tarred board-house stands on the edge of the saltings where marsh and water merge with the horizon on the Essex coast. High tide laps the lowest walls of the outbuildings where we shed our clothes, scrambled down the dry grassy bank, and floated into perfect peace. The sky and sea were one, like the interior of an exotic abalone shell – pastel shades of blue, lilac, green and white, stretching away and away without end. The sun slid over the little silvery ripples which covered miles of warm primaeval mud. Low promontories, covered with marsh samphire and mauve sea-lavender, made fine places to bask like seals and watch the tide slowly rise to fill every creek and inlet. On the far side of the wide estuary ripening fields of corn laid soft bands of toasted colour between the shimmering water and all-encompassing sky. I felt as free as a child, or a fish, floating in the warm shallow water, responsibilities abandoned in this seemingly carefree world. The children dived on and off an old float, pushing each other overboard, while Mally, the black and white collie bitch sat poised on the point of marsh overlooking us, ready to leap into the water from time to time to round us all up.

When my hands turn white I know it is time to leave the water. Janet had already left. I found her sitting on the dry grass bank mixing fresh scones for tea. 'Go and have a hot bath' she said, Shivering slightly, I padded up one of the winding staircases which link rooms on curiously different levels and sank into deep, warm water. It was a startling and exquisite sensation to feel the warmth pass to every part of my chilled skin, until I lay lapped in comfort, closing my eyes in utter relaxation.

Once the tide turns in these shallow saltings the water runs away very quickly as though a plug had been pulled out, leaving shining slopes of soft, grey mud etched with the pattern of parting ripples. Here and there, these are carved deeper by little tributaries, until finally all the water has drained away – except the main channel, which lies like a great silver snake in the bottom of its hollow. Sea birds drop out of the sky to poke about in the gurgling, plopping mud, feasting on creatures hidden beneath the surface that are waiting for the returning tide. Suddenly they all take wing, wheeling and screaming in patterns of flight.

The children had hauled up the float, pulled old jerseys over their tanned bodies and came crowding round the Aga, drawn by the warmth and smell of fresh baking. They carried Janet's teapots and bowls out onto a long balcony, outside the pottery, and with salty fingers ate warm, wheatmeal scones, topped with fresh raspberry jam and drained yoghurt. Back and forth went our tea bowls as we tried different pots of hot clear tea. Peppermint was compared with camomile and fresh lemon verbena which we had brought from the garden for Janet to try. All these teas taste much better when made from freshly gathered herbs rather than those out of packets which may have been kept too long.

Perhaps it was the fresh air which gave an edge to our taste buds or it may have been the magical atmosphere of the place, during that one special week of the holidays when we left behind all feelings of 'should' and 'must' and escaped down dusty lanes to share the sun, the incoming tide and each other.

Now twelve months later, all has changed. Nigel died suddenly one morning this past spring. For Janet, the sun has gone down. Sometimes she comes to warm herself among my plants. The young people will not play again on the rafts as they did, under a cloudless sky.

The spare-room beds are heaped with piles of old-fashioned rose petals in shades of pink and red, white, crimson and purple; all spread out they look like patchwork quilts. It takes a surprising time to dry the petals thoroughly. Among them are rose buds which take longer to dry than the petals but which look very pretty in the finished pot-pourri. When all are ready, they are put into large polythene bags with a sprinkling of Orris root (a fixative), to wait until the rest of the flowers are ready. The floor is also carpeted with dust sheets then spread with the bright blue flowers, like the double rosettes of *Delphinium* 'Alice Artindale'. These, and the double forms of cranesbill, *Geranium pratense* 'Plenum Violaceum', dry perfectly, retaining shape and colour. Marigold petals are pulled off their heavy green centres but still take several weeks to lose that damp sticky feeling.

I am not at all expert in the art of making pot-pourri and hope I shall learn by experience how to improve, but with so much colour and scent in the garden it seems a pity not to preserve a little to remind us of summer during the winter. The evergreen honeysuckle, *Lonicera japonica* 'Halliana', has the most delicious scent, especially in the evening and early morning. I wonder if the scent would be retained if I dry some of the creamy-yellow flowers? A great many would be needed. Some flowers like the white cone-shaped heads of *Houttuynia cordata*, which smell so strongly of Seville oranges, smell of nothing now that I have dried them.

All summer we have looked forward to going to the Sandringham Flower Show. Our own van is not large enough to take everything we need, while the large carrier we hire for Chelsea would be too big. So we hired a van from a local firm. Boxes and trays were carefully packed with a profusion of flowers and fine foliage which had been sheltered from damage in one of our netting-covered tunnels. The site we had been offered was much smaller than our Chelsea exhibit, thank goodness, but to see if I had enough plants or too many, I roughly placed the boxes on the measured area marked out on a flat stretch of gravel.

After lunch, when all was ready, we set off. As this was our first visit we found ourselves a little confused on arrival, not certain of the correct entry. After driving round several times we got out and moved a 'No Entry' sign laid across the most likely looking entrance, replaced it, and were relieved to find ourselves in an undulating meadow dotted with ancient trees and several large white marquees. Carpenters were still hammering and banging display tables into position. We found our site in the Cottagers' Marquee, the longest marquee of all. We parked close to the entrance and, in a fine drizzle, unloaded our plants and stood them round the site. The carpenters came to look and to comment. They were old hands, they knew we were strangers but were friendly and helpful, telling us how to find the village where we were to stay the night.

Beyond the sloping parkland, almost hidden by a fine screen of trees, stood the Royal House. As we trudged back and forth with trays of plants my eye was suddenly caught by the sight of the Royal Standard floating in a gap between the trees where there had been nothing before. It gave us a little thrill of excitement to know that the Queen Mother had just arrived – home for the weekend.

Soon we were installed in a small, local hotel. From my room I looked down onto a rain-soaked garden with deserted tables beneath furled umbrellas. What a summer! After a good meal I was glad to be tucked up in bed listening to the rain gurgling down a pipe onto the cobbled path below.

Next morning we were up early, startling the manager into making us a cup of coffee. Although he was busy putting his bar in order the coffee appeared and we were on site by 8 a.m. We worked till 9.30 then made our own breakfast in the empty van. It felt and looked like November, a cold grey drizzle outside – just as cold and grey inside. But we enjoyed ourselves, staging our exhibit, showing groups of plants for Dry, Shady and Damp situations. As we worked we discussed the reasons which lie behind my ideas for staging, while at the same time I was thinking that I should try to make a list of 'Helpful Hints in Staging'. We have come a long way from the old idea of showing tiered ranks of vases each filled with one variety. This is still the best way to show the newest varieties of cultivars, like *Narcissus* or *Chrysanthemum* but it does not help the viewer to imagine those plants in the garden. It is much more likely to attract amateur exhibitors who see themselves setting up prize blooms for further competitions. My plants are not meant to win prizes. Some are quite modest to set off others more flamboyant; some may be in bud showing a promise of something lovely yet to come. The colour, shape and texture of each plant inspires me to design groups which fit together like a puzzle. It would not be impossible to write down the names of plants and to make a rough sketch, but an exhibit made from a plan worked out on paper would not have the spontaneity which comes from seeing the plants on site, when height, bulk, quantity and quality will all govern the design.

Fortunately my assistant, Stephen, needed no helpful hints on foraging for food. Sent off to find something to supplement our picnic lunch, he returned with apple juice and goats's-milk yoghurt. The rain was now hammering down relentlessly and the inside of the marquee was almost dark. We made a table from boxes and cheered ourselves up with home-made bread and honey followed by fruit and yoghurt.

By 3.30 p.m. we were almost done, and raised our heads to see other nursery firms staging roses, fuchsias and pot plants. Fred Waite, the head gardener at Sandringham House, who had invited us to the show, came to collect us to show us the Royal Gardens. We followed his car and parked our van in the back yard of the house while patrolling guards were informed of our arrival. Everywhere was very well kept – acres of mown grass, clipped hedges and clean gravel walks. It must be strange to be a head gardener in such prestigious gardens which are also, on certain days, public gardens. How much can you let your imagination run riot? Not too far – the cost of new ideas and the ensuing maintenance has to be as critically examined as in our own gardens. Mr Waite was proud to show us the developments which had taken place during his administration. He was particularly pleased to show us his latest enterprise. (Don't we all take our visitors to the newest part of the garden – the latest baby, as it were, to be admired – where tiny bits of plants, still needing our care, have yet to become established?)

Here was a simple stream flowing down a natural hollow, set off by close-mown grass and scattered trees. Dammed here and there, it meandered down the gentle slope, providing homes for bog-loving plants such as Marsh Marigold, certain types of *Iris* and the Bog Arum, *Lysichitum americanum*, in the small beds carved out alongside. Hostas, *Hemerocallis* and *Astilbe* were among the plants to be seen on the less soggy banks. This was planting that any visitor could feel at home with; plants used in small groups, not in vast impersonal splashes. In contrast, I was interested to see the old garden which must have been designed and planted when the house was built. Great bluffs of imported rocks were used to create a spectacular rock garden above the lake, all overgrown now with a profusion of Victorian planting and with evergreens predominating. In summer, gigantic gunneras make fine relief in a scene redolent of the era before the First World War, as evocative as old sepia photographs of that period. These gardens would have looked very different in their youth.

Scores of gardeners would have cherished individual pockets of plants as they waited for trees and shrubs to grow to fit the scale of construction. Today, only the toughest survive – mostly ground-smothering shrubs.

Back at the marquee we had to keep our minds on our own efforts, putting the finishing touches to our 'garden' and cleaning up all the mess – the empty boxes, broken plants, watering cans and other paraphernalia. Throughout the late afternoon and evening exhibitors from the houses and cottages on the Sandringham estate came with their platefuls of shining currants, transparent gooseberries, trays of mixed vegetables and vases of cottage-garden flowers. Old men set impossibly long runner beans straight or placed carefully selected onions on plates of dry sand, while small boys bearing pots of home-made jam or bottles of home-made wine walked behind their mothers who carried perfect sponge cakes. It reminded me of the village flower shows I went to as a child, with my earthenware jam-pot full of wild flowers – but I never won any prizes.

We went to bed and prayed for a fine day. Next morning I awoke early and went to the bathroom to take a shower. I was washing my hair when the head of the shower fell off and, for some strange reason, the water was scalding and could not be cooled. To rinse myself I had to run the bath and put my head under the ice-cold tap. Without further mishaps I dressed and met Stephen at breakfast. He had also had difficulties in the bathroom. (Being a perfect fool with almost anything mechanical, I was relieved that, for once, the problem had not been caused by my own ineptitude.)

We arrived on the showground to find crowds of people assembled. The sun shone, the sky was blue, it felt like a holiday. We made our way to the entrance of the Cottagers' Marquee and had to stoop under ropes to walk down the red carpet which led to the entrance. We felt part of the exhibit! Inside we found judging still in progress. The spectacular floor-to-ceiling displays of roses and fuchsias, one at each end of the marquee, fully deserved their Large Gold Medals, while we were well content to find that we had been awarded a normal Gold Medal. Relaxed now, we went off to see whose runner beans had been considered the best. Part of the fun at a flower show is disagreeing with the judges. But it was not difficult to read the mind of the judge who, in the flower-arranging section, gave first prize to the basket with the biggest dahlias.

Suddenly the sound of a brass band brought us hurrying towards the entrance, and there in an open carriage was the Queen Mother – looking radiant. All around her were calls of 'Happy Birthday' which she responded to with obvious joy, though she must already have heard it a hundred times that week. Escorted by her head gardener, she entered the marquee and was received by Peter Beales. Mr Beales, who is famous for his collection of old roses, lives in Norfolk and has attended the show many times, so he and the Queen Mother knew each other of old.

We stood nearby watching this small, animated lady so obviously enjoying every moment and making everyone else's day. As she walked towards us a ray of sunlight fell through the tent pole like a spotlight onto our flowers. It was a theatrical moment, especially after the gloom of yesterday. She walked round our little garden, asking questions and warming us with her smile before passing on to the sponge cakes. Such vitality, eight-five years young on Sunday, I could not help wondering if I would last so well.

Turning back to our plants we saw the slim figure of Prince Charles bearing down upon us. 'I have become very keen on my garden,' he began, 'but how can I learn to put my plants together to look like this?' 'Ah' said Stephen, coming to my rescue, 'that takes years and years of experience.' We were relieved he had broken the tension, and there followed a very natural and informal chat about some of the problems – and pleasures – of gardening.

The rest of the day was spent answering questions from the crowd and listening to comments about our exhibit. Most people found it a novelty, since many of the plants were unfamiliar. That did not matter. It is not necessary to grasp Latin handles, but to stop and enjoy a new flower or to notice that it is similar, but different, from something you already have at home; that is the beginning of plant collecting. The smallest garden can be packed with interest if, like Prince Charles, you would like to find out more about plants.

AUGUST

THERE still persists a slight doubt in my mind when I am asked if the garden is worth visiting in August. This feeling is left over from my experiences in our first garden where we did not have the wide range of growing conditions we now have and so could not collect such a wide range of plants. Unless you can water your garden efficiently and regularly it is a waste of time to grow beds of Michaelmas daisy or border phlox, especially if you live in a district where drought is a way of life and not an occasional phenomenon. Even heavy clay soils eventually dry out leaving cracks wide enough to put your hand inside.

Efficient watering is out of the question if hosepipes are banned as soon as you need to use them. In such conditions it is much better to stick to drought-resisting plants, predominantly the grey- and silver-leafed varieties. (Plants which flower and then disappear in spring or early summer usually find enough moisture for their needs at that time.)

We have known soil to remain dust-dry until snow has fallen. This depressing state of affairs was my lot until we began our present garden. Now, with many different types of soil, some of it kept moist by underground springs, we have a collection of plants which, without irrigation, keep our interest and enthusiasm going until November and later, because there are then berries, fruits and autumn leaves to add to the surprising number of plants flowering late in the year. Sometimes I think it needs a lifetime of experience to know how to plant the garden so there is a constant ebb and flow of colour – not to have it all at one season, with nothing much left after the wall-flowers have faded. Because I value foliage plants, I find I enjoy the ebb-tides in the garden almost more than when there is a confusion of flowers and I can easily miss individual delights. So I am sometimes relieved when August comes, the abundance subsides, and the quieter pattern of leaves takes over. This is especially so on the free-draining gravels. Here all the artemisias improve as summer passes. Their feathery, whitened foliage stands out among the dark leaves of *Cistus* and thyme, *Euphorbia*, or the fresh green mounds of *Santolina virens* which make such a welcome contrast among many of these ashen-coloured plants. *Thyme, Santolina* and other aromatic plants fill the air with warm, southern scents. Little lizards rustle over the dry soil. Seed pods of spurges explode and pop; bees hum busily in the calamint bushes. *Calamintha nepetoides* is a plant which can become a favourite. It disappears in winter, but in summer it sends up many branching stems which become stiff and wiry, set with small green leaves and covered with clouds of tiny, pale blue flowers. Throughout late summer and autumn they are crowded with stumbling honey bees. They look well in the herb border surrounded with golden or variegated thymes and matt-leaved sages, which all look their best in the latter half of the season. Less well known is *Nepeta nervosa*, but I cannot think why. It is an exquisite plant for the edge of a sunny border with its bright blue and white-lipped flowers held in clustered heads above mats of little green leaves. Near these two I like to plant *Coreopsis verticillata* with its crowds of yellow daisies poised on finely feathered stems.

Several different shades of hardy *Agapanthus* make a lovely show for weeks and are still attractive when carrying their large green-podded seed heads. I have an old cultivar named 'Blue Moon', very pale blue with much larger flower heads than those of the Headbourne hybrids. It does not come into flower until the latter are going over, which is useful.

Outstanding in the Dry Garden during August is the Mount Etna Broom, *Genista aetnensis*, a fountain (15 feet (5 m) high and across) dripping with millions of tiny yellow pea-flowers on thread-like stems, filling the garden with a sweet, spicy scent. Beneath, shrubby potentillas flower all summer long, in creamy-white, yellow, soft tan and apricot.

Diascia is a name which has cropped up in the past few years and now there are several different species available, beautiful additions to mid and late summer. *Diascia cordata* 'Ruby Field' is well named, making wide spreading mats smothered with deep salmon-pink flowers on short stems. *Diascia rigescens* has similar cup-shaped flowers closely set on taller stems. There are others. Only you can tell how reliably hardy they are in your own conditions. I think they survive best in warm well-drained soil but I was amazed to have plants of *Diascia rigescens* come through the hard winter of 1984-5. I think maybe a good covering of snow protected the base of the plants. Two more plants beside them which surprised me by coming through that winter were *Sisyrinchium striatum* 'Variegatum' and *Salvia patens.* I thought the two forms of this *Salvia*, in both dark and light blue, were tender bedding plants, but they have survived several years outside, although we always collect seed and keep cuttings under cover as an insurance.

One of the most spectacular plants in the Dry Garden at this time of year is *Ferula communis*, a gigantic fennel from the southern parts of the Mediterranean. It must be planted when only a few inches tall, looking like a young parnsip with a long, thin, white root and feathery leaves. I usually plant out several in strategic places and, like the squirrels, forget where I have put them all. So I have lovely surprises as the immensely tall (10-12 feet (3-4 m)) stems suddenly shoot up from a base of huge, fretted, non-aromatic leaves carrying great wands of tiny yellow star flowers. They soar above *Cistus* and broom bushes or perhaps appear beside a tall *Eucalyptus* or grey-leafed *Cupressus*. Unlike the scented fennel, this *Ferula* sends up only one branching stem from each individual tap-root; it is as thick as my wrist and is stained purple over green, all softened with pale grey bloom when young.

Elsewhere (and usually impressive) are wide, feathery stands of the aromatic fennel, *Foeniculum vulgare.* Many branching stems, clothed in aniseed flavoured leaves, form a wide feathery column, 5-6 feet (1.5-2 m) tall when in full flower, with tiny starry yellow flowers arranged in flat heads. They are at their best when the hybrid lilies are out. I can never resist cutting long stems of each and dropping them into a tall brown Wattisfield jug to stand on the hall floor against white brick where the pollen drops onto the polished tiles.

It only occurred to me that some people do not share my enthusiasm for sedums when a friend said that she had just begun to notice them. Probably my upbringing in a garden where anything which looked good in August was worth treasuring has influenced me. Next to grey-leafed plants which are protected by wool, fine silky hairs or wax, come the 'Fat Plants'; those which store water in thick, swollen leaves. Sedums are in this class. There are so many; too many to describe in detail, but throughout the growing season they all catch my eye with their attractive leaves. Some are quite large, such as the different varieties of *Sedum spectabile* whose pale, icy-green rosettes draw attention to themselves as soon as they appear, while their wide, flat heads of mauve-pink star-like flowers attract bees and butterflies in September. *Sedum* 'Autumn Joy' comes into this group with *Sedum maximum* 'Atropurpureum' adding chocolate brown leaves and dark red, star-like flowers to make an accent among silver and grey. *Sedum* 'Vera Jameson' is a self-made hybrid of this dark-leafed plant. She is considerably smaller and less self-conscious but has everyone stopping to admire her. Some of the smaller sedums make first-class ground cover on poor gravelly soil looking positively lush with their round chubby leaves in shades of green, blue, grey, brown and mahogany red. Their starry flowers, often arranged in surprisingly large heads for such small plants, can be found in white, yellow, pink and shades of mauve. Sedums have only one disadvantage that I can think of and it is that they are sometimes attacked by a caterpillar – when a plant is thoroughly infected you can scarcely see it for the veils of cobweb the creatures have woven about it, while inside they busily devour every leaf and stem.

Most people know Marjoram, *Origanum vulgare*, and probably the golden-leafed form as well. Both produce tall sprays of tiny, mauve-pink flowers while the young leaves are delicious in soups or sprinkled over pizza. On my warm west-facing raised bed is *Origanum rotundifolium* whose tiny flowers are hidden in large, pale green bracts, resembling hops, but rounder and looser. There are several other relatives. *Origanum pulchellum* has smaller, soft pink hops, while *Origanum laevigatum* has stiff sprays, about 12 inches tall, of tiny pink and green flowers.

From bulbs which can store moisture, or from thick root-stocks, now appear several surprisingly fresh flowers to add character to the Mediterranean garden. *Galtonia princeps* came first with wide, grey-green leaves and smooth stems of pale-green wax-like bells. *Galtonia candicans* quickly follows with taller stems, 3-4 feet (1 m), set with pure-white drooping snowdrop-like bells. Last to flower, and lasting well into the autumn, is *Galtonia viride* whose flowers are as fine as the white form, but are pale, pale green – these are always seized upon by flower arrangers and are an important addition to any garden design.

Despite the frighteningly low temperatures of this past winter the sweetly scented crinums are spilling great trumpet-shaped flowers from clusters of buds sitting on top of thick stalks. This spring, when the ground had thawed and I had pulled away the soggy mess of old leaves, my heart sank as I put my hand into the tops of rotted clumps. I thought they were finished. But *Crinum* bulbs are curiously shaped, they have very long necks hidden beneath the soil, with the bulb itself tucked down very deeply below – more than a spade's depth at the bottom. The bulbs may have had a fright but we have never had so many stems of flower as we have had this summer on both white and pink forms.

Penstemons in shades of pink, red, purple and blue, large-flowered *Scabiosa caucasica*, and a curious plant from the prairies and foothills of the Rocky Mountains, *Liatris spicata*, known in its own home as Blazing Star, are among some of the flowering plants to be found on my drier soils now, in high summer.

If we leave the Dry Garden and go down a shallow flight of steps we come to the cool grass of the lower garden and arrive by the pools. Here the impact of lush green growth is almost overpowering. Huge, upturned parasols of *Gunnera chilensis*, each leaf more than 4 feet across, intricately puckered and crinkled to form a frilled and fluted edge, are lifted above our heads on stout prickly stems.

Sheltered beneath them are the curious flower spikes looking more like knob-kerries than flower stems. In fact, almost stemless, they stand about 2 feet (61 cm) high, thick clubs of closely-packed fleshy fingers, or cones, covered with small green dots which become small orange seeds. These absurdly tiny seeds sown in a pan do not begin to germinate until the following summer when they put out two little leaves the size of cress. But they grow away quite quickly and make a fair-sized plant by the end of two years. They are not nearly so slow to make a saleable plant as *Veratrum* or *Lysichitum*, both of which take at least five years before they would be considered.

More dramatic foliage is provided by great phormiums, or New Zealand Flax, which can be found plain, purple or variegated. None is

Galtonia candicans interplanted with *Artemisia pontica*

187

reliably hardy, the variegated forms the least so. But although all the foliage was cut to the ground last winter despite our careful precautions, the root-stocks were not damaged and all are now sending up fresh leaves. They may not be so tall this year, but they have survived. Ten foot tall stands of *Miscanthus sacchariflorus* with drooping strap-shaped leaves catch the light like a waterfall, while Mr Bowles' Golden Sedge (a form of *Carex stricta*), another lovely grass-like plant, explodes like a bright yellow sunburst by the water's edge.

Too many flowers out at the same time can spoil the atmosphere of tranquillity by the waterside. Colour should be seen to come and go among the rich foliage. Most of the candelabra primulas and water iris are over, but the Giant Himalayan Cowslip, *Primula florindae*, which has stems with pale-green dust, reflects its cool lemon-yellow bells in the dark water with yellow musk nearby; while not far away the colour is repeated in the tall *Thalictrum speciosissimum*, whose small heads of greenish-yellow flowers stand far above stiff fans of wax-blue leaves.

Astilbes are good in August if your soil remains damp. I especially love the small ones like 'Sprite' with its wide spires of pale-pink flowers over dark, finely-cut leaves, and *Astilbe chinensis* 'Pumila', whose 12 inch (30 cm) tapers of soft mauve exactly match the 3-4 foot (1 m) tall spires of *Astilbe taquetii* 'Superba'. There are hosts of others, interesting species and many cultivars in damp or shaded places.

Both in the ponds and in well-prepared sites in cool borders I grow arum lilies, *Zantedeschia aethiopica*. They grow wild in abundance in South Africa, but can be grown here if protected in winter. In natural ponds they are kept free from frost in the deep mud floor, while in the border a thick covering of straw, bracken or cut down autumn flower stems will keep the roots safe. The form known as 'Crowborough' is thought to be the hardiest. It is at its best now, each single petal rolled and spiralled like an old-fashioned sweet bag. In one of the ponds stands a great clump of 'Green Goddess', the flower stems 3 feet (1 m) tall, carrying huge fluted funnels whose green tips disappear into ivory

Himalayan cowslip (*Primula florindae*) with *Gunnera chilensis* on the far side of the house pond

189

View downstream with astilbes, *Lysichitum*
foliage, *Lythrum salicaria* and the round
leaves of *Peltiphyllum peltatum*

throats. The magnificent leaves form a feature in themselves – you have to look twice to see the flowers among them. Beyond the pools beneath the shade of the boundary oaks there are few flowers now. Most shade-loving plants bloom in spring leaving behind a patchwork of different shades and textures of leaves.

Creating bold accents among the small-leafed plants are groups of *Hosta*. One of the most admired is *Hosta tardiana* 'Halcyon' which I have planted to appear like a flood of blue as it flows from the bank above down into silver-painted mats of *Lamium maculatum* 'White Nancy' below. Mingling with ferns are patches of *Trillium sessile* and *Viola* 'Finola Galway', a most delightful small pansy which never ceases to produce a carpet of rich blue flowers from spring until autumn. Where sunlight filters down through a gap in the canopy overhead there stands a beautiful cow-parsley-like plant, *Selinum tenuifolium*. Above lacy mounds of finely-cut leaves there appear to float dainty parasols, formed by tiny white flowers poised on pale struts and fastened onto dark disappearing stems. The effect is so delicate that everyone would like to take a plant home. But this is one of my problem plants. Although I have moved it to several different situations, it refuses to set viable seed after having shown every promise to do so, like fennel, earlier in the season. The other way to propagate it is by division but it is just as reluctant to divide itself into moveable pieces, although I know it can. We consider some of our rare plants to be 'signed copies of limited editions' when only a few can be spared each year, but this lovely plant has so far defied my attempts to 'publish' her. However, I shall keep on trying.

In more open, sunny parts of the garden, where the soil is heavy and retentive, I have been able to indulge in another range of plants that in my early gardening days I stood little chance of growing, such as the bog-loving plants now thriving at the water's edge.

These soils include both silt and clay. They tend to pack down tightly, making it difficult for rain to penetrate in summer, and lie cold and wet in winter. Over a period of years it becomes necessary to remove plants where they may appear to be deteriorating and to refresh the soil by adding plenty of small stone and grit to help aerate and drain away surplus moisture.

Midsummer might not appear to be the best time to do this, but I have two young students tackling the end of the border that badly needed this treatment. We have chosen to do the work now when the soil is neither too wet nor too dry. If we wait till autumn or winter it often becomes too wet and, once again, the job does not get done. Working carefully round trees and shrubs these young men have trenched the rest of the border, removing the top spit of clay, breaking up the lower spit and incorporating gravel. Better soil from elsewhere is mixed with well-rotted farmyard manure, peat and sand waste from nursery pots and this has been piled on top and thoroughly mixed.

191

All this, I admit, is a luxury, but it has taken twenty-eight years of gardening here to learn the value of it, and I have done much digging myself to learn how to deal with many soil problems. During the pioneer days I enjoyed doing much of the digging and came to know intimately the problems involved, but I did not have the muscle power to do well what is being done for me today. When these beds have settled it is a joy for me to replant them with new groups of plants which have been waiting in 'Pets Corner' for a proper home.

Plants which show proper gratitude for all this hard work include the Monkshoods. These are so impressive in well-fed soil but I find they deteriorate quite shamefully if left to their own devices. Simply by digging up and replacing the fattest tuberous roots, in the same place if you have no other, together with a generous helping of garden compost, or anything to enrich the soil, you will please them no end.

Aconitum orientale is a beautiful plant, slightly superior to *Aconitum vulparia* which is similar. Tall stems (5 feet (1.5 m)) clothed in deeply divided leaves carry graceful branching heads of creamy-yellow hooded flowers. A strong piece of twine, or bast, threaded through and around them helps the stems support each other in a loose cluster; it is a sin to bind them together tightly. Beside them a large clump of *Polygonum amplexicaule* 'Album' needs no support while its slim white tapers shine for weeks, to be followed by another leggy plant which produces sheaves of tiny white daisies. This is *Boltonia latisquama*, a North American daisy very like an aster. It is really too leggy and needs to be supported, but is very lovely in late summer arrangements, especially with *Chrysanthemum uliginosum*; just these two alone in a jar give great pleasure. A white anemone from Nepal, *Anemone vitifolia*, which is similar to Japanese anemones, creeps into the front of this pale group. To warm it, I have placed *Polygonum amplexicaule* 'Inverleith' nearby whose raspberry-pink spikes are less than half the height of the white-flowered *Polygonum*, while a third Knotweed, *Polygonum affine* 'Donald Lowndes', provides a foreground with short, stumpy heads of salmon-pink.

In June I love the effect of fluffy powder-puff heads in pinky-mauve and white of *Thalictrum aquilegiifolium*. Now, even more elegant, *Thalictrum delavayi* (*T. dipterocarpum*) suddenly appears supporting itself among neighbouring plants and shrubs. Tall (5 foot (1.5 m), slender stems dressed in dainty round leaves, support wide, airy sprays of tiny lilac flowers filled with dangling cream stamens. In great demand is *Thalictrum delavayi* 'Hewitt's Double'. The flowers are similar but lack the contrast of cream stamens. Instead the plants produce immense sprays of tightly double flowers, their rich-lilac colour accented by dark stems. They are irresistible to cut for the house, but if grown together in a bunch the stems become maddeningly tangled, although this does help to support them as a vast gypsophila-like cloud.

192

I should not forget to mention the white-flowered form of *Thalictrum delavayi*. As so often happens with white-flowered plants, you can tell almost certainly among seedlings that you have a true white by its much paler green leaves. Flower stems are also green, while the stems of the lovely lilac-flowered form are stained with a purple tint.

Veratrum nigrum makes fine contrast in form for these delicate creatures, with its finely pleated hosta-like leaves and tall, branched heads of close-set deep maroon flowers.

A job which takes some of my time is making sure that all the nursery stock beds are labelled. There are several different ways of labelling. (I once had a friend who used to say wryly 'there are two ways of doing a job: my mother's and the wrong way'.) I am not at all certain that my way is the only right way, but our labels last for up to two years, so we continue to make them like this:
We use a galvanised iron metal stake with two holes bored at the top to match two holes punched in a white plastic card. The name is carefully written (all spelling having been checked in advance) with a special nib and special ink which does not readily fade. It is called Rotring Orange Label and it bonds with plastic. The stakes, and the split pins which fix the labels to the stake are made for us by a local firm. These pins must be made of brass (not brass dipped) so that they will not rust. It probably sounds a fussy way to label plants, but the names remain until ultraviolet light causes the plastic to become brittle and to break. The stakes and pins can be used time after time.

On a warm evening, it is a pleasant job to take a writing pad and make a list of labels needing to be replaced. When they have been made I take out a trugful of new labels fixed to stakes, pull up the faded ones and replace them with the new. Then I take the old ones back to have the broken labels removed and have the stakes and pins prepared for the next list of names. Putting the correct names to each different block of plants when you can see what you are doing is essential. It is most helpful to the propagators when they go out to take cuttings or to split plants, and is particularly valuable in winter or early spring when plants cannot be identified with certainty.

Andrew is not well. He has had a fever for two days and is feeling very tired and low. I asked our doctor to call and see him. Now two young doctors have just called and they think he should see a specialist. I stand watching their car disappear down the drive. A large question mark hangs in the air. Before I had time to grapple with it I was called to talk to a coach party of American visitors. Among them were people I had met when I gave an illustrated talk in San Francisco two years ago. As I hurried to greet them I bumped into Janet, who was looking for me and longing to talk about a break she has just had in Ireland. She was

desperately missing the one person with whom she would have wanted
to share her impressions and experiences. 'Do stay to lunch,' I called.
'Fine', she replied, 'I'll make it', and off she went to the vegetable garden
to collect salads.

Revitalised by the warm-hearted Americans, I left them to wander by
themselves in the garden and went to see how my girl-gardeners were
getting on. Because gardening is such a personal thing I like to walk
along a bed with one of these girls to discuss anything unusual that may
need to be done. Garden plants can become weeds if they have seeded
themselves in the wrong place. Usually the girls know which must be
removed, but sometimes seedlings are needed for the nursery. These are
then collected into a polythene bag or shallow bucket of water.

Sometimes summer pruning needs to be done, the shrub roses for
example and early-flowering shrubs, like *Weigela* and *Philadelphus*.
Other plants, like the cranesbills (*Geranium* species), need to be cut
back to remake themselves into fresh mounds of growth ready to flower
again in a very short while.

As I go round the garden I take a barrow with me filled with plastic
and paper bags, labels, pencils and secateurs. Into the plastic bags I put
cuttings needed in the propagating house. Each different variety or
species must be labelled. Nothing is more annoying than having several
hundred cuttings to prepare and finding that some of them are not
labelled. Because we handle our plants so frequently at all stages of their
development we can often make an inspired guess, but with plants like
the Rock Roses, *Helianthemum*, we cannot always be certain of the
colours simply by looking at the foliage. (With plants which are made
from root cuttings such as Oriental Poppies, *Papaver orientale*, it is
impossible.) Great care has to be taken to ensure that a plant of a pink
form has not strayed in among the crimson or the white blocks of stock
plants which lie on either side. Until the new plants have flowered we
cannot tell if a muddle has occurred and, as many plants disappear from
the nursery before they have flowered, we do not always have a chance
to see the error of our ways. But we are usually informed when a
screaming red has thrust its head into someone's well-planned white
border. Sharing our customer's consternation we make haste to put the
matter to rights.

We try to collect cuttings (putting them straight into plastic bags)
early in the morning, but during midsummer there are not enough hours
in the day to do all the jobs which are crying out for our attention, so we
often have to collect them when we can. Withered cuttings are useless
and must be discarded. Wilting will almost inevitably occur and can be
overcome if the cuttings are taken into a cool or shaded building, put
into bowls of water for a short while to absorb water and then taken out,
still damp, and laid as straight as possible in large plastic bags
(supermarket bags or even dustbin liners) for one or two hours, or

overnight, when they will be completely refreshed. If they are jumbled into bags anyhow they will be curved and bent in all directions, making it difficult to insert them tidily into pots or trays. We always use trays for large quantities; pans or pots if we only have a few cuttings. It is a waste of time to insert wilted cuttings; the floppy tips rarely recover, while the whole shoot, if it has lost rigidity, will have far less chance of survival. Sometimes we remove the young growing tips if they are very liable to wilt, but since there is a natural growth-promoting hormone in the tips of shoots we try to leave them on as many cuttings as possible. With some species which root easily it makes little difference whether the tip is there or not. Plants such as *Fuchsia*, honeysuckle, *Clematis* and ivy, will all root and make a new shoot from a piece of stem bearing only two buds at the node.

Propagation from cuttings, whether from stem or root cutting, never loses its fascination. There is not a month in the year when something or other is not being put onto the propagating benches – something which might go equally well into a small windowsill propagator. But from spring until late autumn, when so many plants are making young growth, there is a flood tide for the propagators to handle. In August we can count on three good growing months still to come to establish the young plants once they have rooted.

The paper bags are for seed heads. It still surprises me how early in the year you have to start looking for ripe seed. By August you need to look several times a week. If the seed pods are dry they are snipped off their bulky stems and put into bags which have had the name written on the outside, screwed tightly shut and piled into large cardboard boxes until we have time to shell and clean them ready for sowing.

If, however, the seed heads are saturated with rain, but must be picked or the seed will be lost, they are cut and laid in trays on sheets of newspaper. A special watch must be kept to see that they do not become mildewed. On sunny days we often have several big cardboard boxes containing different kinds of *Euphorbia* standing outside in the sun and air, carefully lidded with more newspaper. As the milky seed heads dry and explode we can hear the seeds hitting the paper covering. Sometimes the boxes are stood on a bench in my little Chelsea potting shed, but we must remember to turn the heads occasionally so they do not pack down and rot. It is most satisfying in a few weeks' time to shake the wilted heads and branches and find a good harvest of seed in the bottom of the box.

Today I have had two very different visitors. The first was a Scottish laird. Tall, slim and very knowledgeable, this man has the eye of a hawk for any new plant which may have appeared since his last visit. For such visitors it is a joy to find a plant which has at last become available after perhaps several years of patient propagation. We hover over the newest introductions, sharing keen anticipation for the time when they, too, will eventually be increased. But it is not all acquisitive. In the garden we linger among old and familiar plants and discuss different ways of growing or grouping them.

It is a help to see the garden through fresh eyes. Sometimes I concentrate too much on the faults: things I have done which I should not have done, like planting two fine shrubs too close and knowing that one must come out; or things which I have not done which I should have done, like replanting the empty bed which was prepared for me last year. At such times it is heartwarming to have my attention drawn from places which look bad by someone who has simply ignored what is unworthy. Sometimes it helps to have an appreciative critic who sees the view as a whole without being bogged down by details. Visitors who come simply to enjoy themselves might be surprised to know how they have contributed to the future of the garden by a casual conversation.

It was towards the end of this warm, golden afternoon that I found the second visitor who caught my special attention. On my way in to tea I saw the tall, spare figure of an old friend sitting bowed on a bench, content to let the sun warm his thin frame as his wife browsed among the potted plants nearby. He was an old tree-felling man we have known for many years who did some work for us in the very early days of the garden. For several years now he has looked so frail I have feared I might not see him again, but here he is once more and I am glad. I sit down beside him. 'Garden looks alright' says he, passing judgement. 'Yes', I reply, willing to admit for once that God was in his Heaven and all was right with my world. But slightly superstitiously I added, 'I have been lucky'. 'What d'yer mean, lucky?' he explodes. 'Yer worked hard haint yer?'

Two different visitors, but both have the same heart for a garden. I went in to find tea was ready; Andrew had made it. He has been up today. I think he is improving although he is still very tired.

It has taken us a long time to decide to make seasonal stock lists of plants that we have for sale. When our business was smaller it hardly seemed necessary; we knew more or less what we had. Now that we have progressed it is impossible to guess our stock and, although it is a time-consuming procedure to compile them, we eventually came to a point where we could not afford to be without stock records. Of course, numbers are changing constantly, visitors come to buy and more plants are propagated. So we decided to make a count twice a year; in August when the bulk of the propagating has been done and our autumn packing season is just ahead of us, and again in January before the spring packing and sales begin. By analysing the orders sent in we know how many plants are needed for the pack and can do our best to see that they are available. Somehow, however hard we try, there are always a few plants that are not available. Perhaps the seed did not germinate. (Did I forget to collect it?) Some plants need very hot summers to make viable seed. The handsome Cardoon, *Cynara*, is a case in point. Another plant may have become too low in stock to be spared, so must be reserved until it has had time to build up again. It is pointless to part with your stock plants to please someone today if, in doing so, you are selling off your future. Some plants take years – twenty years is not an exaggeration – to build up sufficient stock to sell. When I first began my nursery I might have needed only ten or twenty plants of a rare variety in a year. Today that same plant may not be for sale since ten or twenty plants could go in one day if made available. As a plantswoman I have no desire to keep choice plants as a kind of status symbol. When a rare plant comes into my hands my first thought is to make two, and more as soon as I can, as an insurance, to keep that plant in cultivation. If it will set seed there is not much of a problem, the plant ceases to be rare. The plants which must be propagated vegetatively and which are difficult to propagate are the ones which we cannot easily make available. As soon as we can spare plants we do so, and if anything should happen to our stock, we then might have a reserve with a customer on which we could call.

Many years ago I was asked, in an emergency, to take a day-school for gardening in mid-Wales. At the time it seemed a long way to go, but I drove there with buckets of flowers and foliage and with a selection of plants to illustrate my talks. At the end of the afternoon I was joined by a small elderly grey man who sat beside me to help answer questions. Sitting beside me on a hard, straight-backed chair, hands clasped over a comfortably rounded tummy, this stranger began to talk and, with only the gentlest encouragement now and then, went on to entrance us all with a voice, manner, knowledge and, above all, passion for plants, which I shall never forget. Who was this man? He was Percy Picton, who as a young man had been gardener for the famous William Robinson of Gravetye Manor, whose books I treasure. It was a wonderful experience to meet this man who carried his knowledge as easily as breathing. To shake him by the hand was to touch a link which joins us to William Robinson and Gertrude Jekyll. I am ashamed to say that I have seen him only once since, but that too was an occasion. I was taken to visit him and his wife at their home by Joe Elliott of Broadwell Nursery, Moreton-in-Marsh. We never stopped talking and admiring plants all afternoon, indeed until almost sundown and were interrupted only by the most sumptuous English home-made tea.

The point of this digression, to which I have come so slowly, is to relate Percy's comment when we were discussing the problems of propagating certain plants, and the dilemma of pricing them. 'Ah', he said, tapping my knee, 'some plants are like antiques, you can't put a true value on them, you remember that'. I shall always remember him – and his words.

There are about one thousand plants listed in our descriptive catalogue, but we also have an ex-directory catalogue of plants which may be found on the nursery but not in sufficient quantities to list in the published catalogue. Altogether, we list more than two thousand different plants and we fall frequently to the temptation of adding to this number.

Part of the nursery sales area

In the nursery selling area, plants are classified as they are in the catalogue. They are stood out in alphabetical order under appropriate signboards, i.e. Shade Plants, Bog Plants or Alpines. This helps us, as well as our visitors, to find them. When we began our stock-taking we did not realise how valuable it would be to us in many different ways. It is well worth the time which several members of the women staff spend checking and recording. Not only do we know how many plants of each variety we have at the time of the check, but also everyone who needs to know can find out exactly where they are – whether outside on the sales beds, in the reserve areas, or in the tunnels (which are numbered). We know whether there are large quantities of a popular plant, or just a few of a rare variety tucked into a corner for safety. It is these small numbers which are often highly valued but may take ages to find among so many. (Only the sales area has plants set out alphabetically; this is not possible in the stock holding area, although we do now try to keep plants together in families.)

The stock-availability lists have also resulted in closer co-operation between propagators outside and the office staff inside, whose main job is to help postal customers find our plants. Every day, when dealing with mail-order or telephone enquiries, these lists are continually in use. Comparison can quickly be made between the analysis of orders already received for a particular plant and the number we had at last count, to tell whether a customer on the telephone stands a chance ordering one or fifty.

All this talk of numbers, recordings, analysis etc. leads to a big question the reader may already be burning to ask: 'Why do I not have it all on computer?' Such a simple question, but no simple answer.

To begin with, I am of the age group where the very word causes shudders to pass through me. I hate the thought of machinery replacing people, of flashing lights on screens, symbols instead of words, electronic noises; basically factors I cannot handle or understand. That, of course, is the reaction of the uninitiated. We do use some modern technology: our irrigation systems are based on computerised timetables, but we rely on Keith if anything goes wrong with them. We use small calculators in the office and are thankful for them. But knowing that a computer will only return knowledge which must have originally been fed into it, I wonder how on earth every plant can be recorded in a practical way? How many have just been rooted, subsequently died, or been sold? I could not put that extra burden onto my already hard-pressed staff. I would need to employ one, or several persons, to work the computer which might be out of date before we have earned the 'investment' cost. When such a machine is set up it does, with its operator(s), perform a great many valuable tasks. I have seen something of the kind in action – both on the Continent and in the United States – and have been impressed. But I fear that it might require us to jettison those special plants in small quantities which clutter up our ex-directory catalogue and which are such a delight to the plant enthusiasts who, unsuspecting, arrive to find them here.

I tend to say that my staff are mini-computers. Handling plants every day, whether in the garden or nursery, and at all stages from seeds, cuttings and divisions, to saleable plants, they have a very wide knowledge of what we have. Most of them came to me knowing only a limited range of plants. Today many can name on sight every plant we sell, know where it grows in the garden and therefore what conditions it needs.

In years to come many things will change, but I would like to maintain this degree of personal involvement, this feeling of working as a team and caring for our plants and our customers as we do today.

It is the last week in August, and today my grandson Thomas is being prepared for another operation. Everything goes on here as normal. It is a fine warm day, everyone is busy, but listens out for the telephone.

The celery needs earthing up. I am growing the pink-tinted kind this year. The flavour reminds me of my childhood, and of watching my father dig it out of the frosty soil. Cutting off the dirty outside stems, I would breathe in the rich, strong scent as I carried it back to the house. Celery bought in the supermarket is beautifully clean and crisp, but it does not have that mouth-watering flavour. Neither does it suffer slug damage! I save all the damaged and outside leaves to put through the juice extractor or simmer them with other vegetable 'waste' to make vegetable stock. Well-made vegetable stock is deliciously rich in flavour and is ideal as a hot bouillon to start a meal, or to share with a friend on a cold day instead of coffee.

I have now picked the last of the golden butter beans and pulled up the sugar peas which have been spoilt by fungal leaf spot. Slugs are still ravaging the spinach; they are impossible to check in this abnormally wet summer.

I have a very good variety of French Artichoke called 'Gros Camus de Bretagne', given me by Christopher Lloyd. Occasionally I stay with him and am allowed to make salads. He does everything else, being an accomplished cook as well as a distinguished writer. Last winter I feared my artichoke plants would be killed by the severe frosts. They were damaged; the central crowns which should have flowered died back, but side shoots deeper down have appeared and a few of these are showing promise of fine heads. In the early autumn I shall take about twelve or so of the small off-shoots or suckers and pot them to grow on and keep protected as an insurance against the possibility of losing the old plants outside. They will be well-established early in the year to start a new bed and will give me a late crop after the old bed has finished. One could, in a mild winter, take off these side shoots in spring, during a warm, moist spell, and set them out in a new bed. This need not be done every year – only when the old plants appear to be deteriorating.

French artichokes need a sunny situation in well-drained soil that is enriched with a little well-rotted manure or garden compost. They are more likely to suffer from cold in heavy soils. It pays to get a good variety, rather than to grow them from seed, when you'll most likely have heads of spiky scales which are practically inedible. The best kinds have large fleshy scales with blunt tips. They must be picked when young – long before the central thistle-like flower has formed – and to taste them at their best they should be cooked within the same hour if possible, not left in a basket to wilt.

The first dark plums are ripe in the orchard. They are called Czar. I cut them in half, stone them, put them into the oven in a pan with no water and cook them very gently until they are soft, unbroken and swimming in rich dark juice. While they are still hot I take several scented leaves from the Rose-scented Geranium growing outside the greenhouse – this is a small-leafed, small-flowered kind of *Pelargonium* with the most delicious rose perfume. It soaks into the plum juice permeating it, to make something quite different from plain stewed plum. Chilled and served with thick yoghurt, thin cream or a chilled custard made with eggs (not custard powder) they are a summer treat. Preparing more and putting them into the freezer makes a special treat in winter too. You do not eat the *Pelargonium* leaves, but when no-one is looking, I suck each one as I fish them out of the bowl, not bearing to waste a drop of the rich-scented syrup.

The telephone call we had been expecting came as I walked into the house from Friday evening shopping in Wivenhoe. In the village I had met Martine, the young French wife of David, my head propagator, with her little son, Michael, just coming out of the parish church where she had been praying for Thomas. Dropping my baskets I ran to pick up the receiver. It was Mary's voice. Things had gone badly. Thomas had reacted almost immediately to the anaesthetic; he stopped breathing. The operation had not begun. It took several minutes to get him into intensive care and the respirator working. He is alive, but there is fear of brain damage. Cardiac arrest, due to an allergy to anaesthetics, has happened twice before in this little boy's life. How much more can he and his poor parents take? There is nothing to do but wait and pray. Pray for them all, but I do not know what to pray for except strength to accept what is best. Only a few days ago Mary and the two little boys stayed with us. Both were full of excitement to see all that was going on here. The ditch-digging machine on caterpillar tracks was being operated by two young men. Despite his disability Thomas hopped across the rough land at surprising speed, determined not to miss a thing to do with men and machines. The necessary energy is absent as his mother and I walk in the gardens, when he rides like a little pasha on a small trolley, getting down at his favourite places, such as the stack of straw bales, where he follows Jeremy laboriously to the top. Eventually, worn out by the morning's adventures, both boys settled indoors with pencil and paper for amusement. The latest craze is for prehistoric monsters. Thomas is fascinated by them and can draw fairly accurate representations, giving the Latin names of each one, to the obvious delight of his proud grandparents. It is unbearable to think that this bright child, so handicapped physically, may lose the spark which makes life bearable to himself and a joy to his family.

Slowly the days crawl by. Thomas has a chest infection and is running a temperature. I fill the anxious time by tidying the linen cupboard and mending pillowcases. I confess I rarely thread a needle nowadays, but it is comforting to be able to put something straight. Today I have felt too cowardly to ring Mary. What can she say?

After a week of unconsciousness Thomas was taken off the respirator.

His lungs are working but he has been very distressed all day, unable to communicate. There is great fear of brain damage.

The same day we received a letter to say that Andrew has been booked for an operation in a local nursing home. This alarms me. It is too close to the crisis with Thomas. I shall be torn between helping Mary and supporting Andrew, with fifty miles between them. We decided Andrew's operation must be postponed. Knowing I shall be called any day I made preparations to leave home and nursery. Shopping had to be done, food prepared for Andrew and put into the freezer.

For comfort I picked flowers for the house. A few stems of a light wine-coloured form of *Lilium speciosum* look just perfect by themselves. In a mixed bowl of pastel colours I put a pale pink *Verbena* 'Rose Bouquet'. It is much admired just now with its rounded heads of flowers sometimes mistaken for primulas, although its habit – branching stems set with finely divided leaves – is quite different. Bunched heads of tiny white everlasting-daisy, *Anaphalis triplinervis*, were added with a much larger semi-double daisy the colour of raspberry juice mixed with cream. This is a form of the tender *Chrysanthemum frutescens*. Next I added a very pale blue *Aster, A. thompsonii* 'Nanus'. This is another of my 'best' garden plants. A group of perhaps five plants on the edge of a cool border are in flower for more than three months. They need no staking, do not suffer from mildew, and form a low mound of soft-blue made of many branching stems covered with flowers. They are a joy in the garden and for picking. To marry all these soft pastel flowers with yellow eyes I added an unusual Golden Rod, *Solidago* 'Lemore'. Much shorter and prettier than the tall gawky variety usually found in gardens, this plant has soft bunches of pale creamy-yellow flowers. It tends to fade rather untidily in the garden, but it is a very useful colour for flower-arranging, merging into a group with a softening effect. To add height and gracefulness to the group I added a few slender spires of *Physostegia* 'Rose Bouquet'. This summer I have had a change of heart about this plant. I had thought it was perhaps too lanky for the garden, but it is now in a nursery stock bed standing 4 feet (1 m) tall, and without any staking has held itself together well. It has looked attractive both outside and inside the house, for weeks supplying me with a constant supply of spiky pieces. Grouped together at the top of every branch are spires of tubular flowers, almost white but shaded and striped outside with lilac and dotted inside with honey guides. The flowers are spaced in ranks up and down the stem and each rank can be turned round on the stem to face another way. I wonder why? It is called the Obedient Plant.

Just before bed Alastair, Thomas' father, rang. They are feeling more confident. Thomas has become coherent, and has asked for Mummy and Daddy. The old Thomas seems to be lurking there somewhere behind the mists; this evening he was able to reprove the young nurse who was trying to wash his private parts. That sounds very like Thomas.

Next day I said goodbye to Andrew, and the garden, and set off once more for Southwold. It was a beautiful morning, calm and still. Combine harvesters crawled up and down scavenging fields. Almost all the pale-strawed barley was cut. Some fields were already ploughed causing me to feel a little pang of regret; summer has not really come and already the signs of autumn are here. Straw bales stood grouped about the shaved stubble. On some farms were the oblong bales which I can only just lift, while on others there were enormous bales, like rolls of stair-carpet, which need a special machine to move or unroll them. Fringes of whitened grass and seed heads edged the roadsides. There was a warm welcome from Jeremy and the other grandparents whose place I had come to take.

The next day Jeremy was in a ferment of excitement to go to the 'hosstable' to see 'my friend Thomas'. We drove to Norwich hospital and walked through interminable corridors until we arrived at a little room and went in, one at a time. Poor Thomas, he lay on a large sheepskin-covered beanbag still wired to drips. He smiled a big slow smile of recognition. But he could not speak an intelligible word. I felt deeply disturbed by his apparent apathy, at the same time telling myself he was only just out of total blackout. Jeremy acted with perfect confidence, banging toy monsters into his brother's hands, chattering to him – even making the damaged child chuckle. Then, leaving Alastair behind to take the weekend watch, we collected Mary and took her out into the sunshine. We stopped in a pub yard and, finding a seat in a sheltered courtyard, sat with our backs against a knapped-flint wall and drank a long cool beer. There was green grass and the still water of a canal lock. The beer seemed to fall straight down to the soles of my feet, my legs became leaden. Mary smiled. Brave girl. After two days rest for her we returned to the hospital and found Thomas manifestly improved. The drip was removed. A few words struggled to the surface. Jeremy asked where was the toy spaceman he had given his 'friend' and Thomas immediately looked towards a shelf above his head. When we left for home we felt much more optimistic. It may take a long while, but there is hope he will be himself again.

SEPTEMBER

RECENTLY the annual conference of the International Plant Propagators Society was held just a mile or two from here at Essex University. About eighty people attended, drawn from all branches of horticulture. They included nursery men and women as well as lecturers from horticultural colleges and people dealing with associated businesses, such as producers of materials used in the trade. The majority of them would be involved in the production of trees and shrubs to be sold on the wholesale market. Their businesses would be pruned and streamlined to produce the maximum results using the fewest resources in the shortest possible time. For most businesses today this is essential in order to survive. There would also be representatives of smaller, perhaps mixed nurseries, and possibly some propagators involved in research and development.

So I imagined, as I worked, several weeks in advance, preparing an illustrated talk for the first evening of this week-long event. It was in the back of my mind that I had been asked as light relief – understandably – after those seriously intent people had spent an exhausting day absorbing all that was to be learnt from touring around other nurseries, each a very large, efficient and streamlined production unit.

Since neither Andrew nor I have become photographers, we might not have had any early records of the garden. It never occurred to us that what we were hoping to do would be of the least interest to anyone except ourselves. However, quite early on, a local boy (the eldest son of Harry, who has been with us for nearly forty years) started to take pictures which I am now very grateful to possess. Since then, throughout the years, there have been many photographers, both professional and amateur, who have added to my slide collection.

Although it takes time and effort, I enjoy sorting through these slides to ensure that they follow the thread of my story smoothly. When they have been checked and rechecked on my Kindermann projector I can set off with some confidence, backed by the garden and all my photographic friends. It is best to arrive in good time and, if the slides have to be moved into another carousel, to see them run through quickly to make sure none are upside down. I also like to check the focussing, to sit in possibly awkward corners to make sure everyone will see clearly. Standing alone among the tiered seats, the university lecture theatre seemed large, the speaker's table very distant.

After a short walk around the buildings, I returned to find everyone ready and waiting. After the introduction, I surveyed the people in the audience, many of whom had inexplicably arranged themselves at either end of the amphitheatre. There were large empty spaces in the middle. Looking again from left to right I felt quite dizzy. This was going to be like watching Wimbledon for me.

'Is there anything wrong with those empty seats?' I began, to their evident surprise. 'I would prefer to look straight at you', I went on, 'while you can shut your eyes and listen if you like.' Good humouredly, they shuffled into the empty seats.When everyone was sitting comfortably we began in a much more relaxed atmosphere. They shared with me the ups and downs of my professional career; nobody went to sleep noticeably, which was a credit to them, since I do find myself that slides are horribly soporific after a heavy day outside. Before I went home, I met nurseymen from Ireland and several European countries, including Bulgaria and Czechoslovakia.

Two days later two coaches arrived bringing members of the audience to see for themselves what we are doing. I feel diffident about entertaining professional nurserymen. It is not common nursery practice to run a large ornamental garden. However well you run it, it does cost money. Can you really justify it? Well, I do not know how to run a nursery any other way. It is the best way I know to attract visitors to see my plants, to let them see how different plants look when well-established and mature, to see what will grow in difficult situations, which plants look well planted together and what is in flower in the 'difficult' months of the year. It is my living catalogue, arranged first and foremost to please myself but with the hope it may also please others. From a business point of view it could be improved, I have no doubt, as it could be aesthetically, if only I had more time and energy to spend in it.

Well-informed guides would be a great help – my staff cannot always rush to identify a plant although they often do so. A lot more labelling needs to be done, but will never solve the problem, since many people unfamiliar with the plants will ask for a *Galanthus* in May, when you know they have been attracted by the soft blue heads of *Phlox stolonifera*, while the snowdrops to which the label refers, lie buried beneath them. Thinking it might make a change, I invited my experienced visitors to see something very different. As a start I took them to my remaining patch of wilderness, an area of about two acres. I wanted to show them how the garden and nursery looked at the beginning, since the wilderness is the continuation of the same piece of land. I wanted to show them the difference in the soil on these two acres where we have spent the past eighteen months draining and rotavating in all kinds of materials to open up the black peaty soil. Plants such as hostas, primulas, *Hemerocallis* and *Iris* are thriving, the original preparations hidden beneath abundant foliage. Further on we reached the untouched land, overgrown with rank weeds, wet and squelchy beneath our feet. Although I had already explained at length how we had treated the soil, I was quite willing to explain the procedure once more when I was asked exactly how we had transformed such intractable-looking soil to be able to grow flourishing beds of stock plants.

A group of Dutchmen who came to visit me later in the week smiled knowingly, commenting that all of Holland was like this. 'Our forefathers dealt with the soil the same as you are doing.'

Not everyone would consider the effort worthwhile. I did not think the expense excessive for the type of crop I hoped to harvest. Hiring small drainage machines by the day is not expensive in comparison with the time and energy consumed if the job is done by hand. A narrow slit-trench 3-4 inches (7-10 cm) wide is made and the drainage pipes or stone-filling is put in immediately behind it before the sides have had time to cave in.

We did not spend all our time looking at the soil. The rest of the afternoon raced away as we looked at the garden, stock beds and propagating houses, all sharing a feeling of well-being on a warm sunny afternoon as we wandered among familiar and unfamiliar plants.

The climbing French beans are so prolific that we cannot possibly eat enough or give them away fast enough, so I have puréed some for soup. I softened onions and garlic in olive oil added courgettes and beans, cooked them till soft and then liquidised them. Thinned with a little stock it makes a pleasant soup now and will perhaps be a useful base in winter if it keeps its flavour.

I picked thirty ripe strawberries from an old perpetual fruiting variety, and two green peppers from plants in Gro-Bags sitting at the end of one of the tunnels. Because of the dull wet summer they have been slow, but they are fruiting well now. The aubergines have been a total failure. Perhaps the bad summer was partly to blame, but I may not have started them early enough. They need a long season, but my problem is to find enough room in a warm place to grow them on in the spring.

I have planted six rows of garlic, one hundred and twenty cloves. I take out shallow drills, about 1.5 inches deep, with the point of a Dutch hoe and press each clove in firmly upright, about a handspan apart, then pull the soil back over the row. The rest of the harvest of bulbs are quite dry now. They have been cleaned of loose leaves, tied into long ropes, and hung in the utility room where they will not be frozen.

The pot-gardens are spectacular at last. They took longer this summer to get into their stride, as all the plants in them dote on really hot weather and brilliant sunshine. They have had little enough of that. All have made plenty of growth but fewer flowers, so until now the normal intensity of colour has been toned-down to half strength. With warmer drier days (and the onset, we hope, of a late Indian summer), all their pent-up energy has exploded into a riot of colour. In the garden that is a phrase I would hate to be obliged to use, but in the pot-gardens, in groups, on paving or gravel, in sheltered corners close to the whitewashed buildings, I love to see such a rich concentration of colours.

All around the south-facing office window there are climbing, spiralling stems of *Pharbitis tricolor* (*Ipomaea rubro-caerulea*). This morning I counted over a hundred of the large shallow saucers on several plants grouped around the little backyard. This plant is the loveliest reason for getting up early, to see the long furled buds opening a depth of blue which takes your breath away. On a hot day they will collapse before noon, already fertilised by bees and insects which love to visit them. On cooler days, afternoon visitors will stop to admire them. Unfortunately, I do not find them the easiest plants to grow well. I start them in the greenhouse, potting them on and guiding them up tall canes so they will be ready to put out as soon as the weather is warm. But even under cover they will often produce poor whitened leaves caused, I suspect, by too much fluctuation in temperature. In May it can easily plummet from the upper 70's°F (20°C) to 40°F (5°C) and less at night. Once outside, they will continue this tiresome behaviour if the weather is cool, but eventually they get going and chase along the strings I put up for them. Watch needs to be kept for malformed leaves, as closer inspection will reveal aphids, or some other pestilential creature. Any pot plant sitting in a warm comfortable place will be a target for insect pests. Here my scruples about insecticides are quickly overcome ; a small spray-gun kept to hand is used with a safe chemical, like Permethrin, to keep the plants from becoming a revolting mess.

The large Spanish pots hold wide-spreading bouquets of *Helichrysum petiolare*, a plant which grows so efficiently in pots it has to be lightly pruned several times during the summer or it would usurp the whole area, smothering surrounding pots with its whitened stems of small round leaves which look as if they have been stamped out of greyish-white felt. They are the perfect companion for pelargoniums, or geraniums as we usually call them. I grow two forms of a very free-flowering ivy-leafed geranium with single flowers, which are to be seen throughout France and southern Europe draped from windows and old horse troughs. Their names are 'Ville de France' and 'Roi des Balcons'. One has scarlet flowers, the other we call pink – but not the shade of rose one immediately imagines at the sound of the word but rather an electric shade of pink. Intensifying these shades of red are several pots of *Vallota purpurea*, commonly called Scarborough Lily. Why it is called *purpurea* I cannot think, since the large funnel-shaped flowers are the

Pot-garden in the house yard

most brilliant tomato-scarlet. This bulbous plant belongs to the *Amaryllis* family, producing several blooms from the top of each stout stem held high above strap-shaped leaves. This is one of those rare cases where almost total neglect is rewarded with an undeserved wealth of flower usually seen only on the outside of seed packets. About three or four years ago – it could be more, time goes so fast – I put about five bulbs into each of several largish pots. The first year or two I had plenty of healthy leaves, but only one or two stems of flower. This year the pots are crammed with so many bulbs that they are thrusting themselves over the edge. There are ten and twelve stems to a pot, each opening a succession of dazzling trumpets lasting for several weeks. Succulents associate well with these large, simple flowers. Grey-blue rosettes of cool, carved leaves, blue bead-like leaves on writhing stems or green leaves which flush red as coral – there are many different kinds all chosen for the impact they make. Among the species I have are varieties of *Crassula*, *Aeonium* and *Kalanchoe*, but I am lazy about learning the names of non-hardy plants so I am not able to give the exact details. It is enough to say the flowering plants would look sickeningly pretty without these bold leafed plants to set them off. In particular the great agaves, *Agave americana* 'Variegata', add style and relief to the proliferating tubs of colour.

Near to the back door stand great tubs of *Datura suaveolens* set against an east-facing wall so that they are in shade after midday. This is a strong woody shrub which would easily grow 10 feet (3 m) tall if it could have its way, but being tender it must be confined to a tub in a frost-free place in winter so the size of your plant is dependent on the size of the tub you can move. Grouped on a base of blocks, however, my daturas dangle flowers head-high where I stand beside them, while inside, as I wash my hands at the utility room sink, I can see the long trumpet-like flowers against the glass of the window. *Datura suaveolens* has double flowers making a thick frill where the petals spray out at the bottom of the long tube. Even more lovely perhaps, is a single variety which opens palest cream trumpets that become rose-flushed as the flowers mature. The perfume from these exotic flowers is reserved for night time. It is such a pity we seldom have an evening warm enough to sit, surrounded by this wealth of blossom ; the yard is cut off from the comforting warmth of the western sun, but I rarely go to bed without standing among the pots, sharing scented air with the moths.

Between the large tubs I have tucked fuchsias, Cherry Pie Heliotrope and Busy Lizzie, *Impatiens balsamina*, in both single and double forms.

In the greenhouse I have two tender climbers which are new to me and which will, for sure, be added to the pot gardens next summer. The most exciting is *Rhodochiton atrosanguineum*. You may already know it, but I am sure that by the time this book is out it will be the 'in-plant'. It makes an exploring mass of slender, twining stems clothed to the tips with small, heart-shaped pointed leaves. Tiny buds become smallish dangling 'lampshades' in light plum. Not very exciting I thought, until one morning I was startled to find long purplish-black tubular flowers had opened from beneath the modest 'lampshades' which were only the calyces. The effect was quite spectacular. It would be the loveliest idea to train this plant up and around a pillar in a conservatory since, once started, it flowers under cover, long into the winter months.

Maurandia purpusii is another long flowering twiner. Small and pointed shield-shaped leaves are a background for penstemon-shaped flowers, velvet textured and purplish-blue with white throats which peep from the leaf axils. Supported by strands of insulated wire, it has made a column of blue beside my backdoor for weeks throughout the summer. *Maurandia scandens* is larger in leaf and has rosy flowers, but needs a really hot summer to justify a place.

Just inside the nursery entrance is a large group of pots filled with bright and pale yellow flowers, with white-flowered *Chrysanthemum frutescens* among them. I think you need to take care with colour schemes among your pots as you would in a border. The problem is not always that certain colours clash but that sometimes too much colour may be strident where a touch would create sparkle. Most important, I find, are the foliage plants chosen to calm or harmonise startling combinations.

Bidens ferulaefolia, a non-hardy plant, is loved by bees and often mistaken for *Coreopsis*. It has bright-yellow daisy flowers with five broad petals fastened tightly to a boss of pollen-bearing stamens. The petals twist slightly, displaying curved edges and turned-back pointed tips. This is not my favorite shade of yellow but the daintiness of the blooms – indeed of the whole plant – and the fact that it flowers from June until frost destroys it, totally enchants me. Never looking untidy, yet ever increasing, it creates a web of thin, lax, much-branched brown stems, covered with the scantiest finely-cut tiny green leaves. As summer waxes and wanes it becomes more and more floriferous ; as old stems and flowers wither and fade, a host of new ones appear to create a sparkling display, soothed by long trailing stems of white-felted *Helichrysum petiolare*. A paler, softer yellow is provided by one of the many different forms of *Dimorphotheca (Osteospermum)* called 'Buttermilk'.

It is essential to have good watering facilities handy for pot gardens. In really hot, dry times they may need watering every day. 'A little drink' is useless ; the pots must be well filled. This takes time. Most of my pots have large saucers beneath them, bought to fit the size of the pot so that they can soak up the water which has rapidly run down the inside of the pot and the ball of soil, without properly wetting it. In a time of rain-storms these saucers must be frequently tipped out so the roots do not rot. I have not suggested pot gardens are labour-saving, but like families they can be rewarding. Next, of course, plants can become hungry as well as thirsty. About once a month, or every six weeks, I add a dry compound fertiliser to each pot. The quantity varies with the size of the pot, but one has to remember these fertilisers are very concentrated ; too much would kill. About a teaspoon for a bucket-sized pot, twice that for really big pots such as *Datura* and *Agave*, less for smaller pots. Be careful not to let it lie on the leaves or they will be scorched. These amounts seem adequate to maintain good leaf colour and encourage the fresh growth needed to give a long display of flowers and healthy foliage.

I have returned to Southwold. Mary must have a small operation which, it had been hoped, would have taken place when Thomas was in hospital, but because of the crisis it had to be postponed. Now it is to go ahead and I am running the house, helped by two small boys. Thomas has been home for several days and appears to be almost himself. It is unbelievable in such a short time. The normal flood and volume of conversation has abated and his reactions are not so sharp, but it is only eighteen days since he almost died under anaesthetic. Today he rode his tricycle to the little playing field nearby where we played on the swings and the slide. Since he is by no means agile, he occasionally loses his nerve, as at the top of the slide, but he is amazingly determined not to lose face, so it is a triumph when mind overcomes matter. Our last game was on the 'Big Circling Tyre', suspended on strong chains, where we played 'Storms', the sea and Uncle Jonathan's lifeboat being an important part of their lives. I played the part of the howling wind egged on by the 'terrified sailors'. Fortunately everyone else in Southwold was taking advantage of a warm afternoon on the beach.

Halfway home Thomas ran out of puff, so I carried him and his trike till we came to a wooden bench outside the public house, by the lighthouse. Opposite is the sweetshop, but I had no money. Doubting-Jeremy felt in my pockets, but found only a tissue. Back home we all collapsed thankfully into deep chairs and drank quantities of Ribena. We none of us could wait for Daddy to join us for tea.

Mary was brought home from hospital, late one evening, looking frail and tired. Next morning both boys were entranced to find her safely tucked up in bed in another small spare room beneath the gabled roof – timidly touching her, while longing to bounce all over her. We left her to rest and walked to the shops, Thomas making royal progress in his chair. Many people recognised him and stopped to speak. Jeremy helped carry the shopping. When I doubted his ability, he pushed up the sleeve of his jersey proudly showing me his muscles; all of three years old.

It is a novelty for grandmothers to care again for a young family, to have days filled from beginning to end with the needs and demands of young children. But this must be very difficult for anyone who has not had children, to understand both the frustrations and rewards of the young mother who must spend all day and every day with her small charges. Household chores, boring at times, can become a relief from the constant demands for time and attention which the little ones need until they are capable of entertaining themselves. At such times other people's lifestyles may seem more exciting than your own, but unless there are intolerable pressures, being a housewife and mother is one of the least boring ways of passing the time. Tiring, but not boring. It is such a wonderful opportunity to learn to organise yourself, to develop skills, both practical and mental. Within the family, one has endless opportunities to observe the interaction of personalities. Constantly one has to do battle with oneself in order to help others to learn to control themselves. The care and skill needed to balance a family budget is not so very different from running a business.

Warm, gentle September days passed by, healing and restoring body and mind. When Mary was strong enough we pottered together in her garden, picking baskets of beans, cutting down seed heads, tying up the raspberries. Then we just sat in the sun beneath an old William's Pear, the small fruits malformed with patches of black scab but oozing nostalgic flavour – just as I remember from the scabby pears of childhood. Somehow, perfect-looking pears from commercial growers never seem to have quite that hauntingly rich flavour. Or is it my imagination ?

Autumn term begins and once again I walk across the town, over freshly washed pavements, across the little greens, to Jeremy's morning school. His warm little hand is in mine, or else he is racing ahead, stopping just in time at the pavement's edge, uninhibitedly calling out to everyone he knows. Last evening, at bathtime, he thought he might make a scene over who should bath him, Mummy or Grandma ; but as his dark eyes met mine he changed his mind. We had fun as he learnt to squelch water through his teeth – then beaming, he gave me a bear hug. He can be an obstinate misery, then melt you with devastating charm, like any other grandchild. Thomas gets stronger each day, but he has lost the ability to write or draw. This is sad. It was his favourite occupation when he needed rest from physical effort. We pray it will come back.

We are having golden September days. Early in the morning there are spiders' webs everywhere, laced between plants and bushes outlined with dewdrops. The lawns are spread with a silver sheen unbroken except by shadows until my footsteps cross it, or until Harry sweeps it away before mowing. Every leaf is poised, every stem erect and still. The garden is silent, waiting for the day to begin. Seldom is it so still. Later, when the sun has rolled the mists away, the air is saturated with the richest scents of all the year : the smell of the soil, of growing things, of leaves, flowers, fruit and decay. There has come at last the smell of dust and dry grass : before long we shall be saying we could do with rain. The nursery is watered every evening after a particularly warm day. Automatically controlled sprinklers create parasols of droplets whirling above the rows of pots, while blackbirds and thrushes delight in the damp sand on which the pots are stood, hoping to find something to eat.

Each month I try once or twice to make notes of the plants which are

The lighthouse at Southwold

at their best during that time. As the months go by, these lists become longer. When I was young, unless your garden was bedded out with asters, French marigolds, geraniums and petunias, it probably looked pretty threadbare until the Michaelmas daisies and chrysanthemums ushered in the Harvest Festival at the end of the gardening season. Recent years have seen many more gardens growing less well-known plants which somehow maintain a feeling of summer freshness until quite late in the season. Last winter I feared the severe weather would have killed *Salvia involucrata* 'Bethellii' (the name has nothing to do with me), which was introduced from Mexico in 1824. To my delight, it has returned in full glory from deep shoots safely protected in light gravel soil, situated at the foot of a west-facing wall. Now it has made a sprawling bushy plant 4-5 feet (1-1.5 m) high and across. Every part of it is aromatic. The long pointed leaves have thin, pink veins ; a pale echo of the vivid, cyclamen-pink, inflated flowers which are held in long racemes more than a foot (30 cm) long. Each flower spike stands free of the rich mass of velvety foliage and the vivid colour is accented by narrow, mahogany-red tubes which hold each emerging bud and finally house black seeds like tiny grains of rice.

214

It is interesting to see how many different salvias are flowering now. *Salvia rutilans* makes a smaller plant, but needs a really warm situation in well-drained soil as it tends to wait almost too late before producing thin spikes of brilliant scarlet flowers. In the mildest counties these would continue well into winter. *Salvia interrupta* used to be called *Salvia candelabra*. It might have been a synonym or else they are very similar. My plant sits at the foot of a south wall where I like to see its large clusters of crepe-textured leaves. They throw up surprisingly long stems, over 3 feet (1 m), topped with violet-blue flowers marked white in the throat. Elsewhere in the garden, where the soil is more retentive, but not likely to be too wet in winter. the exquisite *Salvia uliginosa* is now in flower. Very cold winters can mean death for this plant, but I have kept it for twenty years, covering the roots with straw or cut-down garden remains. By late summer it has made a. tall graceful plant standing about 5 feet (1.5 m). Many slender stems are topped with clusters of bright, sky-blue flowers, a very unusual colour at this time. Another *Salvia* needing similar conditions is *Salvia ambigens*. Not quite so tall, 3-4 feet (1-1.5 m), this plant holds fewer flowers on slim upright spires, but they have considerable impact, being dark gentian-blue.

Lippia citriodora flourishes against a warm wall. It may be cut to the ground in a severe winter, but the strong rootstock will throw up fine, shrubby growth during the summer. Its strongly lemon-scented leaves are good to use in pot-pourri. The flowers of *Lippia*, held in thin rat-tail spikes, are not at all conspicuous, but nearby is a *Buddleia* attracting a lot of attention. Full of droning bees and quivering butterflies, its soft grey leaves and beautiful heads of buds enclosed in white wool attract visitors to ask what it is long before the large loose panicles of pale-lilac flowers have opened. It is *Buddleia crispa*.

Above the grey- and silver-leafed plants which have all made new growth, generously covering the poor gravel soil, there appears year after year a strange, straggly *Dahlia*. I forget it is there until late summer, when suddenly I see a lax stem pushing its way among clouds of silvery foliage and carrying single, lilac-mauve flowers. It is *Dahlia merckii*. I would not call it untidy and it takes neither room nor trouble ; but it has quite a different habit from the large-leafed hybrids which would wither and die in a normal summer drought on this poor gravel soil, and would look as out of place among most of the Mediterranean plants as a cuckoo in a willow-warbler's nest.

Looking exactly right, giving bite to the delicate flowered *Dahlia*, is *Verbena bonariensis*. Standing 3-4 feet (1-1.5 m) tall, are squared, rough textured stems, scantily branched, supporting flattish heads of deep lilac-blue flowers, extending from minute red-tinted tubes. These plants seed themselves about, but occasionally I move a few seedlings into a void, where their angular, branching stems create a light screen through which to view plants beyond. Sometimes I think it is scented, other days

I think I must have imagined it. Even in the poor soil of the dry garden there are too many good things in flower towards the end of the summer to be able to list them all. *Bupleurum fruticosum* has made a large bush, not unlike a *Cistus* bush, with dark evergreen leaves. The flowers, surprising most visitors, are like yellowish-green Cow Parsley. Walking across to examine them more closely, I found them alive with darting fly-like creatures, enamelled blue and green, harvesting the nectar and pollen.

A member of the campion family, *Silene schafta* makes a rich patch of colour, low at the edge of the path with rose-pink flowers held on a mass of short stems. Another relative, *Silene lempergii* 'Max Frei', also draws attention. A fine plant, spreading 3 feet (1 m) across, its lax stems hang over a wall carrying large heads of rich-pink flowers set in conspicuously brown-stained calyces. This is one of the plants we dare not post since the brittle stems would be smashed.

Gypsophila 'Rosy Veil' still floats a low cloud of tiny, palest pink, double flowers meshed in a tangle of wiry stems. *Lavatera olbia* 'Rosea' flaunts large, pink, silk-textured mallow flowers on wide bushes 4 feet (1.5 m) high. This is another slightly tender plant but well worth trying in warmer counties. It often breaks new growth from the base.

Leaving the open sunny garden on light soil, I walked along an east-facing bed where the soil is similar though the planting different because it is partly shaded by a large oak and holly. I was drawn to a group which glowed like fanned embers. The background was formed by a large bush of *Fuchsia* 'Genii'. Elegant yellow-green leaves, set off by red stems and dangling tassels of red and purple flowers, were surrounded by dozens of stems of *Arum italicum* 'Pictum' holding dense heads of brilliant scarlet juicy fruits. To one side was grouped *Euphorbia dulcis*, insignificant for most of the year but incandescent now as stems and leaves change to fiery tints, while depth of colour was added by several plants of *Heuchera micrantha* 'Palace Purple'.

Beyond beckoned vivid patches of colchicums. Some people mistake these for crocuses. Another name is Naked Ladies, because they flower without leaves. Quite unlike proper crocuses, their bunches of large and shining leaves emerge in spring, build up food reserves in large chestnut-skinned bulbs, then die down in June. These beautiful, goblet flowers are to be found grouped in drifts around shrubs, or between low plants. There are many varieties, large and small, single and double. Some are white, but most are shades of glistening rosy-mauve, dark or light with a wide, white throat, or with none at all. They may have white stems, or dark purple with chequered petals or plain, rounded or funnel shaped ; who can say whether one variety is preferable to another? The colour is brilliant, astounding against the bare earth or vivid green grass. *Colchicum* 'Rosy Dawn' has large flowers slightly chequered ('tessellated' is the correct term), with wide, white throats drawing attention

Colchicum speciosum 'Album'

to yellow stamens. Shafts of sunlight fall through blue-needled pines into these open chalices, while scattered among them are shining scarlet berries of *Arum italicum* 'Pictum'. Out of the blue have appeared clusters of a huge flat fungus, cream coloured with fluted edges each the size of a dinner plate. It may sound a strange mixture, but set against a floor of rough crushed forest bark this autumn group is very exciting.

Tritonia rosea is dangling rose-pink bells from thin wiry stems set among sheaves of grassy foliage. It belongs to the *Montbretia* or *Crocosmia* family but is generally taller, more slender. It is the prettiest thing to add to a summery-looking flower arrangement with lots of white pom-poms of *Chrysanthemum parthenium* 'White Bonnet', a few late roses and *Hydrangea cinerea* 'Sterilis' whose heads of small creamy-white flowers turn pale green as they age.

Among the crocosmias still in flower, I particularly like *Crocosmia* 'Solfatare'. The subtle contrast of soft creamy-orange flowers with smokey-brown leaves makes it very unusual as most of its relatives are brilliant as stained-glass. 'Emily McKenzie' is another, and very popular, opening flat orange flowers twice the size of any others I grow, heavily splashed blood-red.

I always look forward to *Perovskia* 'Blue Spire', commonly called Russian Sage. Each year this plant starts from ground level, sending up many tall, branching stems clothed in small, aromatic grey leaves. The whole plant, stems and leaves, becomes whiter as the soil grows dustier. The main flower spikes are 18 inches (46 cm) long, set with whorls of tiny lavender-blue tubular flowers. They open spasmodically up and down the spikes, so the plants maintain a soft haze of colour for weeks. It is one of the few grey plants to flower late in the year.

I may have said it before, but the point is worth repeating; it is a good idea to group plants in flower together so that they all contribute to the design at the same time, rather than scatter them about like pins in a pin cushion.

So this lovely sage is the dominant plant in a flowering group at the

Scarlet berries of *Arum italicum* 'Picturm' with *Brunnera macrophylla* 'Langtrees' and yellow-leafed *Fuchsia* 'Genii'

end of September. Hardy penstemons, 'Garnet', with light plum flowers, and the dainty fine-leaved 'Evelyn', with small pale rose flowers, can be relied upon for a long flowering period, and so too can *Erigeron mucronatus* which we should now call *Erigeron karviskianus*. At its best, when seeded into cracks or crevices of walls or steps, this favourite plant is in flower for months. Tiny daisies with bright yellow centres open white, fading to deep pink. The wiry stems and minute leaves are so inconspicuous the little flowers seem to float over low-growing grey- and silver-leaved plants through which they thread their way. Near to my back door, among thyme and purple-leafed sage, there is a mixture of these little pink and white starry flowers intermingled with patches of tiny velvet violas. These are a luminous bluish-black, with whiskered faces, and tiny yellow eyes.

The days are still full. Packing is in full swing. The girls from the farm who helped us so well all summer have left, departing with the swallows, and are now busy packing and grading fruit on our neighbour's farm. Janet Crosby has been allowed to remain for a few weeks yet to help us with the pack. She has been Sue's assistant for several years, looking after the sales area as well as plants in reserve. For a newcomer it would be an ordeal to be handed an order full of Latin names and told to go out and find them. Not only would it be unfair, it would be uneconomic. My experienced girls now have the task whittled to as efficient a method as we can make it, but once again, as with the propagation unit, it takes several years of training and experience to ensure that plants are sent out correctly labelled, are of good quality, and comply with the customer's order.

Each order with plant labels attached (prepared by office) is put into a clear plastic envelope in case of rain, the whole being put into a collecting tray. A trolley is filled with trays, then each girl picks up individual orders, knowing where every plant will be found. When the packhouse floor is full of trays the packing begins. Our motto is : 'Do not pack anything you would not be pleased to unpack yourself.' If a plant we know is badly wanted, is smaller than we would wish but viable, a note is usually put in with it to this effect. Each tray of pots is emptied, the plants are checked for quality, then wrapped, labelled, boxed and weighed for postage. A record book is kept for the Post Office to invoice us. Meanwhile, visitors are still coming to the nursery, so between us we must attend to their needs. It is sometimes very hard to refuse a plant to a visitor who can actually see it here, when all the stock has already been bought by postal customers.

The vegetable garden is the best place at the end of the day to calm frayed nerves or to settle ruffled feathers. With a barrow and bucket I remove all the dead and mildewed leaves of spinach and Chinese cabbage. I cannot remember seeing mildew on them before. Emptying the barrow on the compost heap I refill it with my crop of red-skinned onions, a variety called 'Nordhollandse Bloedrode' (not a difficult title to translate). They are an extraordinary colour, very like the rich, purplish shades of red cabbage. They are dry enough now to be hung in bunches under an outside roof before being stored in the garage where they will hang from a high wooden shelf. I have filled a wooden trug basket with vegetables and salad for the house. There was spinach, parsley, cabbage and mint to be put through the juicing machine to make a brilliant green drink added to fresh lime or lemon juice. Tomatoes at last are turning colour fast, both red and yellow varieties. There are pale green peppers, green and yellow courgettes, purple-podded climbing beans and purple-leafed basil. A bronze-leafed cabbage-lettuce, a few tight heads of calabrese and the delicious autumn sprouting broccoli are just asking to be picked. Last of all, using a rhubarb leaf as a plate, I picked a handful of strawberries. What luxury to live in the country and be able to pick such a feast for the eyes, as well as the stomach, and put it straight onto the table. Well, almost. For supper this is what I made :

Tomato cocktail on crushed ice – easily made in the juice extractor. I used small tomatoes with a little garlic, two small peppers, several fresh leaves of basil added to fresh carrot juice. Season to taste.

219

Gougère with courgettes
(Sarah Brown's *Vegetarian Kitchen*)

Choux pastry

150ml (0.25 pt.) water
50g (2 oz) butter or margarine
50g (2 oz) wheatmeal or 85% wholemeal flour
2 eggs
50g (2 oz) Gruyère cheese, grated
Pinch of mustard powder

Bring water and butter to boil. When water and butter are boiling take pan off heat, shoot in flour and beat until glossy. Mix in one of the eggs, beating thoroughly until amalgamated. Repeat with second egg. Stir in cheese and seasoning. Put into four medium-sized greased pans. Bake for about 20 minutes in pre-heated oven Mark 7, 220°C (425°F). Reduce heat to Mark 5, 190°C (375°F) and bake for a further 10 minutes.

Prepare filling :

1 medium onion, chopped
25g (1 oz) butter or margarine
2 cloves garlic, crushed
1 green pepper, de-seeded and chopped
About 1lb courgettes, diced
20g (0.75 oz) wholemeal flour
150ml (0.25 pt) milk
½ teaspoon grated nutmeg
1 teaspoon chopped marjoram
Salt and pepper
25g (1 oz) Gruyère cheese grated

Sauté onion gently in butter or margarine until softening, add garlic, green pepper, courgettes, cook for a further 3-4 minutes, sprinkle flour over, stir well. Cook gently for 3-4 minutes, stir in milk, bring to the boil, simmer and stir for 2-3 minutes. Add nutmeg, marjoram and seasoning. When the gougère is cooked, spoon filling into centre, sprinkle with grated cheese and put under hot grill till cheese browns.

With such a variety of food you may think it sheer gluttony to dwell on the pleasure of eating fungi. I enjoy eating everything in season. While the deep freeze is invaluable to prevent waste and provide future delights, I prefer to eat the fruit and vegetables of each season as they come : warm blackberries with apple while your skin still smarts from nettle stings and prickles (there are always nettles among blackberries, they like the same rich damp soil); quince *compote* while you still remember the pale fawn fluff on golden skins as you held your face over a basket of nose-prickling tingling scent; the crunch of sweet chestnuts freshly rubbed out of their prickly cases found hidden in long grass – or better still fresh English walnuts.

I have just found a Giant Puffball in the garden. They appear every autumn, rarely in the same place. When just right to eat, they are almost as large as a football. Cut in half they should be firm and white as curd cheese, not at all yellow as they will be when they are preparing to burst into a cloud of yellow spores. They have no gills as mushrooms have, but are solidly white throughout. I cut them into slices about half an inch thick and fry them, like slices of bread, on both sides when they quickly turn golden brown. Sometimes I cut them into cubes and fry them like croutons to add to salad. They are delicious. It is a treat if we can find one when the family is home since one is too much for two people.

Diana, our elder daughter, taught us to eat parasol mushrooms and blewitts, while with Lett Haines we ate crêpes and chanterelles cooked in a little olive oil laced with crushed garlic and chopped parsley.

Our knowledge of edible fungi is very limited but I feel safer with those which are easy to recognise than with some which look like mushrooms and of which I am not absolutely sure.

The tilers have come to strip the roof, find out how much damage there may be to the timbers, add more insulating material and replace the tiles. It is going to take three weeks of hammering, banging, wrenching and clattering above our heads. Scaffolding is being erected along the west side of the house which will reach the long sloping roof overlooking the ponds. The tiles are large flat sheets made of thin concrete in two sizes, bought originally in mixed shades of earth colours. They are laid to form a double layer, their rough texture and the slightly irregular pattern they make when laid creating a more pleasing effect than the very regular pattern and smooth texture of more conventional tiles. They remind me a little of the flat, split pieces of rock used to roof mountain houses. They have weathered attractively over twenty-eight years, being now covered with various kinds of lichen, including large sponge-like mosses which add a look of antiquity but are 'up to no good' according to the roof man. They may eventually weaken and rot the tiles, so they must be cleaned off. You need to find skilled people to lay the tiles. Such a team is Mr Ironman and his son. They methodically lift the heavy tiles, scrape them clean and stack them. Then the original supporting laths have to be ripped up creating a horrific tearing, rending sound, followed by clumping, clattering and hammering. Poor Andrew has been driven from his study to find a marginally more peaceful room at the furthest end of the house.

Outside, I am far less bothered, but was startled one evening to see that silver lines had appeared in my living room between some of the

221

dove-tailed boards of the polished parana pine ceiling; it was daylight! Thank goodness we have had no rain. Occasionally I climb up the ladders to see what is happening, glad to know the roof will be secure, the house dry and cosy in winter after all this effort. It is fun to have a sparrow's view of the garden; the five linked pools stretching the whole length of the shallow hollow, now smoothly carpeted with grass walks weaving between rich patterns of foliage and flower.

I have just spent a day or two tidying my little Chelsea potting shed. All summer it has been used as a dumping place for seeds. Now it needed sorting out to make way for sowing several hundred pans of seed. Piled up trays of seed heads like *Alstroemeria*, late flowering euphorbias and *Veratrum* needed to be shaken into labelled packets or bags ready for sowing. The earlier euphorbias have already been sown in rows in the open ground and are now pushing through the warm soil. Many seeds germinate much more readily if they are sown as soon as they are ripe, but you have to discover which will stand winter conditions as young tender plants. *Morina longifolia*, although perfectly hardy when established, is as tender as a young seedling. Sown in autumn every seed germinates quickly, but all die in severe winter weather. Such seeds we keep until spring, but by then the seed cases will have hardened, making germination slow and difficult. We soak the larger, very hard seeds for a few hours in warm water before they are sown. *Salvia argentea* can also be a problem. This beautiful grey-foliage plant with large round leaves (so heavily coated with white, silky hairs that each might be used as a powder puff) will germinate like cress when sown in late summer, but in spring, even after soaking, when the round black seeds are surrounded by a jelly-like mass reminiscent of frog's spawn, they are erratic. We therefore sow them, when fresh, into large pans and keep the young seedlings protected during the winter. Once established outside they are hardy in well-drained soils.

After I had cleared the broken sticks and seed cases from the bench I came upon boxes of last year's seed. This has to be carefully checked, for we must keep anything we may be short of, or may have missed this year. Most of this year's harvest has been packeted and put into boxes, in alphabetical order, so we can quickly check whether we have it or not, or add seed which ripens over a long period to the labelled packets. By the end of the season a list will have been made of every seed collected during the year, and this must be checked with the master list of everything we should have collected.

In a few cases we do not always have enough seed of our own. Recently I was delighted to receive in the post a packet containing the pearlised blue-black seeds of *Paeonia mlokosewitschii*, the lovely single, lemon-yellow paeony, sent to me by Christopher Lloyd. He has a stock row, set out in full sun, in heavy soil, of long established plants which set good seed. Years ago I needed only the seed from a few plants in the garden, but two years ago I planted a stock row specially for seed. It will be several years yet before I have more seeds than I can count. This is the kind of plant, like veratrums, which takes years to make saleable plants. The seeds we have just sown in the ground of *Paeonia mlokosewitschii* will, most of them, not germinate for eighteen months. Next spring there may be nothing, or maybe a dozen or so tiny seedlings to mark the row. The following spring the bulk of them will rush up, each making one pair only of true leaves above a long, thin tap root. They will stay in the seed row another year, then in the third year they will be rowed out into well-prepared soil, a handspan apart. Here they will stay a further two or three years before they have made a fat rootstock and the first flower bud may appear. After five to six years they will be saleable.

Each year we sow seed to have a succession of plants coming on. This means we have a piece of land taken up by one crop for a very long space of time. It does not take so long to produce a shrub or many trees. So is it economical to grow them? Probably not. This is the kind of consideration which makes some plants scarce because growers have not the time or patience, nor can they afford to have land locked up producing no income. The sale of more easily grown plants helps towards the cost of the long-term plants, but generally speaking the price asked for these long-term plants bears no relation to the time spent producing them. It was with relief that I came across a bag of the seed of Cardoon, *Cynara cardunculus*. This huge artichoke-like plant looks spectacular in the dry garden, as effective as *Gunnera* in the damp garden. With any piece of planting, if the foliage is all much the same size, with leaves no larger than privet, the overall effect will be fussy. By the introduction of a plant which is spectacular in form, such as the fine grasses, *Stipa gigantea* or *Miscanthus sinensis*, or very bold foliage like *Acanthus*, *Cynara* or the large leaved hostas and bergenias, a more restful design emerges, depending on long-lasting foliage rather than occasional splashes of colour. By the use of bold forms to outline or add weight to the design, the effect of flowering plants will also be increased. The seed of *Cynara cardunculus* is precious because our plants only set viable seed in really hot summers. Needless to say there is none this year. They are very deceptive. When you cut open the hard, thistle-like heads there are plenty of fat-looking seeds at the base tucked among the stiff, hairy choke. If they are dark and blackish, and rattle like a stone as they drop into your tray, they are properly developed and will germinate. If they are white you can be sure they are empty husks; just press with your finger and thumb to prove for yourself. There will be no need to press them all, only the dark brown seeds are viable. The seeds I have now were harvested after our last hot summer, every seed head then being emptied of good seed and saved for the lean years when we would have none. We are now wondering how many years these seeds will continue to germinate.

223

Standing in tall flower-buckets are decorative seed heads which caught my eye during the summer, which I thought might 'come in useful' for dried flower arrangements. Most of them were chosen for their carved or sculptured form and texture. There are tall stems carrying rich, brown, short-branched heads of *Veratrum nigrum*, 3 foot (1 m) stems of *Gentiana lutea* encircled with clusters of upturned pale capsules, stuffed with flat papery seeds; alliums of many kinds, spherical shapes in all sizes, from golf balls to the star-spangled airy globes almost as large as a football, of *Allium christophii*. There are fritillaries, foxgloves and several kinds of Sea Holly, *Eryngium*. Hanging from the roof are bunches of papery *Hydrangea*, white everlasting *Anaphalis* and bright yellow *Helichrysum* 'Sulphur Light'. Trails of hop and silvery seed heads of *Clematis* add to the confusion.

In years gone by there would have been buckets, bowls and tin cans containing dark collections of shrubs for foliage – laurel, *Rhododendron*, *Cotoneaster* and many others for experiment – all soaking up through their crushed stems a mixture of glycerine and water until the leaves had turned the desired tone of brown. (The mixture is one part glycerine to two parts of hot water.) I find glycerined leaves of *Fatsia japonica* invaluable as they make bold centrepieces to hold the arrangements together visually. These glossy evergreen leaves, fingered more elegantly than a fig, add drama without being too heavy and can be found in several sizes on the same shrub. However, they take a very long time to change from green to a dark blackish-brown. By putting them to dry in the sun, even pegging some to the clothes line so they did not blow away in the wind, I found the colour lightened to softer, paler shades, like polished leather. The leaf stalk becomes weak after the glycerine treatment, so a few fine flower wires are needed to strengthen them, but the leaves last for ever when well dried and kept flat in boxes.

A shrub which naturally turns to a soft creamy-fawn, the colour of chamois leather, when given this treatment, is *Choisya ternata*, the Mexican Orange Blossom, but all leathery-leafed shrubs like laurel and *Cotoneaster* will lighten attractively if dried off in sunlight. I found *Cotoneaster salicifolius floccosus* made the prettiest sprays of small, pointed leaves.

For large arrangements the seed heads of the Cardoon are exciting if they are collected when they are at their best, not battered and damaged by wind and wet. They must be cut while the large thistle-like head is firmly attached to its stalk. Pull away the dirty remains of shredded blue petals and you will see the beginnings of a shiny, straw-coloured centre. Stand the head in a dry room and rows of scale-like bracts will turn back to look like silvered petals. If picked too early the scales will not open properly; if too late, the head will disintegrate and fall off the stem.

Sword-shaped leaves of *Crocosmia* were hung up in tight bunches to dry, picked in all stages from yellowish-green to warm brown, all the different shades making useful variety.

Sometimes I have bleached the large prickly heads of *Eryngium giganteum*, known as 'Miss Willmott's Ghost'. They need to be at the right stage, not yet beginning to disintegrate, but with the cellulose between the fine veins partially broken down. They will probably look a dirty straw colour. (Some years they dry beautifully in the garden, when they are lovely, more natural than when bleached.) With a skewer I poke out the large, dark seeds which will not bleach, then fill a zinc bath or deep bucket with water, add bleach – you will find out by experience how much – put in the heads and hold them down with something heavy like a brick or large stone. After a day or two they will have become ivory white. All kinds of firm, partially fretted seed-cases can be treated like this.

These cream-coloured pieces add sharp contrast to the warm tans, russets, dark brown, fawns and faded greens of all the other pieces you may have collected. Grasses cannot be overlooked; nothing looks prettier than a mixed bunch picked along a headgerow, but in the garden I use the tall golden heads of *Stipa gigantea* or the shorter, quivering stems of *Melica altissima* whose papery seed cases are stained purple, threaded together like strings of flattened beads. Hairy caterpillar shapes hang from the fine wiry stems of *Pennisetum orientale*, while best of all, perhaps, are the delicate feather mops of *Miscanthus sinensis* 'Silver Feather'.

Some years I collected leaves late in the year, when they had lain for some weeks on the damp soil, and had been partially eaten away by moulds and micro-organisms scavenging among the waste, reducing it until it became assimilated back into the soil. I collected many different shapes and sizes with the vein structures still intact and soaked them in diluted bleach. Not all were whitened completely. According to the stage of decay, they were speckled or marbled with fawn or brown. Dried between newspapers, even ironed sometimes with a very cool iron, they were delicately beautiful, as ghosts, preserved in boxes, wired onto stems for arrangements or used in pressed flower pictures.

The tough, leathery leaves of *Magnolia × soulangiana* I left to soak until spring in a bowl of rain water, when the green, slimy part could eventually be scrubbed off under the tap and the remaining skeleton bleached. It was better not to press these delicate lace-like leaves but rather to let them dry naturally, assuming more natural curves and twists.

One of the most beautiful dried arrangements I ever saw was in a fine old house where I had been asked to lunch. It was a cold, raw day in early May. The entrance to the dining room led, unexpectedly, down a short flight of steps facing the long refectory table, with a fire blazing at the far end. Dominating the room, and lit by a high window, was a dried masterpiece that seemed to fill the corner from beamed roof to brick floor. It appeared to have grown there. In fact I'm sure it had, pieces being added as they turned up, rather like a Dutch painting, but in soft muted colours.

This is the art of dried flower arrangement, whether you use skeleton shapes, preserved leaves, or treated flower heads like *Delphinium*, roses, immortelles, or anything else you care to try. The individual pieces must have good shape, must not look as if you had raided the rubbish heap for them. Graceful, curving tendrils, twisting ribbons of grassy leaves will be needed if you are not to find yourself struggling with little more than bare stems, stiff as stair rods. Good foliage, whether dried naturally, preserved by glycerine, or pressed beneath the carpet, is essential. Once you are hooked, doing 'drieds' can become an obsession. I used to make them, when we first arrived here, to furnish my empty, white-walled house. Against a tall, narrow space I used to make a large design of leaves and seed heads suggested by wood carvings I had seen in cathedrals or great houses. I am ashamed to say how many years it lasted, with few replenishments, until it was replaced by a painting.

Eventually, it seemed, I would need a house just for drieds – where there would be a drying room where material never went mouldy, with endless shelves and drawers filled with dried flowers, buds, grasses, pressed and bleached leaves – all the precious pieces collected from year to year. By then, however, I had started my nursery, and the craze for doing drieds died. But not entirely. There are still these buckets to be decided upon in the potting shed. I picked out those pieces I knew I would use. The rest, with all the mess from seed sorting, was swept into a barrow and taken to the bonfire.

Finally, I sprinkled the floor with a fine rose on the watering can and swept it clean. In any confined space this is the rule. The job is more pleasant, more efficiently done, and prevents the sweeper inhaling dry dust.

OCTOBER

In February I wrote about preparing a book for publication. Two or three years before, I had been asked by the editor of the Telegraph Sunday Magazine to write each week a short description of any garden plant that took my fancy. At the end of two years there were one hundred and four essays describing mostly plants, with the addition of a few trees and shrubs, that could be found in the garden throughout the year. They are not my one hundred and four favourite plants; they are just ones which caught my attention at the time. There are many others I would have liked to write about, which had to be left out.

These essays were illustrated by Joy Simpson whose delicate paintings attracted readers to the little word portraits. To our delight letters of appreciation began to arrive. Some readers said they were pasting them into a scrapbook. Thus came about the idea of publishing a book under the title *Plant Portraits*. This meant more writing had to be done. The essays had to be rewritten to make them longer, each to fit a page. When writing them for the first time, I had often had to pare them down, to reduce the flood of description and information I felt bound to give, into a concentrated teaspoonful. The original 'portraits' were the result of seeing the plants growing around me, feeling the atmosphere of the day, seeing the petals wet with rain, chilled by arctic blasts, or basking in dusty heat. It took several weeks of winter to unpick my trimmed and tailored phrases, to recall the purple patches I had thrown away. In both cases it was an interesting and necessary discipline, but I found I write better from life than from memory. I had mislaid an essay on erythroniums. Feverishly I hunted for it, without success. Finally I wrote another. Because I love these delicate, lily-like flowers very much and have studied them carefully, I thought I had written a fair account of them, until the original essay surfaced from among a mass of papers.

Collecting these essays in book form, we felt that here also was an opportunity to show the talent of two more artists. Jill Coombs and Christine Grey Wilson, both of whom do work for Kew Gardens, were chosen to paint and draw from living specimens. This is not always as easy as it sounds. One difficulty is to find the plants. Several times the artists drove considerable distances to visit the garden here, sometimes to stay a while, sometimes taking plant material or even plants home, to plant in their own gardens, to paint when they were in flower. The final pictures show the concentrated effort each has made to portray faithfully the plants as they saw them. Each stem or petal seems to breathe on the page. Plant photographs are easier, take far less time, but as yet, for me, do not have the life that a really fine artist creates whether in colour, half-tone or black and white.

Many people were involved in finally collecting all these individual efforts together, making decisions – on paper, typeface and above all quality of printing – before the whole could at last be stitched together between hardback covers.

I wrote a few letters and tidied my desk

Finally the day of publication drew near. An evening party had been arranged in an unusually stylish garden-centre in Chelsea. Several weeks previously I had been asked to send a guest list to my publisher. I confess I was dilatory in getting on with this task since several old friends I would have dearly loved to come have now departed this world, or else live too far away and would not, I considered, bless me for inviting them to spend good money travelling to London for a glass of wine. Then I came to my senses and realised we were supposed to be selling the book and didn't I know anyone who could help to promote it?

London was not the only scene of activity. Scaffolding had now been removed from my living room windows and re-erected along the bedroom wing, including the bathroom. On the morning of the book launch I dressed before a view of dungareed legs (veiled by net curtains), passing back and forth across the window. They belonged to the tiler's son, a blond young fellow who was removing and scraping tiles from the back half of the roof. The builders too had returned and were replacing rotted facia boards.

The girls were packing, the men were spreading grit and bonfire waste on the newly drained land. It is still very wet and peat-like, despite the fact we are now in a period of drought, but the new drains all run well, washing little piles of fine silt into the main ditch.

I wrote a few letters, tidied my desk, signed some papers for Rosie, and wore a summer dress. The days I have done so with comfort this summer could be counted on one hand. This was one of the hottest.

My twin brother, Seley Little, who lives in Wivenhoe, the next village, came to lunch as he was to be my escort in London. (Nothing would induce Andrew to go to a party of any kind.)

We drove to Wivenhoe where we were to take the train. Although I have lived in this district for most of my life I had never before travelled on this little riverside branch-line. We parked the car, and instead of walking along Station Road we slipped through a short, bushy lane behind the backways of cottages, slithering down a steep, sloping bank onto the station platform. Waiting for the train in the hot sun, in my summer dress, it suddenly felt like a holiday. So sleepy was the little station that there was no one in the ticket office, so we boarded the train without tickets, feeling like felons! The train curved away from the village, the rails running alongside the bank of the River Colne. From the window I saw the familiar salt marshes stretching on either side of the broad band of sparkling water, saw gulls fly up, and a pair of swans with outstretched necks, whose feeding ground, with dozens more, is the wharfside at Colchester where cargo ships load and unload. As we came to the town we rattled across the level crossing and stared back at the cars where I normally sit waiting for the gates to be opened, and wonder at the two or three lonely passengers in the passing train; who they are, where are they going? We stopped at Colchester North where more people joined the train, then rattled through undulating Essex farm-land, much of it already ploughed and planted for next year's harvest. Barn-yards, clustered around red-tiled farmhouses, were stacked with straw for winter-feed and bedding. Flocks of black and white plovers flew up, wheeled around, then resettled themselves to their systematic searching between the furrows.

Despite the assurance of other travellers on the platform that we could buy our tickets on the train, no ticket-man appeared during our journey to London and we finally paid our way at the barrier on Liverpool Street Station – after considerable delay.

We found our hotel, our rooms and with gentle persuasion a pot of tea in time to take a little rest before I must get ready to appear as 'The Author'. I am not good at preparing myself for auspicious occasions. For anything else I have to do I am prepared to devote all the time and effort it needs, but for myself the preparations are usually left until the last minute. There are always so many things that seem more important than clothes. It is not that I do not care how I look, but shopping for clothes today needs not only money, but time and a large slice of luck (unless it is your hobby). Sometimes I have walked round a store and thought I would not wish to carry one item away, not even if it were given me. In another shop I may love almost everything but I know at a glance it was not meant for me but for dazzling young women structured like giraffes. I go home depressed with my lack of the right image, but fortunately I forget all about it when I have climbed back into my jeans and shirts. The few special-occasion clothes I have, I like, but they tend to turn up again and again, like good perennial plants.

For one of my first appearances at Chelsea, on that special evening when the royal parties are shown around, I wore a simple Chanel-type suit. Several Chelseas later, I went one evening, in the middle of May, to visit my mother, a tiny bird-like creature over ninety years old, who still sat firmly upright in her chair. I went to see her wearing a new dress I had just had the luck to find. It was of soft, finely-tucked cotton, sprigged with tiny flowers and leaves, with narrow frills at the neck and wrists.

'Dear child!' exclaimed mother, who was neither a devotee of fashion nor wordly inclined, 'I am so relieved you have at last bought a new outfit to go to Chelsea. If you had worn that suit once more the Queen would have thought "My goodness – that girl is taking a long time to get her business off the ground!"'

While I imagined myself to be an independent young woman, I often resented being called 'child' by my mother, but as we watched my children grow into young women, and the great grandchildren were brought to her lap, it became a precious gift. To her I was forever young.

My brother and I took the tube to South Kensington. I was glad to be guided through the unfamiliar streets till all at once we arrived at the

'Chelsea Gardener'. Crossing the road, we came face to face with a window decorated entirely with covers of *Plant Portraits*. I was astonished and delighted, of course. The dust cover is pale primrose-yellow, the perfect shade to set off the portrait of *Papaver orientale* 'Cedric Morris', a large pink poppy with crumpled petals, shadowed with purple-black blotches. This plant was bred by my old friend and mentor, Sir Cedric Morris. I chose it for the cover, proud of the lovely painting, but proud too to have Cedric's name to keep me company. If only he too had been alive to come and share the fun.

Inside we found Jill Coombs, Christine Grey-Wilson and their husbands, our friends from Dent's and many others. Another book called *The Winter Flower Garden*, by Sonia Kinahan, was also being launched, and there was an exhibition of stylish garden-furniture and ornaments. It was a spacious place to hold a party, rather like a huge conservatory; a lovely setting in which to have the pleasure of meeting old friends and making new acquaintances.

Soon the artists and I were signing copies of *Plant Portraits*. I found myself in a whirl, greeting people I knew and being introduced to strangers whose names I never quite catch on such occasions, but my brother fielded for me, carefully noting whom I had promised to contact or might need to know at some future date. He guided other people together who wished to meet but who felt uncertain how to go about it. When we all became dehydrated with unseasonal warmth and endless talking, he was there before the waiters with glasses of cold drinks. For me he is the perfect P.A.

Eventually we left, still feeling elated – but hungry. That was no one's fault; I cannot eat, drink and talk all at once. Nearby, we found a little bistro where we sat by a large window and could watch London life pass by. We ate a deliciously fresh meal – calabrese and almond soup, cold duck stuffed with orange and nuts and a simple green salad, while my insatiable thirst was wetted with iced tonic water, faintly flavoured and slightly pink with Angostura bitters. No alcohol. I was quite high enough without it.

Back at our hotel, it was so warm I could not sleep. I threw off all the bedclothes and propped up the pillows to sit and write my diary, isolated in my small, safe room, yet feeling part of the London roaring around me. Vehicles of every kind, their head lamps gleaming like great eyes of nocturnal animals, rushed through the night on nameless errands. If only they could be as silent.

Next morning we went shopping. I needed wallpaper for two small bedrooms. We went to Sanderson's in Berners Street. It is always disturbing to see so many ideas. It is good to be open-minded about new designs or unusual colour combinations, but demoralising if it makes you want to discard everything you possess. I have had less opportunity to practise the art of interior design than garden design. Both can take a

231

lifetime if you wish to speak the language fluently – to put plants or objects, fabrics, colours and styles together so that they look inevitable, not ostentatiously contrived. I have tended to keep to the well-tried and simple, rather than put up with extravagant mistakes, but these bedrooms had deteriorated to the state where simplicity had become downright spartan.

Gradually my eyes became attuned to the bewildering display. I began to eliminate the impossible, to pass by near-misses, not to be fooled by the spaciousness of showrooms which can sometimes distort one's sense of scale. Finally I chose two papers, one of which reminded me a little of an old house we used to live in when we were children. Later we looked in other shops, but saw nothing to make me wish to change my mind. In Liberty's the rich patterns seemed to ask for dark and stately rooms, mediaeval at least; ideal for Great Dixter, but we did find a pretty embroidered cushion, worked in wool, from India. It pleased us both, because during the war my brother was in India, had seen such work being done by hand and had sent several pieces home to me.

On the second evening of our book-launch I was pleased to meet two friends whom I had originally met through Cedric – Mary Grierson and Margaret Davies. Mary Grierson, internationally famous for her artistic and sensitively faithful botanical paintings, has always felt indebted to John Nash and Cedric Morris. Their teaching and encouragement changed her whole life. Now, when her contemporaries might be tempted to take life more easily, Mary sparkles with energy, still welcoming new projects, illustrating new books and having exhibitions of her work. Her enthusiasm for her work is infectious.

It was Cedric who first told me of Margaret Davies. When I wrote *The Dry Garden* I had no idea how to set about finding an artist to illustrate it. I had drawn plans for different types of borders, and roughly sketched the profiles, but they were neither finished nor stylish enough for publication. Margaret transformed them with her exact and delicate black and white drawing. When we came to *The Damp Garden* she not only transformed my plans but added several of her own highly individual illustrations and painted the striking dust jacket.

There were many people to meet: journalists, representatives of the book trade and people from radio and television. It was exciting and quite exhausting.

I enjoy being in London with my brother. I do not care very much for shopping, but I do like looking around with someone who knows where to go and how to get there. We spent most of the morning browsing before going home. We went into several bookshops, including Foyles. *Plant Portraits* was not yet on the shelves, but it is still a thrill to see the dust-jackets of my other books on public shelves.

Eventually we came to the offices of Chatto and Windus, just round the corner from St Martin in the Fields in William IV Street. This publishing house was originally started by my husband's grandfather, and as we stepped inside I saw, directly ahead of me, the large framed portrait of Grandfather Andrew Chatto, easily recognised from the old sepia photographs in the family albums. The young receptionist was friendly and patient, but light-years away from an era which died with the Great War.

We meandered through theatreland and arrived in Covent Garden where we spent the rest of the morning enjoying the restored buildings and the little narrow streets with no traffic but a lot of small and fascinating shops. We bought tea in a dim shop selling nothing but tea – dozens of different kinds – and other things related to making tea : pretty tins, caddies, trays, cosies, teapots, delicate bowls and cups and saucers. We also went into David Mellors to look at fine kitchenware. I was tempted to buy all kinds of things there, but after forty years of cooking none were really needed. However, I did buy a small wooden salad-bowl just right for two.

We watched street buskers, singers, a mime artiste and story-tellers amusing little groups of people who sat at small tables, eating and drinking, taking a few hours holiday. I bought little gifts I thought might please my grandchildren. The one that pleased me was a large flat seagull, beautifully designed and simply made of painted wood. It is a large mobile. By pulling a string it flaps lazily. It now hangs over the bath in Thomas and Jeremy's house by the sea.

Since the few days spent in London I have found myself with a curious huskiness in my throat and chest. I do not appear to have a cold. Perhaps I should put the blame on all the talking I have done recently. With less energy than usual I try to 'tread water' for a bit, just pottering about the nursery. There are always a dozen little jobs just waiting to be noticed, and they ease the mind considerably when at last they are done.

We need rain. The recent high temperatures with drying winds have caused unsightly browning and wilting. I wanted to repeat the large arrangements of white daisy flowers which I had made before I went away, but was disappointed. Their petals are disfigured, spoilt by drying wind. Quite suddenly, like the flowers fading in the garden, I wilted too and took to my bed, aching from top to toe. What a relief to lie flat in bed, prostrated by a leaden weariness, that was induced, I suppose, by a kind of flu. Threats were made to call a doctor, but I was not in need of drugs. Bed and rest, with plenty to drink and no heads appearing round the door, are the best medicine for minor ailments. Large jugs of fruit juice, diluted with spring water, were all I needed for two or three days.

As soon as it became boring to stay there, I left my bed and went outside, thankful to be up and dressed, but with legs as weak as a newborn lamb's.

Everything has run smoothly without me. As well as the routine work

233

there was the organisation of our stand for the Red Cross Sale at Cressing Temple. This plant sale has been held for about fifteen years and has become part of the autumn calendar, both for us and the visitors who come from miles around. It is held in a magnificent Tithe Barn which has stood since the twelfth century when it was a meeting-place for crusading Knights Templar. It is an experience to enter this huge, cathedral-like building with its vast timbers perfectly preserved, to think of all the generations of people, the successions of harvests, of kings and queens, of musicians and writers who have come and gone while this building has remained. To this day it is not a museum piece but is used for the purposes originally intended by the farm on which it stands. For the sale it is emptied and the floor swept clean, with room for us to drive in with our vans ready to furnish our stalls and to set the whole length of the barn in bays between squared pillars. An enormous amount of plant material is collected by a regular band of hard-working volunteers whose task is to persuade, cajole, or threaten gardeners to pot up seedlings, cuttings, divisions, runners, bulbs, trees, shrubs and herbaceous plants – just anything saleable that can be gleaned from gardens and greenhouses. Some of it arrives straight from the garden. It is tipped onto the barn floor and must be quickly sorted, wrapped, priced and labelled. Many other plants are carefully potted and grown on for the occasion.

At one end on a raised platform is a scene reminiscent of the Women's Institute, with tables of jams, jellies, chutneys and pickles, cakes of every description and freshly made flans, scones and bread. All the rich colour and fruitfulness of the countryside is here. Tables are heaped with marrows, pumpkins, walnuts, hazelnuts, baskets of eggs, apples, quinces, pears and medlars, all lovely to look at, irresistible to buy.

Various crafts are tucked into the dim recesses. Someone mends chairs with cane or rush, another makes corn-dollies or spins and weaves naturally dyed wool, with soft, gentle-colour skeins heaped all around.

We have our usual site, tucked between the structural pillars. We cover three trestle tables with brown hessian draped to the ground, to hide our boxes of plants beneath and keep off our legs the draught which comes straight across from the great double doorway opposite. The day before, we have taken our plants and arranged them on the tables at the front edge of our site, putting the rest on tables against the wall behind us, so they will also be seen. Among the plants we take are golden-variegated Pampas Grass, sky-blue *Salvia uliginosa*, scarlet and pink Kaffir lilies, purple-spotted Toad lilies, boxes of glowing colchicums, tiny cyclamens in flower, creamy-white 'bottle brushes' of *Cimicifuga* and late-flowering asters. We will also have brought ornamental vines, *Clematis* with fluffy seed heads, ornamental grasses and plants with beautiful leaves for those who have learned to use them.

We have all gained by experience since we attended the first sale, learning to select plants with more care and to display them more effectively. The first time I attended there were far too many plants, inadequately prepared. It is no use having great heaps of mixed border plants thrown on to the floor by a generous donor who has just decided he cannot cope any more, stuffing them into a fertiliser sack and offering the lot for twenty pence. It might seem like a lucky dip, but more likely the buyer already has the plants. It seems to me unfair to the donor – who, after all, has spent considerable time caring for the plants to have enough to give away, and unfair to the beneficiaries, be they the Red Cross, Wild Life Fund, or any other good cause. The charity does not benefit from rubbish being offered for a few pence. It is always best to offer good quality for a fair price. Bargains should be available for people new to gardening, while the rare plants will be snapped up by enthusiasts who have come hoping to find them. By carefully sorting, wrapping, labelling and grouping the plants, potential customers can see all that is available and are given the chance to find what they need. Careful attention needs to be given to innocent-looking yoghurt pots and cocoa tins, usually found on the 'Odd Plants' stall. Just give the occupants a gentle tug to make sure you are buying a rooted cutting, not a stick which has only recently been pushed into the soil. There are times when you are only too pleased to buy an unrooted cutting, if it is of a plant obtainable in no other way, and if you know how to look after it and will subsequently root it, but I myself have been caught unsuspecting. It is a pity to feel soured having paid fifty pence each for ten rootless sticks taken at the wrong time of year, even if it is for the Red Cross. I would rather give the five pounds than find myself deceived.

On the morning of the sale we arrive in good time, usually with a few extras for friends who have asked if we could bring this or that. Everywhere is swept and tidy. We make time to have a quick look round to see if we can find any unsuspected treasures: anything we have lost and could replace, or something that might have turned up out of an old garden. One year we were very short of *Sisyrinchium striatum*, a useful foliage plant with grey-green iris-like leaves, topped with stiff spikes of small creamy-yellow flowers. Left to itself it usually seeds generously, but occasionally my gardeners are a little too prompt in their clearing up· doing their best to avoid a mess of plants in the wrong place, they sweep off the seed heads before I have had time to collect them. So we were glad to be able to buy a handful of seedlings clamped into newspaper. Our stock of Eau de Cologne scented mint came out of a yoghurt carton, while the beautiful white flowered *Crinum powellii* 'Album' I found, one year, at the end of the sale, lying in a discarded heap, its large elongated bulbs unrecognised. They were about to be thrown into the rubbish cart when I came upon the scene and thankfully offered ten pounds for the lot. They were worth far more than that to me.

235

This is often the case in gardening ; we put a high value on what we do not possess and maybe have little chance of growing. But I knew I could grow the crinums in my warm, well-drained gravel soil. They are now established in a stock bed in the open (not sheltered by walls), but protected with a mulch. They have survived the recent cold winters (despite the necks of the long bulbs becoming mushy) sending up several stems of large, perfumed, trumpet-shaped flowers. They look sumptuous on the south or west wall of a house, their sweet scent drifting through the air for weeks during late summer and autumn, while the sheer size and stature of an established clump is architecturally impressive.

At 10 a.m. the heavy bar across the great black doors is lifted and the crowds surge in. For the rest of the morning we are engulfed, with time to do no more than wave to old friends over the heads of the crowd. Everyone knows what they want, hoping to catch our eye next as we struggle to serve each one in turn. The smell of hot soup and coffee from the Refreshment Bar nearby is tantalising, but there is no time to stop. Then suddenly, as if a plug had been taken out, the flood of enthusiasm subsides, becomes a trickle and then dries. After lunch a few late shoppers wander in, more curious than enlightened, but the main business of the day is over. We stack the empty boxes, sweep out our space and fold up the hessian to be put away for another year.

Now and then I take a little canvas stool into the garden and make notes. There never seems time to do as much note taking as I would like. Often, when I am rushing round, I see a plant or combination of plants I would like to record, but the fine descriptive phrases that float into my mind quickly float out again as I am pulled by something more pressing and practical.

A plant new to me is *Elscholtzia stauntonii*, not to be confused with *Eschscholtzia* which seems very like in spelling but is a very different plant, the well known Californian Poppy. I first saw *Elscholtzia* as a seed head in the gardens of the Arnold Arboretum in Boston, USA. *Elscholtzia* belongs to the mint family. It makes a tall 3 foot (1 m) stiffly erect plant. Branching stems hold thick flower spikes, densely set with tiny, bright mauve, fuzzy flowers. It is the same glowing colour as we see elsewhere in the garden at this time, in colchicums and the Obedient Plant, *Physostegia virginiana* 'Vivid'.

In dry gravel soil is a plant of *Glaucium phoeniceum*. I am not certain of the name, but the plant is unmistakeable. It is similar to the Horned Poppy (*Glaucium flavum*), which can still be found growing on shingle beaches along the coast of East Anglia and differs in having pale yellow flowers. Both produce a large basal rosette of blue-grey leaves, but the leaves of *Glaucium phoeniceum* are much more blue. By late autumn it has made an interlacing mound of grey branching stems about 3 feet (1 m) high and across. You cannot help noticing the long curved seed pods, yet the whole plant still has a sprinkling of furled flower buds while, overall, the bluish background of foliage is still alive with glistening poppies of the most intense orange-scarlet. This spectacle has gone on for months as the abundance of seed pods shows. The seed pods are long, slender and curved, reminding me of the bills of curlews seen on our Essex salt marshes. As they ripen, they split open along the whole length to show quantities of tiny jet-like seeds, each embedded in separate woody recesses.

The same vibrant red is to be seen in the Hummingbird Trumpet flower, *Zauschneria californica* 'Dublin'. Long scarlet tubes flare open at the mouth, to form a frill of cut petals from which extend scarlet threads bearing pollen-filled anthers. Extending further still is the tiny knobby pistil, the whole making two inches of dazzling brilliance. Behind them stand a majestic clump of *Agapanthus* leaves, narrow, strap-shaped, still perfect in form, fresh green in colour. The scarlet flames of *Zauschneria* will still be flickering around the edges of the scene when the *Agapanthus* leaves have turned to shades of honey and amber before collapsing with the onset of winter.

The cooler parts of my garden (where heavier soil means better water retention) provide most colour in autumn. All soils have their advantages. The art of gardening is to know your soil intimately, to treat it well and select plants which will make any soil seem like an asset, not a problem. You may not be able to grow all the plants you would like to possess, but by choosing plants suited to your conditions you can carpet the bare earth with contented plants rather than endure the effect of a moth-eaten rug where too many plants have given up the struggle. It would be a waste of time to try to grow Michaelmas Daisies where *Zauschneria* and *Glaucium* flourish, but on heavier land they have been in flower since August. Now they are mostly past their best, but *Aster* 'Esther' is still lovely on the edge of a border and good to tuck into small flower bowls. She is an *ericoides* type, low-growing and dainty with light heads of small pale-rose flowers. *Aster* 'Violet Queen' is an old variety with no faults that I can see. Rich violet-blue daisies are accented by dark, rigid stems 18 inches (46 cm) tall.

A very unusual aster is *A. lateriflorus* 'Horizontalis' which makes such stiffly branched plants that it can be used quite dramatically to form a low summer hedge, but one plant alone catches the eye. By September, small dark green leaves become tinged with purple, harmonising with thousands of tiny silvery-lilac flowers densely set along horizontal branches. As the weeks go by the colour intensifies, the central boss of each little flower grows larger in deepening shades of rosy-mauve. As winter comes the leaves fall but the stiffly twiggy plants are still smothered with tiny straw coloured stars, exquisite when outlined with frost.

Two more names I cannot omit are *Aster* × *frikartii* 'Mönch' and

Aster thompsonii 'Nanus'. These two blue-flowered asters are without equal. They bloom for at least three months, never suffer from attacks of mildew and need no staking. They each make, in effect, a dome of blue, drawing you across the garden to admire them. *A. thompsonii* 'Nanus' is the smaller of the two, about 15 inches (38 cm), with slightly paler flowers. I use it in mixed posy bowls for weeks on end, until the first frost spoils most flowers for picking.

A rich blue flower which keeps us waiting till almost the end of the season is *Aconitum carmichaelii* 'Arendsii'. It is a tall Monkshood 4-5 feet (1-1.5 m), sometimes taller if the fat tuberous roots are dug up from time to time and replanted in refreshed soil. These roots are poisonous, but that need not discourage you. The tall blue heads look well above the fiery tapers of *Polygonum amplexicaule*. The polygonums are a versatile family, offering plants to suit almost every situation. Many provide flower from midsummer until autumn frosts. There are low carpeting plants like *P. affine* and *P. vaccinifolium*, both ideal as edging plants, better still if allowed to tumble like a curtain over a bank or rock. *P. amplexicaule* on the other hand makes an impressively large plant, 4 feet (1-1.5 m) tall and as much across. It is a wondrous sight increasing in size throughout the summer and autumn, covered with narrow tapers of tiny crimson flowers. There are several forms in pale pink, white and a bright red form called 'Firetail'. If you feel deprived because you have no room for such a giant, then you will be delighted to find *Polygonum amplexicaule* 'Inverleith'. This is very similar in miniature, not more than 2 feet (61 cm) tall, providing a display of raspberry-red tapers for many weeks in late summer and autumn. Suitable for the small damp garden is *Polygonum sphaerostachyum*, a choice plant whose poker heads on 18 inch (46 cm) stems are composed of wax-textured flowers crowded into finger-thick heads. They are a luminous cyclamen-pink, a quite exceptional colour. I surrounded my plants with a carpet of *Ajuga reptans* 'Burgundy Glow' since the flower-heads seem to be an intensification of the pink tinted leaves of the *Ajuga*.

Making a change among the wealth of daisy flowers at this time of year are Toad Lilies, *Tricyrtis*. They have been in flower for weeks, yet still look fresh. They produce many graceful flowering stems from a tangled mass of white roots, need retentive soil in sun or part shade and are lovely among ferns and hostas. From a distance, their colour appears subdued, but close to, they are curious and appealing. *Tricyrtis formosana* comes from the forests of Taiwan. Shining leaves deeply veined and freckled with deeper green are set alternately along upright stems. The strange flowers are supported on dark maroon stems which emerge from the axils of the leaves on the upper half of the main stem, extending over many weeks into an open head of flower. The buds are dark purple-maroon, opening small upturned, lily-shaped flowers. Each consists of white petals so densely freckled with reddish-purple that they

238

Strange lily-like flowers of *Tricyrtis formosana*

appear purple overall. A complicated arrangement of stamens and stigma, protruding from a gold circled centre, adds to the strange charm.

There are others; taller, shorter, paler, in white, and even yellow. *Tricyrtis latifolia*, found in woods of South West Japan, has flowers much earlier, in August. They are pale creamy-yellow finely spotted with maroon. Setting off their delicate colour are pale green leaves, matt-textured and curled at the tips.

For many years I turned my back on tender plants, growing only hardy perennials which did not need a lot of fuss, bringing in, or planting out. On the whole this is sensible since the garden does not rely on plants being set out like garden furniture. But being sensible is not always fun. Now, as well as making thoroughly artificial, yet captivating, pot gardens, I indulge in planting out a few impressive foliage plants which are not hardy, like cannas. The most dramatic, reaching 5-6 feet (1.5-2 m) tall by the end of the summer, is *Canna indica* 'Atrosanguinea'. I love its bold simple leaves – dark, mysterious purple, held upright on stout stems. They make a deep rumbling bass beneath high notes of taper-lit polygonums and can be used to fill a void, make a focal point, add colour and interest, where late in the year there might be nothing. All this effect without any head of flowers, but flowers do appear eventually as an afterthought, spikes of close-set buds open broad, furled petals savagely contrasting in orange-scarlet. I have a slightly different variety whose leaves are less consistently purple, smoothly elegant, green above, shaded purple beneath with conspicuous parallel, purple veins. As I turn a leaf in my hand, it has a shot-silk effect, changing from purple to green. *Canna iridiflora* makes an even taller plant with huge smooth leaves, rather like banana leaves, pencilled with fine veins running from the leaf edge into the broad central channel. From the top of the gorgeous column of foliage emerge slender flower stems clustered with slim buds, protected in brown sheaths. Slowly, one at a time, they unfold dangling deep rose, lily-shaped flowers. Place it well, not muddled among uncongenial neighbours, and your friends will gasp with admiration, hoping you might one day have a small piece to spare.

Scarlet tapers of
Polygonum amplexicaule
beneath statuesque plants
of *Canna indica*

The variegated grass, *Arundo donax* 'Variegata', is another star performer. It is rarely seen in British gardens because it cannot take frost. My plants, like the cannas, are dug up by the end of October and housed in a frost-free greenhouse. In a good summer they stand 4-6 feet (1.5-2m) tall, with long fluttering ribbon-like leaves, ivory striped with green, falling from cane-like stems. This is a plant I would grow in a cool conservatory if I had one.

My garden diary for October lists too many treats to mention them all, but I would like to share a few. *Campanula burghaltii* dangles a second crop of large pale bells, opening from long pleated indigo buds. Dazzling white bottle-brushes of *Cimicifuga simplex* pierce the gloom under the shade of ancient oaks. *Vernonia crinita* is spectacular in warm sunshine. Massive clumps of strong stems 6 feet (2m) tall are topped with flat, clustered heads of tiny, brilliant, magenta-crimson daisy flowers. Scrambling over a low wall by the entrance to the nursery is *Clematis rehderiana* with clustered heads of small greenish-yellow bells, smelling like cowslips. Opposite to it the variegated form of Jasmine, *Jasminum officinale* 'Variegatum', tumbles from the roof to the ground against the west wall of the packhouse, twining green stems garlanded with pinnate leaves tinted cream, pink and green. *Solanum jasminoides* beside the south facing door of the packhouse, survived (to my surprise) last winter's destructive weather, sprouting just below ground level from a

White bottle-brushes of *Cimicifuga simplex* 'Elstead' partner a dainty
flowering grass, *Panicum virgatum* 'Rubrum'

strong root-stock; it has now reached the roof. Pure white flowers, similar
to those of the potato, hang in dainty clusters from thin inter-twining
stems. This is a plant that does well in my imaginary conservatory.

Today is a sad autumn day; overcast, slightly damp, not actually
raining. It suits the soft changing colours and matches my mood. Kazu
left today. We shall miss him. He has worked well and became a good
team mate.

When I came home I went through the tunnels with Madge, to see
how many plants she could safely put out to fend for themselves and so
make room for plants which must be brought in to ensure we have small
stocks of everything at risk under cover. It is often not the cold which
kills, but alternate wetting and freezing, especially on plants which
keep their leaves. There is also the danger outside of freezing wind when
the chill factor becomes much greater than it would be if the air was
still. Although the temperature drops well below freezing in the single
skin tunnels, the protection they afford is usually enough to keep plants
alive which would have died outside in the full icy blast.

For several years I topped the seed trays with sharp sand bought from
the local gravel pit. On the whole, it worked well enough, but I noticed,
particularly on the empty pans where the seed had not germinated, that
the layer of sand was lightly cemented together if the surface became at
all dry. At a touch it crumbled into flaking pieces, but this could be
enough to stop a tiny seedling struggling to reach the light. It would give

241

up the struggle and die, smothered, while I would be left wondering why the seeds had not come up. I had thought about using grit, as I know the growers of alpines do. This is usually bought ready prepared as ground granite or limestone chippings. Would my gravel grit be suitable, especially for tiny dust-like seeds, or would they feel buried under 'boulders'?

Then I met Peter Hutchinson from Brookside Agricultural College, Leicestershire. He appeared one day on the nursery and I discussed the problem with him. Provided I washed the grit thoroughly to remove all the fine sand which would still act as a cementing agent between the small pebbles, he said it would work, and indeed it does. The grit placed in fine, mesh-lined trays, is well washed with a hose, dried thoroughly in the wind and sun, and then stored ready for use in winter and spring. Seeds which once germinated poorly now spring up between the little pebbles which must slide aside like tiddly-winks as the small but strong seedlings slip between them, searching for the light.

When I received an invitation from Mr Hutchinson to give a talk to Leicestershire gardeners I felt indebted to him for giving me such a simple solution to one of our problems, so I accepted, knowing the three-hour journey would take me within an hour's drive of my elder daughter's home and her family of four children.

I collected root artichokes, sorrell and spinach for soup and bundles of fresh herbs – tarragon, rosemary, thyme and basil, knowing that Diana would be pleased to have them. On the way I stopped at a fruit farm, collected a bucket and picked apples. First, 'Egremont Russet', rather flat, yellow-skinned apples overlaid with fine russet, solid in texture, somewhat spicy in flavour. Then 'Bramley's Seedling', large crisp and green with a red cheek, the best of all cooking apples. It was calm and relaxing in the old orchard. The ancient trees were much too large and not well cared for by modern standards. Pruning had been minimal, if at

A visitor finds Madge in a tunnel

242

all, for several years. That, combined with a cold summer, resulted in too many small fruits, many of them lying on the ground. Someone must be concerned about the poor crop being taken from this patch of land, but I was free to enjoy the peace of the empty orchard, the cidery smell of rotting fruit – the responsibility was not mine.

Stowing away my boxes of warm, scented apples, I rejoined the stream of cars and lorries relentlessly surging northwards until it was time to leave the main road and turn towards Melton Mowbray, passing through the small town where I sometimes stop to buy Stilton cheese made in the neighbourhood. I meandered through five or six miles of by-roads sunk between the heavy clay fields of Leicestershire, finally arriving, while it was still daylight, before the pale stone buildings of Brookside Agricultural College.

I had been told Leicestershire was not a gardening county and I had imagined red-faced fox-hunting farmers galloping over solid clay fields but, as usual, generalisations are easily disproved. The room was filled with the reassuring buzz of enthusiasm which quickly dispelled my blues. I hope I helped them as much as they did me.

Next day I drove to my daughter's house. She was busily mopping the kitchen tiles, careful to have everywhere spick and span for Mother's visit. It is a very old house, situated in the middle of a large village, with the stern faced Presbyterian church opposite the front door, while the parish church stands just beyond the back garden gate, the spire and gilded clock face dominating the view. The low, dimly-lit living room is cluttered with plants, books, and childrens' activities. We sank into deep leather chairs designed to take the battering of tiny feet and talked before the doors were flung open and the family was home – Julia and Daniel, who had swum with me in the estuary at Landemere, and Lucy and Emily.

Next morning two small girls, with icy feet, crept into my bed for a cuddle and chat. As I watched them I recalled the night of Lucy's birth seven years ago, early in January. It was bitterly cold, the streets clogged with snow, vehicles unable to climb the steep hill outside. As I peeped out through the curtains looking for the midwife crunching through the snow, assisted by my son-in-law, the scene was like a Christmas card or a scene from Dickens. Snow lay thickly everywhere, several inches piled on the two or three steps leading to the door of each house. The street lamps blinked blearily through curtains of silent, sifting flakes. For several hours I sat wide awake in my room while the midwife bustled about the house. I tried to read my Christmas present, Sir Kenneth Clarke's *Civilisation*, but the words floated off the page without entering my head. At last I went downstairs, made tea and tapped on the door of my daughter's room to find her still battling, as she said, to pass this child round the S-bend. While I was thankful for the midwife's training, she seemed to me uncommonly detached. Remembering vividly the birth of my second daughter, in my own home, and the strong support I had received from a warm and dedicated midwife, I sat by my daughter's head, momentarily shaken to see in her face the child she once was. Then she tightly closed her large dark eyes and the struggle began again. I had never before seen a woman in labour, but did not stop to wonder if I did right or wrong. There seemed no way we could get further help, being cut off by snow and slippery slopes, so I did the only things I could to encourage her – held her hands tight, bathed her face and prayed all would be well. It was a hard, long night. Just as I was beginning to wonder if the exhausted mother could take much more, Lucy arrived. Fear and pain fled with the dark. Day had come, the room was full of joy.

Diana's house reminds me of a bus station, all coming and going. Small children dash in and out, or stay and play games of dressing-up with Lucy and Emily. Teenagers, taller than I am, pass up and downstairs accompanying Julia or Daniel. When they have all vanished on individual errands or outings their places are taken by young wives, who sink into the deep armchairs to continue instalments of their colourful lives, tottering marriages or less-defined relationships. I do not envy the young, buffeted at the height of life's emotional storms. Are they being forced by the media, or by the lack of any real conviction, to chase will o' the wisps – to expect a state of emotional well-being that cannot be, perhaps never has existed? I do not know, but I feel deeply disturbed by some of these young people who have so little power to help themselves. Some have had nervous breakdowns, have left or should have left their husbands. What about the husbands? I cannot comment – I have not heard their stories.

From such imponderables we turned to the ever-comforting kitchen. While I made salads and soup, Diana quickly made deliciously light bread rolls, raising the dough in her oven turned very low. It worked perfectly. I must try that when the kitchen temperature is too low on cold winter days and when the heating is turned off till late afternoon.

We tend to think it is a hardship now to economise on heating, but when we were children there was no heating until the fires were lit. The bedrooms were icy to dress in but I also remember dashing to the window to enjoy the patterns of frosted 'ferns' which covered the glass.

The builders have at last returned to replace the white-painted boards on the west wall of the bedrooms with brick, and to enlarge two of the windows.

It sounded pretty simple, but as usual there had to be a long discussion to sort out the possible from the impossible, ensuring the finished effect would look right. As most of the house walls are white-painted brick, we decided to repeat this for the new wall but to build the lower third with warm-toned, hand-made bricks as a kind of plinth for the white wall

244

Watching the dredger at work

above and to form a practical background for plants to be grown in the raised bed at its foot. The men went off to order the materials needed, but I was caught by Keith to come and meet Mr Crees, who had arrived to discuss the dredging of our ponds which, over the last twenty years, have become silted up. In some places the water is not more than a foot deep. Although I have been worried for several years about the deteriorating state of the ponds and knew something would have to be done, I dreaded the thought of the mess that must be made. It is one thing to put up with the sight of oozing black mud when you are starting a water garden, but what would visitors think who had motored many miles in the hope of seeing an established water garden? Would there be an appalling smell from rotting vegetation which has fallen and drifted in over the years? What about the grass? What would happen to the fish?

These weak-kneed thoughts had to be pushed firmly aside. We had planned to start dredging by late autumn, when the land should be dry and firm if we had our typical late Indian summer. Then the caterpillar tracks of the drag-line would do least damage to the lawns. There had been no rain for over a month, so we decided to start as soon as everything was ready. We possess one dumper truck and have arranged to hire another, so the waste from the ponds can be transported to the far end of the wet nursery. The silt and rotted vegetation will be spread on the surface to dry out; the clay we dig out to deepen the ponds will be stacked to form a boundary bank.

We also had to consider access for the long arm, or crane. There has to be space for the machine to stand by the edge of the water, to swing the long arm across the pond and then swing round to empty the bucket into a waiting truck. Here and there a branch must be sawn off a tree and some bushy willows cut to the ground. While my reason tells me the butchery will be kept to a minimum, that some will be beneficial and the rest will quickly grow up again, the thought of three great machines snorting and scavenging like dragons throughout the length and breadth of my water gardens deeply disturbs my peace of mind.

I do not find the more choice varieties of common primrose *Primula vulgaris* the easiest plants to grow. I find the truly bog-loving primulas, which include the lovely candelabra types, easier, probably because they are healthier, as most of them are grown from seed. The common primrose in all its forms, double and single, seems to do best on heavy clay soil, provided a little leaf-mould is added. It must on no account be water-logged, nor must it dry brick-hard in summer. This can happen only too easily in long periods without rain. But there is more to the problem than finding the right soil conditions. With the choice double varieties in particular, the plants will deteriorate after a few years if left to themselves. They must be dug up when you find they will fall apart into many pieces, each with a long warty-looking base with white roots attached. You must remove as much of this base as possible, cutting just below the leaf bases where new roots will be seen emerging. Reduce the leaves by about a third in length, discarding most of the old, outside ones. Plant the trimmed pieces into pots or trays and stand them in a sheltered place until they have recovered, made new roots, and are strong enough to be planted out in the open. It is essential to take this trouble to retain the beautiful old varieties which seem, over generations of vegetative propagation, to have lost some of their original vigour and now seem prey to all the pests and diseases which lie in wait for them.

We have learnt to watch during the summer months for signs of attack by Red Spider mites. These are practically invisible to the naked eye, but the loss of colour and vigour in the leaf caused by these little pests sucking out sap from the undersides is very apparent. We have just planted a partially shaded section of our newly prepared wet nursery, hoping it will prove to be a suitable site for my remaining stock of primrose varieties. I hope it will be sufficiently drained in winter, yet heavy enough to be retentive in summer. Next spring, a mulch of finely pulverised bark will be spread over the soil to imitate the protecting habit of fallen leaves in woodland. We shall wait to see whether the small pieces we have planted will be lifted by frost, or whether any need to be replaced. When we can see a full bed of healthy plants becoming established, they will be lightly hoed and then the weed-suppressing, moisture-retaining carpet of bark will be put around them.

The ornamental gourds have done well, despite the cool wet summer. Small ones, smooth as marbles, or warty, plain green and striped, or white as birds' eggs, are grown up the wire-netting fence which keeps rabbits out of the vegetable garden. There should not be any rabbits inside the garden or nursery, but occasionally gates are left open or an undiscovered hole appears in the boundary netting. We are rarely able to shoot or chase every last one. I collect all the ripe gourds in a wheelbarrow and take them to the house where I wipe them clean and dry, then pile them into large shallow baskets on the floor where I think they look best. It helps to have as many different shapes and sizes as possible. In one of the largest groups, in a round shallow bowl-like basket, there is room for one or two Turk's Cap gourds. During the long winter, when the old year slides into the dark, I am reminded of sun warming my back as I bent to turn the heavy fruits on their bed of straw so they would colour evenly. As they ripened they developed broad stripes of cream and orange, sometimes flecked with red like a Sultan's silk-swathed turban. For years I used them only as decoration then discovered, unlike many ornamental gourds, that they are edible. Their bright orange flesh makes a good base for vitamin-packed soup, or spiced baked custard.

In my baskets they need the contrast of smaller gourds: dark green oval ones boldly marked with longitudinal orange stripes; others, the size and shape of an orange, but bitter-green, are beautifully sectioned with pale green. Just one on the table beside me gives me pleasure; to see it, to feel its roundness in the palm of my hand, to follow the lines of subtle colour running over the smooth surface ending in an upward spiral of withered stem. I cut the ripe gourds from the stems taking care not to snap off the stalks (this would leave a wound, moulds would enter, and the gourd soon disintegrate). The curving 'tails' add character to the whole basketful, as well as to each individual gourd.

It is the last Saturday in October; the clocks will be put back tonight; summer-time ends. The garden party is over; a chill in the air sends a shiver down my back. As if to stave off the inevitability of short days and long dark evenings, I fill a last, summery-looking basket of flowers for the house. Although they are all truly autumn flowering plants, the colours are light and fresh. This weekend I use no flaming reds nor oranges of autumn but have found still the soft pinks, mauves and white of high summer. For tapering spires I use the mauve-pink, mint-like heads of *Elscholtzia*. Providing totally different texture are the long elegant sprays of a pink berried snowberry, called *Symphoricarpos* × *doorenbossii* 'Mother of Pearl'. This unusual shrub makes a lovely show in the garden when long wands, heavily weighted with berries, bow to the ground. From a distance you might think it was a mass of pink flowers. Closer, you will see each marble-like berry is flushed rosy-pink above, still white on the undersides where the sun has not reached. To produce the best effect, regular pruning is necessary. By cutting out all the previous years fruiting wood new long growths are produced, closely set with berries. If you omit to prune, you will not find these long graceful sprays. They will have branched, leaving you with short twiggy pieces, less attractive in the garden and useless for cutting. There are still armfuls of the invaluable *Chrysanthemum parthenium* 'White Bonnet'. When I first heard of this plant I imagined (in my ignorance) it would be a cultivated garden chrysanthemum, but it is a double form of Feverfew, a wild European plant, with composite heads of small white daisies.

The individual flowers of *Chrysanthemum* 'White Bonnet' are larger than the wild form, about the size of a thimble, filled with snow-white centres that are surrounded by broad ray-petals. Clustered into sprays, they are a joy tucked into small bowls or allowed to hang gracefully from the edges of larger arrangements. If you cut some plants down in midsummer they will have time to make strong, fresh growth to ensure a final crop in late autumn; but whether you do or not, there is scarcely a week from midsummer onwards when you cannot find a spray of this lovely fresh flower.

The small, pale pink flowers of *Aster ericoides* 'Esther', crowded into dainty sprays, fill in the background behind tight pom-pom flowers of *Chrysanthemum* 'Anastasia'. This hardy old hybrid brightens the last, dying days of the gardening year; dense and tidy mounds, covered with small dark green leaves, making a background to other flowers all summer. Then, throughout October and November, the whole mass is smothered with small, tightly doubled mauve-pink flowers.

The arrangement still lacks something bold to calm the fussy effect of many small flowers. It is transformed by a few sprays of *Chrysanthemum* 'Emperor of China', large enough to be dramatic yet delicate in effect. Crimson in bud, the quilled petals are tightly incurved. As they unroll in layers from the outer edge each quill splits open and palest pink petals are shadowed with rosy-lilac. An unusual feature is the way the leaves on some shoots become almost beetroot-red, while others turn yellow with crimson veins. Just one or two sprays in a narrow-necked vase are perfect in themselves, but in mixed bowls they are large enough to enhance the arrangement without subduing the smaller flowers.

For many years glass vases remained in the back of my cupboards while I concocted elaborate arrangements in wire netting or oasis, concealed in cut-down copper lamps or stone urns. Today, much simpler arrangements please me and take far less time. Clear glass bottles, jugs and vases show the balancing effect on stems, but the glass must be clean. When I see a layer of green algae has formed on the bottom or sides, I take the vase into the garden, gently drop in a layer of sand and pebbles, half fill it with warm soapy water and swirl the lot around until I can see the glass is completely clear. It is the only way I know to clean very narrow-necked vases.

It is interesting to make pot-pourri using mostly leaves, preferably picking them when they are at their best: usually before the shoot has run to flower. I am thinking of plants like Lemon Balm, *Melissa officinalis* plain or variegated, and *Calamintha nepetoides*, whose wiry little bushes are covered with strongly-scented foliage. It is worthwhile nipping many different plants to see if they have a perfume or not, and also to dry a little at a time to see whether it retains its scent. You can keep the leaves in separate polythene bags when they are thoroughly dry until, by the end of the season, you have accumulated a good selection.

Before long the first frosts will destroy many aromatic leaves, including the rose-scented geraniums. These plants have made large, leafy masses. Pulling them by the root and shaking off the dry soil, I hang them from the cross-beams of the office ceiling where the wood-burning stove has been lit to take off the autumn chill. Already there are bunches of Lemon Verbena, *Lippia citriodora*, smelling sharply of lemon peel, Sweet Bay, Eau de Cologne scented mint, Sweet Basil, and Lad's Love, *Artemisia abrotanum*. It is important not to over-dry the leaves as you will lose the essential oils. Once they become brittle, take them down. I strip mine into a shallow clothes basket lined with newspaper where there is plenty of room to crumble the tiny pieces. I put some into separate bags for use in cooking or in herb teas. Small amounts are put for everyday use into glass containers ; they look attractive, but I have read that the flavour deteriorates after long exposure to light, so I keep my reserve packets in a closed box. The bulk of dried leaves I mix together in a large earthenware container and add spices such as cardamon, cinnamon, cloves and coriander crushed in a pestle and mortar. Do not make the mistake of using too much spice – the mixture could smell like mincemeat rather than pot-pourri. Dried peel of Seville oranges, tangerines and lemons, adds perfume and also acts as a fixative to the other scented oils. Peel the fruit as thinly as possible, let it dry on a tray, then pulverise it in a liquidiser. It will grind almost to powder and must be kept airtight until you are ready to use it in your mixture. The dried and ground root of Sweet Rush, *Acorus calamus*, can be used for the same purpose. We grow the handsome variegated form of this plant whose leaves and rhizomes are powerfully scented. Orris root is sometimes mentioned in recipes. This is the root of *Iris germanica* or *Iris florentina*. The rhizomes of either may be used. It is said that Orris root emits a faint perfume of violets when dried and reduced to powder form, but I cannot smell it. To add a little colour to the leafy pot-pourri I add a handful of dried marigold petals.

The art of making pot-pourri is a little like the art of cooking. The more experienced you become, the better the results. You learn how to blend, to preserve the best perfumes, to retain the bright colours. I am not an expert as I have only tried making it the last few years, but with so many scented plants in the garden it was only a matter of time before they found their way, via the kitchen, into the sitting room and linen cupboard.

My prettiest pot-pourri is based on old roses. During June and July, their petals and rosebuds are spread like patchwork counterpanes over the spare room beds, retaining many shades of pink and purple. For contrast I add the vivid blues of delphiniums and hardy cranesbills. These have no scent but add enormously to the appearance. In each case I have dried the double forms. They keep clear colour and good shape. Unfortunately, *Delphinium* 'Alice Artindale' is not easy to come by. It has perfectly double flowers, like a double buttercup, in brilliant pure blue. The double *Geranium pratense* 'Plenum Violaceum' has deep violet-blue flowers, darker than the *Delphinium* and making perfectly formed rosettes. Handfuls of dried lavender flowers are also included.

There are many flowers I have yet to try. *Philadelphus*, in all its forms, would surely be good. The scent from 'Beauclerk' has everyone's head turning as they search for the source of the heady perfume drifting across the garden. I have been given cuttings of some old fashioned clove-scented pinks. Will they keep their scent when dried I wonder ? Not all flowers do.

Finally, although I feel it is cheating, I add a few drops of aromatic oils. Concentrated flower scents for the flowery pot-pourri, wood and fruit scents for the leafy one. When all are well-mixed, I put them into 7 lb sweet jars with screw-topped lids and keep them in the dim recesses of wardrobes until I need to refresh my bowls and jars. The scent remains longest if kept in sealed containers, but small open bowls placed conveniently near armchairs give off a faint, old-fashioned fragrance as you go near, are pretty to look at and tempting to turn with your hand as you pass by.

The orchards surrounding the garden are noisy with starlings. Great flocks are feeding on the windfalls and discarded apples left by the pickers. They have come to the feast from far and wide, joined by friends and relations from surrounding parishes, chattering and clattering continuously, noisy as a playground. All day they feed; then, in late afternoon, as if a bell were rung, there is a moment of silence, followed by the startling sound of ten thousand wings immediately overhead, slightly menacing, like a great black cloud. Now they are swirling high and silent as if scooped up into a great billowing net flung across the sky. Now they dive, swoop together and then, against the wind, stretch away in long undulating lines far into the distance. They are heading for their roosting place, some secret woodland haunt, where they will descend and darken the tops of burdened trees keeping up their noisy gossip long after sunset. I watched them go, then picked up some of the fallen apples, took them home and scrubbed them to make into juice for supper.

For the past few days the wind has been in the right direction, blowing away from the house, so Harry has lit the huge pile of waste material that cannot be composted. The heap burns and crackles for days, rounded up from time to time using the fork loader on front of the tractor. Occasionally at night, when only a large heap of ash and burnt soil remains, I see a tall column of flames and shimmering sparks suddenly shoot up into the empty blackness, as the heart of the heap comes to life. With no-one there to tend it, the flames are soon spent and the night becomes dark and featureless once more. In the morning I find a caved-in crater on the side of the heap. It will be several weeks before the ash is completely cooled and can then be spread to add potash and other trace elements, as well as to improve the texture of heavy soil.

NOVEMBER

IT IS always spring in the propagating house. There is the exciting smell of green growing things while enervating warmth flows over you as you pass through the door. Here the temperature is several degrees warmer than outside on a chilly November day, although there is no additional heat, apart from soil-warming cables buried beneath the sand on the two main benches. The least bit of warmth in the atmosphere outside seems to be quickly absorbed and held for some time by the fabric of the building, polycarbonate sheeting, which looks rather like corrugated cardboard made of clear rigid plastic.

From autumn, and throughout winter, we need to take extra care in protecting newly rooted cuttings not only from cold, but from attack by moulds, a state of affairs aggravated by reduced ventilation and slowed-up growing conditions. Ventilation is more difficult in the propagating house in winter, because we seal as many openings as we dare in order to retain as much warmth as possible, but condensation can be a problem. To control this we spray the inside surfaces of the propagating house and all our plastic tunnels with a material called 'Sunclear', choosing a warm day for the job when the plastic will be dry. This substance alters the behaviour of the plastic surface, encouraging water to form a thin overall coating which runs down the curved sheeting to the floor of the tunnel. If water drips regularly onto tender foliage it rots the leaf or shoot on which it is lying, fungus spores enter and the whole plant may collapse in a heap of grey mould.

Throughout winter it is particularly important to remove dead or damaged leaves to reduce the risk of infection. In addition, we carry out a fungicide programme at intervals of ten days. Fungicides protect new leaves by destroying the fungus spores as they drop from the air onto the sprayed surface. They do not kill the puffs of grey mould you see already attacking the plants. These are fruiting bodies about to explode into a cloud of new spores. In trying to treat fungus diseases we are dealing with two living plants. The safest way to treat the problem as yet is to protect the host plant before the parasite has a chance to develop.

It is dangerously tempting for me to spend half the morning dreaming over pans in the propagating house when I might be better employed doing other things. I tell myself I need to make certain all is going well, but I am largely motivated by expectancy, as keen as that of a new parent visiting the maternity ward, only in a plant nursery there is much more variety and it is blessedly quiet. Any day there could be new arrivals. A cutting may cause excitement because it has become viable after months of waiting; another will astonish us because it has made new roots in a matter of days.

Sometimes I stay to water the trays and pans standing on raised benches, using one of the long hoses with spray heads attached which are to be found looped over a hook at either end of the house. The appearance of sand or grit on top of the trays can be deceiving. It may look moist but be dry underneath. The spray from the automatic mist jets is regulated to maintain only a damp surface to the leaves of unrooted cuttings so they do not wilt. It does not soak into the compost in the trays. This will gradually dry out if it is not watched. Only by poking down into the pan with a finger or little knife, kept nearby for the purpose, can one tell for sure if the compost needs watering. On the other hand, benches without mist may show trays with dry surfaces, but underneath the soil will be moist because the person responsible has regularly done his job and there is no need for me to interfere.

It is very satisfying to look across the benches and see trays of cuttings, at all stages, responding to care and attention. In spring and early summer I hang over the seed frames watching for new seedlings to appear, but newly rooted cuttings are a joy every month of the year, as thrilling now, after millions, as were the first. It still seems a miracle to take cut stems or bare pieces of root, put them in trays with faith, hope – and a little help from rooting hormones – and then after days, weeks and sometimes months, to discover fresh white roots or shoots have been formed and to hold new life in your hand.

It is even more miraculous with root cuttings where you do not have the encouragement of an already formed green shoot. When I began to be interested in root propagation I found most gardening books that mentioned the subject advised winter as the best time for the job to be done. However, in practice I have found that although it may be more convenient in winter to dig and prepare suitable plants, conditions generally are not encouraging to plant growth. We found too many little chopped sticks of root rotting in cold conditions. The growing medium needs to be warm enough for plant cells to reform themselves, for the pieces of root to callous over their wounded ends so they may more quickly produce new roots and top shoots. Now, having been prepared in September, there are trays of oriental poppies, sea-hollies and pink chicory cracking the surface as freshly formed shoots struggle into life. As soon as they are well developed they will be removed, so that the warm benches can be used all winter to bring on other plants propagated from roots, such as *Catananche caerulea*, *Crambe*, *Stokesia* and *Verbascum* hybrids. By early spring we can see which plants have been successful and which have failed, and still have time to take more root cuttings if we need them.

I have two grape-bearing vines: *Vitis vinifera* 'Purpurea' with purple leaves and *Vitis vinifera* 'Dusty Miller', also called 'Black Cluster', whose young foliage is dusted with white meal, giving a pretty silvery effect to the light green leaves. Both these vines bear clusters of dark purple grapes on warm south-facing walls. 'Dusty Miller' has the better tasting, sweeter grapes of the two. Sometimes I pick a bunch from the vines over the pack-house door on my way back to the house for lunch. I enjoy the sharp-sweet taste, but since we do not attempt to thin them they are small and I have a tedious time spitting out pips and skin. This prompted me to think of using my juice extractor to make fresh grape juice.

Two large basketfuls of ripe grapes had been picked. I sorted them, pulling them individually off the bunches, avoiding any mouldy ones usually found in the centre of the bunch. After washing them well I put the grapes through the juicing machine – this was only partially successful, but it smashed them so I could put the remaining pulp into a nylon sieve and press the juice through with a wooden spoon. (I think another year I might put them through the Mouli sieve as I usually do blackcurrants, using the finest sieve, but the result would still need to be strained – perhaps hung up in muslin to obtain clear juice.)

Into a large bowl of rich purple juice I added a small bag of concentrated elderflower syrup taken from the freezer (originally made this summer to put with strawberry pulp, but somehow I never found time to go to the fields to pick enough). The mixture was pleasant but still seemed to need something else, so I added a pint of orange juice. Now it was better, strong by itself, better diluted with bottled springwater and ice. Not having small cartons available, I poured the mixture into small freezer bags and stored it away for winter when it will be a pleasure to serve unfermented juice from the vine flavoured with that tantalising hint of muscat, provided by the English elderflowers.

It is many years since I have grown fruit so I am not up to date with experience or information. For almost forty years my husband Andrew grew top fruit – apples and pears – professionally, which both prejudiced and discouraged me from growing fruit in the home garden. I feel

255

disturbed by the increasing numbers of sprays used on commercial orchards but, at the same time, am aware of the demands on the fruit farmer to provide clean, good quality fruit. If I were younger I would attempt to grow top fruit knowing I would face considerable loss if I did not take a few limited measures to control problems like Scab, Sawfly caterpillars, Codlin Moth, not to mention mildew and Red Spider.

Soft fruit seems to fit more easily into my plans but suffers just as many predators as do apples, especially since the thrush and blackbird population has increased over the years as suitable nesting sites have matured in the garden. A few rows of strawberry plants among the vegetables have regularly surprised me with little servings for supper, but recently I have been encouraged to do more by the handfuls of fruit I have found on lusty canes of the raspberry 'Zeva', running about in a frame where they had no business to be, having been heeled-in two years ago in the hope of a fruit cage being built. They have fruited continuously these last weeks of autumn, such large well-flavoured berries almost entirely neglected, yet with no sign of raspsberry weevil maggots in them. They deserved better treatment. Now, at last, a fruit cage has been erected alongside the vegetable garden. Timber supports painted with wood-preserving Cuprinol have been sunk into pockets of cement in the ground to keep the frame rigid, but with gravel at the base where the timber meets soil level. This is where it rots. The sides have been clad with Netlon fixed with wooden battens, while the top cover has been measured, cut to size, labelled and stored, ready for use when the fruit blossom has been fertilised by insects. Before the cage was built the soil was deeply dug and plenty of well-rotted manure was added. Finally, several loads of nursery waste containing peat, sand and plant remains was forked into the top spit to try to achieve the light humus-rich surface raspberries and strawberries – both woodland plants – prefer. The 'Zeva' raspberries and four bushes of blackcurrant are planted.

I intend to add a summer-fruiting raspberry and a bush of red and white currants; largely because they look so attractive, with dark seeds showing through almost transparent skins. I must also have a few bushes of dessert gooseberry. All of these I remember from the garden of my childhood, where I lay, imagining I was unseen, beneath dessert gooseberry bushes searching for forgotten fruits ripe to bursting. Does any fruit taste better than thoroughly ripe gooseberries? Do you ever have the chance to tell?

Preparations for the next Chelsea show can never be allowed to slip far out of my mind. Previously I have commandeered part of one of our growing-on tunnels to over-winter some of the large potted plants that help give an established look to the centre of my exhibit. This summer I decided we must build something specially for them. We bought a few extra tall tunnel hoops to form a tidy, plastic-sheeted shelter high enough to accommodate the taller plants and to allow two rows of irrigation nozzles to be erected well above our heads so we can move pots around without hanging ourselves.

All the plants are hardy when established outside and planted in well-drained soil, but exposed in pots to alternate wetting and freezing would reduce them to a sorry sight by the end of winter. Before setting them out in their new home I went through them all, pruning and trimming, removing thick wodges of dead leaves beneath the canopy of fresh shoots such as you see on shrubby salvias. This blotting paper-like clutter is a breeding ground for moulds, especially when the plants are put into a sheltered environment where foliage may remain damp.

There have been a few light frosts this month, but nothing severe or damaging. We expect frost in November and take precautions, making sure that a selection of all plants at risk, in particular nursery stock in pots, has been put safely into plastic covered tunnels. Stock beds of plants from warmer climates, such as *Schizostylis*, *Nerine* and *Crinum*, are covered with extra deep layers of crushed bark to protect them from being frozen in the soil. I have a particularly good variety of Globe Artichoke 'Gros Camus de Bretagne', given me by Christopher Lloyd. Growing artichokes from seed is rather like growing dessert apples from seed: they do not come true; inevitably the offspring will be inferior. New varieties are the result of years of trial and selection – and sometimes accident. Needless to say we make sure the artichoke bed is protected. Any dry material can be used to make a deep mulch – some of the cut-down remains of herbaceous plants are just as effective as straw or peat, and are easier to come by. Do not worry if you think it looks untidy to see mini compost heaps about the garden. They will all be removed in spring as soon as the danger of severe frost is gone and before new shoots emerge. Particularly damaging winters have recently taught me to remove about a dozen side-shoots from the parent artichokes while we still have warm growing weather. We trim off the largest leaves then pot them up to let them grow on in a frost-free shelter. This is to make sure we do not lose our stock. The old crowns will produce edible heads earlier, in July, while the young plants set out in spring will crop in September.

The long season is coming to an end, with almost the entire cast stepping forward for the last grand act. Background trees and shrubs take it in turn to present their contribution before they retreat into winter rest. Flower colours glow like freshly squeezed paint, undiluted by summer's overhead spotlight. There are mornings of 'mist and mellow fruitfulness', buckets and baskets of fruit, berries and intricately curved seed cases – too much to see or write about in one chapter.

The many shades of green that furnish the garden change slowly over a long period so the feast of autumn foliage is long and lingering. Among the varied shades of autumn red none is more brilliant in my garden than *Malus tschonoskii*. Most crab-apples are planted for spring blossom or autumn fruit, but I scarcely notice either on this crab, so inconspicuous do they seem to be. The value of this tree lies partly in its strong vertical line – its branches turn sharply upwards like a Lombardy Poplar which is useful when you need height but not the breadth – but mostly I value this tree for its astonishing red colouring in autumn. It never fails, even in bad years when very little else colours well.

Prunus sargentii has to be visited regularly or every leaf will be down before you have noticed, but this year it was a sight for over a week, among blue-needled *Chamaecyparis* 'Triomf van Boskoop' and bottle-green brushes of *Pinus ponderosa*. The tall, flaming torches of these two deciduous trees are repeated nearer the ground with *Rosa virginiana*, a suckering rose with small polished leaves now turned bright crimson and yellow with young wood enamelled crimson too. Big shrubs of *Rosa rugosa* provide a sharp contrast, their handsome, deeply-veined leaves have turned bright yellow.

In the heavier, moisture-retentive soil around the reservoir my tree and shrub plantings, begun about ten years ago, are beginning to make effect. *Liquidamber styraciflua* 'Lane Roberts' is slowly making itself into a fine feature. Its vine-shaped leaves have turned dark burgundy, relieved here and there with light crimson, while others inside the tree are yellow, faintly flushed pink. Nearby a group of *Viburnum betulifolium* arches over the grass walk – long branches wreathed with bunches of tiny redcurrant-like fruits. Many years ago we saw magnificent specimens of this shrub in the Royal Valley Gardens at Windsor and felt we must not delay planting to achieve such an effect here. The shrubs were not difficult to obtain, but it was very discouraging to see, year after year, a fine crop of flowers persistently drop off without setting fruit. Now, after about twenty years, we feel we have earned the pleasure of seeing our shrubs weighed down with clusters of berries. It seems they take many years before they crop well.

The little crab-apple, *Malus* 'Golden Hornet', looks prettier than a Christmas tree, its bare branches hung with small, bright yellow apples – lovely against a blue sky, or sweeping down to meet autumn-green grass. Another crab-apple not frequently seen is *Malus* 'Hillieri'. It is a delight in spring when its arching boughs are smothered in rich pink semi-double flowers ; but what a bonus it is to now have such a fine crop of small red apples hanging from the branches like clusters of large cherries. They last well on the tree until Christmas when they make an attractive arrangement, just two or three loaded branches, held together in a narrow necked vase, or stone jar. You could add a few leaves of ivy and spray the lot with 'glitter' if you feel they need it. I do not.

The leaves of a mountain-ash from China, *Sorbus hupehensis* 'Rosea', have turned crimson and yellow, but its bunches of small rose-pink berries have been stolen by birds. Some years when they have been spared and the leaves have fallen the effect from a distance is as if the bare branches were covered with pink blossom. The bare branches of *Viburnum × bodnantense* are loaded with sweetly-scented clusters of pink and white flowers, but I dread to think of the destruction that must come with the first sharp frost, when every bunch will be shrivelled and browned. Behind this spectacular shrub *Viburnum tinus* is dressed in modest lace caps, while beneath them *Polygonum affine* 'Superbum' carries rose and crimson spikes, bringing the colour down to the ground.

At this point it might be a relief to take a rest from looking and go back to those great bushes of *Rosa rugosa* which, in September, carried large clusters of plump, round red hips, rather like small tomatoes. For years I have regretted seeing them go to waste, although it suited the blackbirds well that I should be so dilatory. But this summer I found a recipe in a book called *Companion Planting* by Gertrud Franck. There are many sensible and helpful ideas in this book dealing with vegetables, herbs and fruits. This is how I made Rose Hip Pulp from her recipe:

Tomato-like fruits of *Rosa rugosa*

I picked a large bowlful of hips and we removed as many seeds as our patience allowed; Andrew being drawn, understandably reluctant, into this operation. I was not too fussy about removing every seed, but took care not to use any mouldy pieces. It was a sticky business as the inside pulp is very moist. Then I poured over them a quarter of a pint of wine (you could use water) and kept the bowl covered in a cool, dark cupboard for a week, stirring occasionally. I expected the whole mass would ferment, but it did not. At the end of the week I pressed the soft sticky mess through a nylon sieve with a wooden spoon.

I melted about one pound of pale raw cane sugar in a quarter of a pint of water, (this can be varied according to taste) then added the rose-hip pulp to the melted sugar and brought the mixture back to the boil. At this stage I swirled several sprigs of rose-scented geranium leaves around in the hot pulp until enough of the perfume was absorbed. It made all the difference, as it also does to stewed plums. Now the mixture was the colour of finest apricot purée and tasted exotic. It is delicious dribbled over thick yoghurt, baked Bramley apples, or eaten by the spoonful. The blackbirds and I continued to watch with greedy eyes the remaining clusters of hips slowly turn from orange to bright tomato-red. There were enough for us all ; and several bowlfuls were eventually hoarded away in little containers in the freezer.

Many years ago I collected various kinds of Barberry berries, sowed them, rowed out the seedlings to grow on for several years, then selected those whose berries I considered best to plant in the garden. Now some have long, drooping clusters of fruit, like fashionable ear-rings, others are tightly bunched along branches bowed to the ground with the weight. Some berries are round and scarlet, others long and pointed. I cannot give them names as they are all hybrids of Chinese species. One very striking bush is roped with berries, as bloom-coated and purple as grapes. The extraordinary colour of the close-packed berries is repeated nearby in a large shrub of *Berberis* × *ottawensis* 'Purpurea'. The dark dusky-purple summer foliage is fading now, highlighted reddish-wine as low rays of the sun penetrate the shrub. All these shrubs hold their colour – both berries and scarlet leaves – until late into winter.

Wide sweeps of border beneath the barberries are filled with stabilising stretches of *Bergenia*. They give me much pleasure, loyal and valued friends all the year round except for a brief spell at the end of winter when I gladly forgive a little tattiness while they remake a fresh suit of clothes. Their bold, handsome leaves improve the scale of planting by offsetting the tedious, somctimes uncomfortable look of small-leafed prickly barberries. There are many varieties available, many of them coming from German nurseries, selected both for good flowers and rich winter colour. From now until spring, it is cheering to meet these bold groups massed on the curve of a border, and be heartened by the dramatic red colouring. Two of the best German hybrids I have are *Bergenia* 'Admiral' and *Bergenia* 'Wintermärchen'. They both have oval, upstanding leaves with polished bronze surfaces and bright carmine undersides. An old Irish variety, *Bergenia* 'Ballawley', produces some of the largest leaves, beautifully waved, cabbage-like, and well coloured in winter. But *Bergenia* 'Eric Smith' is, in our opinion, the choicest variety we have. It was bred by Eric, so it would be fitting for the great plantsman to be remembered by such a fine introduction.

I have not done justice by half to the wonder of trees and shrubs around me. November is a symphony of leaves: the main theme of russet, gold and amber surging through the garden – fading, falling and re-emerging as the weeks go by with variations, subtle touches, or sudden upstarts of violent colour. The Golden-Leafed Poplar and Great

Bold leaves of *Bergenia cordifolia* beneath
seed-heads of *Crocosmia* 'Lucifer'

Maidenhair Tree, *Gingko biloba*, brush splashes of warm yellow high
against the sky, while on a lower level the large sprawlng willow bushes
of *Salix sacchalinensis* 'Sekka', covered in sharp yellow leaves, are
doubled by shimmering reflections in dark water.

Betula jaquemontii, with almost all its leaves littering the mown grass
below, stands isolated, off-centre, like an ivory fan sprinkled with the
last yellow leaves. These brilliant but transitory performers are partnered
by the deep tones of many evergreen trees and shrubs. Dark pines,
slender cypresses, bulky columns of yew, shining hollies and large-leafed
laurels form a background and lift the eye and mind to the tallest trees
in the garden, as necessary to the landscape as church towers rising
above roof tops. Smaller evergreens like *Elaeagnus*, *Mahonia*, *Cistus* and
Skimmia anchor mixed groups firmly to the ground. When all the leaves
are down from the deciduous trees and shrubs, the bare outlines of bark
and stems in great variety of shades, textures and designs, together with
the evergreens, will create a winter garden.

Mary, my younger daughter, was 'doing the flowers' for a wedding and
wondered if there might be anything in the garden to animate pink and

white chrysanthemums. As the arrangements did not need to be large, we were able to find a few unusual plants for highlights. There were glistening sugar-pink heads of *Nerine bowdenii* and a few of the white form 'Alba', not strictly white but a faintly flushed shell-pink. The truly white *Nerine flexuosa* 'Alba' has green shadows left from the opening buds and it flowers latest of all with rather smaller flowers, but it is something to treasure, flowering so late, beneath a warm south-facing wall. Like many other good things it takes years to make a really impressive clump, but then you will go down on your knees to look closely at such cool perfection so late in the year.

One late autumn day *Rosa* 'Bloomfield Abundance' still flaunted large open bouquets of tiny, button-hole roses, each delicately-rolled bud surrounded by long, twisting calyces. Put into a narrow-necked glass vase, with a few heads of lily-like nerines, it looked as if it had strayed from a June wedding, pink and white lilies and roses, in this autumn season of bronze and red chrysanthemums. The effect delighted me.

Dark-toned flowers or leaves take away the effect of a fruit sorbet when one has too much pink and white, so Mary and I added dark heads of *Sedum* 'Autumn Joy', now dark mahogany-red, to add weight to slender spires of Kaffir Lilies. These rich crimson, cup-shaped blooms continue to open until Christmas if the weather stays mild. Exciting to put with autumn flower and fruit arrangements are the pale green alabaster-like bells of *Galtonia viride*, similar to the white flowered Cape Hyacinth, *Galtonia candicans*, but flowering considerably later. We also added to our collection elegant branches of juvenile *Eucalyptus* leaves. There were plenty of these springing from the bases of trees killed to the ground by last winter's severe frosts.

Wide ribbon-like leaves of *Hakonechloa macra* 'Albo-aurea' are boldly striped with yellow

The most unusual addition to our barrowload of wedding finery was a flowering grass, *Panicum virgatum* 'Rotralbusch'. It is one of the most beautiful of autumn grasses. Sheaves of needle-stiff stems support long slender leaves, transformed now from green to ruby-red or dark burgundy, beautiful in sunlight or lamplight. They are topped with large sprays of tiny, millet-like seeds suspended on dark thread-like stems. A few stems of this lovely and unusual grass add elegance to a flower-arrangement, delicate as *Gypsophila* but with more style.

No other plant creates the same effect as a grass, whether it be large and imposing, dwarf and tufty, or gracefully fountain-like. Grasses and grass-like plants can be found to suit many different soils and conditions, adapted to drought, shade or boggy places. Most of those we grow are well behaved, forming dense, non-invasive clumps. Those that wander, like the blue-leafed Lyme Grass, *Elymus arenarius*, could well be used to bind steep sandy slopes. *Carex riparia* 'Variegata' and *Glyceria maxima* 'Variegata', both vigorous colonisers, do no harm at the edge of a lake where their large patches of pale white and cream striped foliage provide cover for fish or duck, beneath a selection of catkin-bearing willows.

More ornamental grasses could be introduced into natural landscaping projects like roadside banks or areas in public parks where wide mown walks might run between 'meadows' of selected grasses and species plants. These might include achilleas, cranesbills, sea-hollies in summer, with rudbeckias and polygonums to follow, while the foliage of grasses adds contrast in form and outline, changing in movement and light. Seed heads of *Eryngium*, *Rudbeckia*, *Lythrum* and many other species plants would add to the flower heads of many grasses with their feathery plumes, oat-like awns or cloud-like sprays of tiny seeds.

As a child, I loved the lanes around our village on the Essex-Cambridgeshire border: minor roadside verges where I could find a patch of harebells on a dry bank, yellow Toadflax, Field Scabious and purple-leafed Knapweed, all mixed with flowering grasses and tall umbellifers. We could put fennel, *Foeniculum vulgare*, into our imaginary 'meadow' (in some sandy seaside districts it has become a roadside weed) and bold groups of *Angelica* where the soil was better. Many of these plants are to be found in wild flower mixtures being sown by enlightened authorities along some of the new motorways. In Germany I have seen, in two successive summers, a steep grassy bank covered with the yellow flowers of Black-Eyed Susan, *Rudbeckia fulgida*. It looked so right among flowering native grasses and was obviously successfully established.

Some years, by late November, severe overnight frosts will suddenly switch off this grand end-of-season performance. We turn from summer to winter in the blink of an eye. The ground is littered with leaves. Those which remain hang like dirty rags, and flowers are reduced to withered ghosts. It is a relief to cut down these bedraggled remains, to be strangely inspirited by the ascetic look of the winter garden. But this mild autumn has caused many flowers to prolong the feeling of summer, both in the house and garden. It is tempting to write about all of them but such details can become tedious to read – rather like sitting through too many slides. They may be captivating, but after a while the eyelids droop and the mind is saturated.

At the end of the day I go as usual to the vegetable garden with a knife, a fork, and a basket to collect vegetables and salad for supper. On the way, beside the gravel path, I notice that the huge old clump of fennel by the water tank has sprouted a mass of tender young shoots, already several inches high, as if it were spring. They will soon be cut down by frost, but meanwhile they are delicious to eat raw, chopped into a mixed salad. Several weeks ago we harvested the seed, then cut down the tall stems as wind and wet would blow them into a ragged untidy heap. The seeds are well dried, then stored in a screw-topped jar. They are pleasant when nibbled by themselves (unless you dislike the flavour of aniseed) or used to make tea. This is an improvement on the taste of hot water if you are fasting to rid yourself of a cold or flu, and it comforts the stomach if you have indigestion. I also put a teaspoonful into the water when I boil dried beans. It is supposed to help prevent flatulence, but it also improves the flavour.

There are still many delights for the salad bowl. Both Dill and Coriander are in flower again, flavoursome and pretty to decorate side salads. Weeks ago I cut the fine leafy stems of these herbs and hung them to dry, but they were not successful; both lost their flavour, so obviously I had not dried them properly. This cool, damp summer has not been ideal for drying; perhaps they took too long. Many herbs are dried commercially with heat, but I have not mastered a method of using the oven. It is true, however, that quick drying is essential to preserve the essential oils of any herb.

A patch of Rocket, *Eruca sativa*, with its very distinctive flavour, has

Tidying up in autumn

Baskets of freshly picked vegetables

produced fresh shoots all summer, but now is trying hard to make flowers and set seed. I pick off some flower shoots, sprinkling both leaves and cream- and brown-veined crucifer-flowers over our salad plates. By constant cutting, thus preventing it from making seed, new shoots are continually growing. The old plants have served us well. They will not survive the winter but I shall sow seed again as soon as the soil is warm enough in spring.

American Land Cress is another hardy salad crop. From rosette-like plants, taking up little room, you can continually crop a few dark green leaves to add the peppery taste of watercress to bland lettuce or Chinese Cabbage leaves. Garlic planted in September has produced leaves several inches through the ground. I have never known it to be damaged by cold after more than twenty years of growing, but I do need to protect it from pheasants. After it was planted we laid wire netting flat over the bed to prevent them hooking out the bulbs with their strong claws.

The Chinese Cabbage does very well once it has grown away from attack by Flea Beetles at the seedling stage, and if it has not been turned into lace by small black slugs. It is a luxury in November to be able to cut a firm big head, weighing several pounds and providing enough salad for a week if it is washed and drained carefully, examined for slugs and then stored in the fridge in a large plastic bag.

Chicories do not appear to be appreciated by slugs. Both 'Sugar Leaf' and 'Crystal Head' make large heads, rather like loosely folded Cos lettuce. They are beautiful to look at when you unfold the leaves under the light in a warm kitchen. How can such a delicate-looking leaf

265

survive outside? It has large, wide leaves of palest green, with a wide central vein and radiating veins, glistening like pearl. This chicory is delicious when freshly picked – just as it is for lunch when you have no time to do more – but in the evening, decorated with the last nasturtium flowers and a few incurved leaves from red-leafed chicories, all tossed in a garlicky dressing, it is a luxury easily available if you have the good fortune to be able to grow your own.

Calabrese has become available in most vegetable shops and super-markets. What a good thing, because it is delicious when steamed for only so long as it takes to make it tender. Once it has lost its brilliant green colour and become yellow in the pot, it is ruined. From two short rows of plants we have been picking fresh heads since July, and are still picking handfuls twice a week. The plants take up far less room than spring sprouting broccoli, and crop for much longer. If we become weary of eating it hot, I let it cool and dress it for salad or make soup, simmering the stems together with a little lightly fried onion and garlic and a handful of blanched almonds to make a liquidised base, adding at the moment of serving a suspicion of nutmeg and finally the brilliant green heads, lightly steamed.

Twelve young cabbages intended for the spring gap are heartening up. Will I need twelve? I think it is unlikely. We might stop to consider other vegetables like cauliflowers, taking up more room than they deserve, especially if half of them end up on the compost heap. Of such things plant only as many as you know you will eat.

The mixed patch of salad (sold in packets as Saladisi) including lettuce, various forms of chicory and herbs like Rocket, takes up a patch of ground about 4 ft × 4 ft. The lettuce have faded away now, but since midsummer this patch has continuously provided tender salad leaves by regular picking, taking up far less room than two or three rows of lettuce where most would have probably run to seed before they could be eaten. Early in the autumn we could not eat the leaves fast enough and cut half of them down to the ground. In no time at all fresh leaves were produced from the base – much better than letting the original ones become tough and bitter.

The leek bed looks magnificent with squeaky, blue-green leaves above thick white stems. This year I have grown a variety called 'Molos'. Whether it is the variety or the weather, I have never had such long thick leeks. Small slender ones can be very delicious, but I do like decent-sized leeks. They are a staple winter vegetable, taking up a considerable piece of land, so they need to be worth digging. I just cannot imagine what people do with the vast inflated vegetables one sees at shows. Just remember to listen to the weather forecast so you can dig what you need before the ground becomes frozen.

The same applies to Jerusalem artichokes. This is another vegetable that is easily over-planted. By the end of the summer, each tuber planted will have developed a clutch of new ones, rather like a root of potatoes. I prefer a white-skinned form 'Silver Skinned', which makes less knobbly tubers than the purple stained variety I used to grow ('Fuseau'), making them easier to clean. With both leeks and artichokes, do not dig more than you require to use and wish to keep perhaps, for a week, in a cool place. Flavour and food value deteriorate if they shrivel.

Artichoke tubers are good scrubbed (peeled only if you insist), then eaten raw like a crisp apple with bread and cheese, or grated into a bowl and quickly stirred around in a little French dressing. They can also be steamed, skinned, cut into slices or cubes and combined with rice, nuts and sultanas for a main dish salad. Cooked in milk and water they can be strained and puréed, the stock being reserved for soup. Finally, artichoke soup makes a most comforting bowl on a cold winter's day. I used to wonder why 'Jerusalem' as this plant is an American sunflower, but it appears that the name is a corruption of the Italian 'Girasole'.

As much as possible, the soil of the vegetable garden is covered, partly with broken down straw used in summer for mulching, and partly with the old bean haulms and outside cabbage leaves. Yellowing leaves from brussels sprouts and spring sprouting broccoli, snail damaged leaves from spinach and the tops of leeks – anything we remove from vegetables before taking them to the kitchen – is now spread over the soil as surface compost. By spring it will all be rotted and can be lightly forked into the ground. Some people practise this method on narrow beds where they do not compact the soil by constant trampling, with the result that the soil rarely needs digging. The abundant humus encourages soil organisms to keep it aerated.

Sometimes I tend to enthuse over a plant which might appear slight, especially if planted among the wrong companions. *Gaura lindheimeri* would not turn heads if it were lost among a wealth of strong colour, but for the past three or four months it has bewitched passers-by with its grace and delicacy. Slender, branching stems carry white flushed flowers, not unlike Willow Herb, opening from pointed, red-stained buds. Standing tall and isolated above mounds of soft, grey-foliaged plants, they float like flights of moths above the quiet garden.

Nearer the house are a selection of half-hardy plants that have given pleasure for months. In recent years I have learnt to bend my principle of growing only hardy plants as I now can use a little heated greenhouse to protect these frivolities in winter.

Of all the dimorphothecas I grow, only one is reliably hardy. (The correct botanical name for *Dimorphotheca* is now *Osteospermum*.) *O. ecklonis* 'Prostrata' came to me years ago from the garden of the late Cedric Morris in Suffolk, where he had grown it outside for many years. Its sprawling stems carry strongly aromatic leaves, while the white, blue-backed daisies with navy centres become flushed with pink as they age. The other varieties with rich pink, purple, and even butter-yellow flowers are all treated as bedding plants, adding soft colour in gaps among the grey-foliaged plants. The variety called *Osteospermum* 'Pink Whirls' is still full of bud, with quilled spidery petals in shades of pink, magenta and blue. Nearby, that unusual wall-flower *Erysimum linifolium* 'Bowles Mauve', still carries soft mauve-violet flowers, while the bracts of *Acanthus* seed-heads repeat the purple tints. The warm weather has woken up *Iris unguicularis* from dreams of desert sand in North Africa. Already there are several silk-petalled flowers in shades of purple-blue to add touches of spring to this late autumn colour scheme.

It is a pity *Coronilla glauca* is unreliable. For several years, when we had comparatively mild winters, I had these shrubs in sheltered positions where their sweetly scented, yellow pea-flowers smothered the light bushes in spring, and often again in autumn. Recently I have become enchanted with *Coronilla glauca* 'Lutescens'. It has flowered most of the summer and autumn against a west-facing wall, but I do not think it will survive the winter. We keep a few reserve plants in the greenhouse to have the pleasure of its sweet, lily-of-the-valley scent, and pale creamy-yellow flowers. It would be a perfect small shrub for a conservatory.

Several clumps of *Eucomis punctata*, usually described as greenhouse bulbs from South Africa, appear every year beneath a warm wall. Large heavy cylindrical spikes are packed with star-shaped apple-green flowers, edged with maroon. Each head is topped with a pineapple-like tuft of leaves. They have been in flower for weeks and now, among tumbled stems, one good flower head is still standing.

Completely hardy, *Geranium sanguineum* is always an autumn delight, although its main flowering season is in June. I suppose it is partly the light and partly the lack of competition that makes these bright, magenta-rose saucers so magnetically appealing late in October and November when they provide deep accents among the shell-pink of nerines.

Many of these autumn flowers with jewel colours are set among grey and silver plants, now at their best, many as white as hoar frost. Soft felted *Ballota*, matt-leaved *Salvia*, whitened *Artemisia*, wax-blue sprawls of *Euphorbia myrsinites*, all set off by dominating shrubs of *Euphorbia wulfenii*, whose curving stems are spirally-set with dark, blue-green leaves. What invaluable plants these are in warm well-drained gardens. They are too handsome to be described as background plants, yet their colour and form throw into prominence lesser plants – as now, for example, orange seed-packed pods of *Iris foetidissima*, together with a few tissue paper-petalled flowers of *Papaver rupifragum*, transparent tangerine.

Two unusual salvias flourish in warm, but not dry situations. They are *Salvia ambigens* and *Salvia uliginosa*. The first, standing about four feet tall, has spires of kingfisher-blue flowers, individually larger but fewer than those of *Salvia uliginosa*, whose small electric-blue flowers are held on taller stems in dense nodding clusters. Both are rare colours in late autumn, worth treasuring by covering the crowns with piles of cut-down remains or a bucketful of peat before frost penetrates deeply to kill the resting buds. Remember to remove this protection in spring once the likelihood of damaging frost has passed. Sprawled at their feet is a different blue. The shallow saucer-shaped flowers of *Geranium wallichianum* 'Buxton's Variety' are blue, warmed with fine red veins running into the cool white centre, giving the flowers a look of open-eyed innocence.

My favourite *Anthemis* 'E.C. Buxton' is still full of pale lemon-yellow daisies, lighting up a background of grey-leafed Cistus. On the opposite side of the path the colour of her petals is repeated in clumps of *Yucca filamentosa* 'Variegata'. A plant I do not make enough of is *Serratula tinctoria* var. *seoaneii* (formerly *S. shawii*, of gardens). It is a small knapweed, doing its utmost to attract attention before the curtain falls. Thin wiry stems, about 15 inches high, are dotted with little powder puffs of soft mauve. Each head is made of individual flowers, each thrusting out a long-pronged stigma to produce a soft hazy effect.

If we took another path we could fill our basket with many more flowers, the notebook with many more names. Among them we would find a form of *Saxifraga fortunei*, with sprays of white flowers and blood-red leaves, astrantias still in flower, *Liriope* with light violet heads of unopened buds like *Muscari* in spring, a patch of *Physostegia virginiana* 'Vivid', brilliant purple against the green grass edge.

Ornamental gourds

DECEMBER

My PRATTEN greenhouse in which I have spent many happy hours, sometimes in retreat, is an old friend. It was put up about two years after the nursery was started. Before that, seeds and cuttings had been raised in a row of simple frames built of railway sleepers and covered with plastic sheeted lights. This might encourage anyone who is thinking of propagating hardy plants to realise they do not necessarily need a range of automatically heated and ventilated glasshouses. One of the most important things plants need is tender loving care – at weekends, as well as during the week. I have never tried talking to my plants; we seem to get on well without speech. Yet they would notice if I, or my staff, ignored their needs.

As the nursery expanded, protective plastic tunnels were erected and a new propagation house was built so the function of the greenhouse gradually changed. It is now used to house tender plants, primarily those I use to make my pot gardens. This is a luxury on a working nursery, but if there is a choice then I would rather meet the cost of heating my greenhouse for the winter than toast myself for one week in the Bahamas. And for me it is much more fun to spend a couple of days at the beginning of December, sorting out the greenhouse.

Several weeks ago, in preparation for winter, all tender pot plants were brought inside, and now I found them crammed onto every shelf, every square foot of staging and floor. It was a jungle. Tall plants hid smaller ones; many were redundant; all required attention.

As the weather was mild it was a relief to be able to stand half the pots outside and make a space on the bench where I could work: pruning, cleaning and repotting. It is important to remove all dead or drying

271

leaves, especially those hidden under the fleshy rosettes of succulents. House plants, rejuvenated by their summer vacation, were carried back into the house to take up their winter duties. Anything which could be severely pruned was reduced to make room and allow more light to reach its neighbours. Plants were placed with taller ones at the back and small ones at the front so everything could be easily seen and cared for. These plants will continue to grow slowly during the winter months; many will need to have their tips pinched out to prevent them from becoming weak and floppy. We need to be able to reach everything for whatever service it may require.

There is a hose for watering when necessary, but most pots stand on sand-filled benches, kept moist with water supplied from a header tank similar to the cistern in the lavatory. As we set the ball-cock inside the tank, so the water flows into perforated pipes hidden in the sand until it reaches the required level. Then it is automatically switched off. It is vital to cover the holes in the alkathene pipes with something which will allow the water to trickle out, but prevent sand from blocking them. We use short pieces of Dexion (perforated angle iron used for supporting the shelves) to hold a piece of glass wool-fibre close over the holes which are about eighteen inches apart.

Stock plants of heliotrope and *Felicia*, the lovely climbing *Maurandia* and *Rhodochiton*, which gave so much pleasure this summer, are all here with many (too many) more. The invaluable grey-leafed *Helichrysum petiolare* and its yellow-leafed form are growing away well in pots, newly grown from cuttings this autumn. More cuttings will be taken from these fresh young plants before spring. The same applies to the French balcony geraniums. Young plants for next summer are already established in individual pots.

To use as much of the heated space as possible, we have put up narrow slatted shelves above the sand benches, to take extra plants, mostly succulents. These need less water in winter than some other plants, but the soil ball will shrink away from the sides of the pots, letting water run straight through, if they are allowed to become too dry. I make sure all the pots on these upper shelves stand in plastic saucers so that the water will be retained and gradually soaked up into the pot. The soil will slowly expand again to fill the pot tightly, but do not forget to check later and empty out any water not absorbed.

Beneath the benches are the big Canna plants, dug from the garden, their tops removed. Dormant now, they rest in plastic fertiliser sacks until spring when they will be divided and grown on in pots until it is safe to put them back in the garden. The giant agaves stand in their pots on the floor, their tops swathed in Netlon, so this year I have not been so savaged by their wickedly prickly tips as I push past them.

During the summer I have been worried by my inability to control Red Spider Mite on the big tubs of *Datura*. I did not want to destroy the plants, particularly the pink-flowered one given me by Ed Carmen, a good nurseryman friend in California, but this was not the only plant affected. By now Red Spider Mite had obviously made its home in the greenhouse. Other plants showed tell-tale symptoms as their leaves became pallid and finally spotted with white as the sap was sucked away by these minute pests. They are very, very small, mere dots, slowly moving on the undersides of the leaves. I wrote to the Royal Horticultural Advisory Service at Wisley and was promptly sent all the information I required. We all are very fortunate, as members of the Royal Horticultural Society, to have the benefit of this service which offers advice and information. We have been most grateful for their help on numerous occasions and for the help we have also received from ADAS, the Agricultural Advisory Service.

During the winter one can do little to tackle the Red Spider because the mite is hibernating in cracks and crevices, and among those dead leaves if you haven't removed them. But as soon as the temperature rises in early spring something must be done. There are a number of sprays available, but since the effective ones are unhealthy for the user, as well as for the pest, I prefer not to use them. We will try a biological control: a predator called *Phytoseiulus*. This creature requires a daytime temperature of at least 70°F (21°C) and must be introduced after the Red Spider Mite has become active but before heavy infestations have developed. For years I have been able to control most pests in the greenhouse with smoke. Many years ago I bought a large tin of Campbell's nicotine fumigating shreds which has lasted so long that the tin is falling apart with rust, but the compressed flakes are still as new. They look like damp strips of brown paper. If I see any sign of White Fly or aphids I wait till sunset, close all the fan lights, put two or three piles of fumigating strips on the floor, light each one, put my foot on them so they only just smoulder, then retreat quickly as the columns of smoke rise to the roof, closing and locking the door behind me. We have bought a smoke specifically for Red Spider, based on Pirimiphos-methyl, but these creatures need constant surveillance. In three weeks from the egg they are breeding. They also have the capacity to evolve strains resistant to a chemical if the same one is used for a considerable time.

Although we have had a few frosty mornings with the grass remaining white for an hour or two, the temperature has not fallen very low. There has only been the thinnest film of ice on the ponds.

On a crisp, sunny morning I walk out of my back door into the little Mediterranean garden and see good foliage all around me. Although we are at the lowest ebb of the year, there is almost total ground cover in this part of the garden. The sky is blue; the colour and texture of every leaf stands out clearly. The main spines of the borders are made with

Rosemary, Lavender, *Cistus* and *Phlomis fruticosa*. A sea-green shrub of *Bupleurum fruticosum* is still covered with umbellifer-like seed heads. Beside it a blue-leafed cypress which we bought as *Cupressus arizonica*, but which might be a form of *Cupressus glabra*, dominates this border while nearer the house *Libocedrus decurrens*, like a dark green totem pole, towers above the roof line.

Bold foliage in the Mediterranean garden: *Yucca gloriosa, Euphorbia wulfenii*, and *Galactites tomentosa* in the foreground

Most handsome of all at this time of year, *Euphorbia wulfenii* adds substance and character as nothing else can. There is much confusion regarding the identification of this plant. It is in fact a variable species occurring throughout southern European countries. From Spain and Portugal we have *Euphorbia characias* ssp. *characias*. When found fairly pure this plant is a tougher, more sinister looking plant than the form we usually call *E. wulfenii*, with short narrow leaves, red stems and baleful black eyes. *Euphorbia characias* ssp. *wulfenii* comes from the eastern Mediterranean, from Greece and Albania, and makes much larger plants with large rounded heads of bright lime green flowers, almost gold sometimes. Variations of these two are to be found in gardens. All these euphorbias do well in poor gravel soil, indeed they rely on it, if they are to survive a hard winter. Average winters do no harm, but exceptionally low temperatures with frost lasting several days and nights can kill large old plants, although the young ones usually survive. I just hope and pray we shall be spared such weather since the effect of this handsome spurge in flower will be spectacular from March until July.

The dominant bushes and shrub-like plants are linked to lower areas of mats and cushions by pale groups of felted *Ballota*, or purple sage, whose young tips are lightened with patches of rosy-mauve and cream. Sturdy dark green bushes of Bowles' Mauve wallflower, *Erysimum linifolium*, carry clusters of brooding buds, one or two, just opening an eye to take a look around. *Thymus* 'Golden Carpet' makes low wiry bushlets covered with tiny ochre-yellow leaves, lovely with a scattering of pale *Crocus tomasinianus* opening among them on a mild day in February. Some thymes form low dense bushes with dark green or variegated leaves; others spill like water over low brick walls.

Sprawling shapes of *Euphorbia myrsinites* are topped with terminal flower heads which already show pale green buds. Here and there, seeded into bare spaces or into the gravel path, are sharply pointed, deeply-cut rosettes of *Galactites tomentosa*, each leaf heavily veined with silver and outlined like fine lace ruffs against the dark earth. This very attractive thistle is an annual; much daintier than the better known *Silybum marianum* sometimes called Virgin's Milk Thistle. *Galactites* takes up very little room on the ground, but in summer appears like dainty bouquets above lower plants with open branches full of nodding, soft-pink thistle flowers.

Among all this variety of foliage, bare-branched trees and shrubs pencil in lighter tones and textures. The purple-twigged Judas Tree, grown from a seed taken from the tree we planted in our first home, is slowly becoming a feature, while the Mount Etna Broom throws a fountain-like tracery of delicate branches against the cold sky. Behind the low, white-washed house, a wide-spreading oak embraces the scene, its last, lingering leaves blown away. Its warm-tinted twigs echo the rust haze of *Potentilla fruticosa*, pretty buff seed-heads of *Caryopteris*, and tall pagoda-like outlines of *Acanthus*.

At this time of year the most handsome *Artemisia* is *A*. 'Powis Castle'. Bright silvery mounds of finely-cut leaves stand out among other grey plants, but all contribute to the jigsaw puzzle of tones and textures that make this little winter garden. I am patiently watching the progress of several young plants of *Yucca glauca*. Three years ago I brought them home from a nursery I visited in Connecticut. They still do not make much impact, but one day, when they are fully grown, each one will look like a pale grey porcupine rolled into a ball. Their leaves are very narrow, grey, edged with white, and stiff as knitting needles. *Yucca recurvifolia* has made a great pile of sword-like leaves, outlined against the white sunlit walls of the house – a much needed contrast among ashen piles of small-leafed plants.

Both shrubs and plants are grouped so they complement each other in shape, texture and colour, nudging into one another to form large, well-knit groups rather than being dotted about in draughty isolation. But I do not mind a few bare spaces between groups at this time of year, where plants have retired beneath the soil. They help to create a breathing space, as it were, between sentences.

On the raised bed beneath a west-facing wall there is the same variety of foliage, even though it is winter, but with plants of smaller scale to suit the setting. Most look much the same in winter as they do in summer, except for the lack of flowers, but that is not detrimental. I can dawdle along the wall, enjoying the succulence and colours of many different *Sedum* and *Sempervivum*, flat mats of a minute-leafed thyme, prim rosettes of *Androsace*, mealy-coated, petal-like leaves of *Primula auricula*; I lose myself in the alpine lawn of *Raoulia* where squats the boulder-like shape of *Hebe* 'Boughton Dome' and think of my mother who, in her eighties, would take an hour to scan this sheltered bed, reluctant to miss a single plant.

Walking past the ordered ranks of nursery pots, I come to the reservoir garden, maturing now after ten years of planting. Wide emerald-green walks curve around large island beds and borders, grouped with mixed deciduous and evergreen trees and shrubs. There are dark black-green shapes of *Pinus radiata*, grey-leafed *Eucalyptus*, columnar *Cupressus*, soft curves of purple tinted *Cryptomeria*. None of these would look so well without bare-branched trees and shrubs for contrast. There are the warm-toned barberries, still holding leaves and berries, enamelled red stems of *Rosa virginiana*, great shrubs of purple-twigged *Rosa glauca*; we used to call it *Rosa rubrifolia*. Outstanding are the white boles of Silver Birch and the snakeskin effect of *Eucalyptus niphophylla*. Great slivers of old bark have dropped to the ground, leaving new bark, petal-smooth and dove-grey, while older bark left behind forms islands of khaki, deeper grey and green, creating a marbled effect.

Buff, feathery heads of *Stipa calamagrostis* sway gently in the slight movement of air while on the edge of the reservoir 12 foot stems of Pampas Grass, *Cortaderia argentea* 'Sunningdale Silver' carry silky pennants, silhouetted against the wide expanse of water. Many kinds of willow grow at the water's edge; some fill the sky with fan-like shapes, others arch and tumble, finally spilling a cascade of yellow-tinted stems into the water. The dark outlines of hollies and tall columnar cypress are reflected in the blinding, glittery surface of the water.

I turn away, dazzled by the low winter light, to face the Reservoir Garden, an area of large island beds with trees and shrubs already making a pleasing pattern on the skyline. As with all my plantings, they form the spines or centres of beds, holding together the mixed groups of smaller shrubs, herbaceous plants, bulbs and ground-cover plants which surround them. Years ago this was part of the wilderness, an area of poor gravel soil covered with broom, blackberry bushes and scrubby grass. Now it has become a reason to go out on a winter's day. There are so many things not to be missed. I love the spreading cushions of grey-leafed *Helianthemum*, which make a good contrast with wax-blue *Hebe pinguifolia* 'Pagei', and I make no apology for drawing attention again to *Bergenia* 'Eric Smith'. All winter it stands out among its neighbours, outshining other bergenias. They all make a contribution to the design, but are not able to hold a candle to the splendour of this special plant. You need to see it planted in a group, on the curve of a border. As you approach with the sun behind you, the light catches the rich crimson-backed leaves, glowing against the short turf of the grass walk. Further along, on the opposite side, a second group catches the eye, leading you on as effectively as any flower in summer. Purple-leafed phormiums tone with these plants, while *Yucca concava* 'Variegata', a small-leafed *Yucca* with vividly-striped yellow and green leaves, makes a small repetition of *Phormium* 'Veitchii', an old variety with brightly-striped yellow and green foliage. It is a little hardier, perhaps, than some of the modern introductions from New Zealand like 'Dazzler' and 'Cream Delight', but none are reliable in severe winters. Sometimes I feel sad as I remember the splendid clumps I had growing here in mild winters past, but I wonder if they suit the gentle outlines of an English garden.

Beneath the trees, in shady places, the ground is furnished with patches of *Epimedium*. The old remaining leaves on deciduous forms have assumed soft shades of coral and russet, warming the edge of a border I can see from my desk as I write. Elsewhere, evergreen forms show bright, lively green sometimes flushed with red, set among carpets of *Vinca minor*, that most useful little periwinkle which already is winking a blue or purple flower to greet me. *Euphorbia robbiae* colonises poor soil beneath the trees, with large rich-green rosettes, while my favourite *Iris foetidissima* 'Citrina' provides contrast with its beautiful vertical lines. The marbled leaves of *Arum italicum* 'Pictum' seem to have spread everywhere in cool shady places. They make perfect partners for snowdrops in late winter. I have established both success-fully now in rough-cut grass beneath a little stand of oak trees.

Euphorbia amygdaloides will grow in sun or shade. This native spurge is sometimes seen in hedge bottoms, or on the edge of a rough piece of woodland. The selected form, *Euphorbia a.* 'Purpurea' is very effective in winter as the leaves immediately behind the flower head flush turkey-red, standing up like a cockscomb behind the down-turned cluster of buds. As the wide head of lime-green flowers opens, this crest fades and pales to green. We grow all our plants from cuttings – from a well-coloured form – since seedlings vary. Some may be worthless. It is only fair to say that the effect of this plant can be ruined by mildew, but it is a simple matter to preserve it from such disfiguration by using a suitable fungicide. Then the display of coloured foliage lasts for months, from late autumn until late spring.

Finally we cannot pass *Tellima grandiflora* 'Rubra'. It is a perfect clump-forming plant for cool, dim places. All summer its rounded leaves, with scalloped edges, are green, slightly bristly and covered with tiny hairs. But with the first November chill they turn dark mahogany-red on the surface, while the glistening undersides become bright carmine-rose. Huddled together in neat clusters, both sides of the leaves can be seen making a palette of reddish hues, from light to dark, all winter. One year at the Chelsea Flower Show a moist parcel was put into my hands and a voice murmured 'Do you have this? It is a scented form of *Tellima*.' No, we did not have it, but now we are grateful to that kind visitor for a stock bed which sends showers of perfume through the little woodland nursery where it thrives. 'What is that scent?' said one of my girl gardeners busy some distance away. 'It smells like pinks but there are none nearby.' She was right. The scent of this *Tellima* drifting across the garden smells very like old-fashioned scented pinks. We have called it *Tellima grandiflora* 'Odorata'.

It raises my spirits to see so much life, form and colour developed over these past years, creating scenes and sheltered areas where not so long ago the ground was bare, poverty-stricken or covered with scrubby rubbish. I am pleased to see new empty spaces waiting for me to plant around the edges of beds where the turf has been removed and used to repair last winter's damage to the lawns caused by the pond dredging. The turf we bought and laid to make quick repairs was not a success. It was a much coarser grass, growing faster and darker than our original lawn, which we sowed. From this experience we have learned that we must sow and maintain a spare 'lawn' of mown turf to repair areas worn by the passage of many feet, by plants flopping unnoticed too long over the edges, or sometimes by an inexplicable accident with oil from a mowing machine.

Walking back past the water gardens, I hear the water splashing over the slip-way between the pools and notice the leaves of the very large Marsh Marigold, *Caltha polypetala*, have not yet been wiped out by frost. I touch the caramel-coated bark of *Prunus serrula*, the cinnamon flakes of *Acer griseum*, and stand for a while pressed against the snow-white trunk of the Great Himalayan Birch, *Betula jaquemontii*, looking up at a blue sky through a canopy of whitened boughs and branches till they thin to tiny twigs forming a fringe of purple around the perimeter. In the distance I see the little nursery pond, edged with shining stands of bare-stemmed dogwood, crimson and olive stems making fiery reflections, while just beyond them, like a pall of smoke, I can just make out tangles of Ghost Bramble (*Rubus cockburnianus*) beneath ancient, tumbled Crack-Willows.

I walked back across the nursery feeling well-pleased with its cared-for appearance. Throughout late autumn and early winter we all keep looking and checking to make certain we have taken into shelter sufficient samples of everything which is not completely reliable when left in pots outside. It is very satisfying to walk through the tunnels, a little like reviewing troops on parade. I like to walk slowly, assessing the stock block by block, admiring the fresh foliage of young plants, noticing

White-barked *Betula jacquemontii* with evergreens and
Iris foetidissima in seed

that small quantities of scarce or special plants have been stood in little
blocks near the edge of the central path where they can be watched.
They are not lost in long single lines where they might become buried by
more vigorous plants on either side.

Every inch of covered space is precious, so all 'dead' pots are removed
and spaces are blocked up to make room for other plants coming in later.
As I walked slowly, my head down, taking note of all the special things I
had asked to be done, I suddenly came upon a block of *Schizostylis*, the
Kaffir Lily, crowded with tall stems of crimson flowers. Just beyond
them lay pots full of the lavender-blue blossoms of *Iris unguicularis*. The
December day suddenly took a leap into spring as these flowers made me
gasp with delight, autumn and spring standing side by side, the old and
new year bridged in this sheltered environment.

By half past three the sun has dropped behind the view I see from my
desk – ancient oaks and planted evergreens, shielding us from the
windswept acres of bare farmland beyond. Blackbirds, thrushes, wrens
and robins are creating waves of alarm calls. I look up and see a man
with a gun and his dog, busily searching among the plants and bushes.
He has come to deal with rabbits that have penetrated the boundary
fence. Sometimes a gate is left open; sometimes, as netting becomes
rotten with time, an entrance can be forced. Recently we discovered
that a compost heap had been piled against the netting in such a way as

to make a highway for the pretty little wretches. Now that the collapsed heaps of foliage have been removed, there is less cover. It is easier for man and dog to disturb the rabbits, but sometimes you can practically step on one, so still do they sit, like a clod on the bare earth, or tucked camouflaged into a tussock. Their instinct for self-preservation urges them to remain motionless until the last minute. With luck, the hunter might pass by.

Blackbirds and thrushes have the sweetest, most melodious tones, filling the morning and evening of these last mild days of the year with nostalgic sounds of spring. Not in the least musical is the old cock pheasant, but the sound is as seasonal as mince pies. I love to hear his cracked croak as he makes his winter patrol of the boundary wire. Sometimes I meet him unexpectedly and he explodes at my feet, squawking with indignation as he heaves himself into the air, resentful of my intrusion into his territory.

Some days in winter I sit and write, some days I just sit. After months outside, closely involved with plants and the soil, my thought processes become rusty. I struggle to find an end among the tangled threads of my mind, to find one which will run smoothly for a while. Another day, free of interruptions or tempting alternatives, finds me no better. I feel all used-up, as my grandmother used to say. Recently there was such a day. Giving up the struggle, I left the house and walked into the cold clear air of the garden and crossed the bridge that spans the little brook running into the reservoir. Down I went among the meticulously pruned trees of my neighbour's fruit farm, past a towering wall of poplars, pale-twigged in the sunlight, and came out onto Leyland's Farm overlooking a wooded slope in the distance. It was good to rest my eyes on wide slopes of smooth arable land, rib-rolled, showing mixed shades of brown as the texture of soil varied, the corn just about to sprout. Seed sown on other fields in the distance had already germinated and was well up, making bright green patches in the quilted landscape. Little drifts of lilac-grey clouds hung like a frieze above the purple-shadowed alder wood.

I walked, not across the plough, but along the ditch edge. The water which flows through my garden pools continues through a small alder copse just below the garden, emerges at the far end in a steep drop and then hurries on down through well-maintained ditches until it joins Tenpenny Brook, meeting the estuary of the River Colne about three miles away. Here fresh water meets the incoming salt water of the tides. It is at this point that young eels, spawned in the deep Sargasso sea, enter our streams and rivers having floated slowly for three years across the Atlantic as little leaf-shaped creatures. Arriving at the mouths of rivers, they change to the normal shape of eels, or 'elvers' as they are called at that stage. They wriggle along Tenpenny Brook and struggle up the well-kept ditches until they arrive at the reservoir; finally, some arrive in our garden pools. Here they live peacefully for many years.

When they have become adult they change into their sea coats of silver and black, their eyes enlarge and they set off along the ditch I have walked beside, back to the Sargasso Sea where they breed and die – provided they have not been turned into smoked or jellied eel.

On my walk I came across lesser ditches, not well brushed but cluttered with blackberry tangles; long trails of the past summer's growth sprawling among frost-withered grass. Many held bold leaves, some of them flaming orange and red. Further along there had been festoons of bryony, ropes of shining crimson berries. Now was left a knitted tangle of pale, string-like stems draping the hedge like an old frayed bedspread left behind by gypsies. A pair of bare, red-brick cottages stood on the contour of the ploughed field where it touched the sky, dwarfed by a wide black barn crouched beside them. With so little cover I saw no animal life and very few birds. The redwings and fieldfares I had left busy feeding on the last fallen apples in the orchards. Thinking of them reminded me it was time to go home for lunch.

Since the beginning of September, my women staff have been busy packing orders sent in by our postal customers. Each order is collected individually until the packhouse floor is filled with trays of plants. They are then checked for quality and identification, wrapped, labelled and packed. Twice a day there is a trolley-load of parcels weighed and waiting for the arrival of the Post Office van. It is concentrated and skilled work; only occasionally are we told the wrong plant has been sent. Handwriting may sometimes be more of a problem. Many different styles must be interpreted and instructions are sometimes muddled. Those who clearly print their names, addresses and plant requirements are showered with blessings since they help the whole process to flow smoothly. With regular customers there develops a feeling of rapport. Their names and addresses ring a bell; often the kind of plants they choose create a personality. They become familiar characters, as much as the faces we recognise in summer whose names we often do not know. By the end of the first week in December we stop packing, since we do not want our plants to be buried in the avalanche of Christmas post.

Like children let out of school, everyone is glad to be outside again, making the most of the mild weather and the short time left to get everywhere tidied and to find shelter before Christmas for every plant that needs it.

I would prefer to leave more of the border plants standing than we do, since many still look attractive. The brittle brown stems of *Aster corymbosa* still carry multitudes of tiny beige stars, glistening among the *Bergenia* leaves, while *Aster acris* is covered with pale fawn fluffy heads, like miniature powder puffs. Other plants, *Rudbeckia*, *Lythrum* and *Phlomis*, have strong rigid outlines, wonderful to see when seed heads are changed into snow flowers formed by softly fallen snow. But I

A busy pack-house

have learnt we must make the best use of our time, when we have it to spare, and that is now. There simply is no time in spring, so most herbaceous plants are now being cut to the ground and carted to the compost heap. Where it is needed, extra straw or crushed bark is added to mulches already holding weeds in check. For the last time this year the grass edges are trimmed.

Much of the vivid winter-green grass is covered with a rich russet carpet of fallen oak leaves. These are raked and carted away in the dumper truck to make a new heap in the shelter of Badger Wood. Each year a separate heap is made. The leaves take about three years to rot down into crumbly leafmould and then they provide the perfect top-dressing for shade-loving plants. Other well-rotted heaps of garden compost, hidden around the perimeter of the garden, are being dug out and spread over the surface of the soil. A few weeds may germinate from the compost in the spring, but hopefully we shall catch them in time. Then a new covering of bark will be put down on any bare spaces; these become fewer as the plants themselves spread and cover the soil in summer with their leaves.

It is fascinating to see how sunlight falls into the house in winter, touching objects it rarely reaches in summer. Today my room has looked pretty all day, simply because the sun has lain in it. Yesterday it was plain and lifeless. It is not be wondered at that most of us are sun worshippers – not necessarily the kind who prostrate themselves unclad – for when the sun shines new life is given to everything, to ourselves and our surroundings.

Today the low winter sun has crept round the house peeping in each window. First it caught the few remaining leaves of a vine curved around a corner of the house wall. From inside the house each leaf glowed like Burgundy wine as the sun shone through it and fell across the table onto small bowls and baskets of flowers and fruit, turning them into a still life. Later it dipped below the bare boughs of the big Magnolia and fell the full length of the sitting room floor. Only in winter does sunlight move across to Cedric Morris' painting of rooftops in Portugal, at the far end of the room. New shadows and highlights appear among the warm sun-baked tiles. We can sense the glare from white-washed walls around the little parapet where he sat, imagine voices rising from the hidden street below, smell the cooking, the sizzling of onions and garlic, the mouthwatering aroma of wine spitting into the air as it is sloshed into the hot pan.

Back in my room each plant has been drenched with light as the sun moves around the room, passing slowly over the weighty begonias immovable as armchairs, the spider-like babies of *Chlorophytum*, and a pretty little succulent I have just brought in from the greenhouse, whose name I do not know. The pot is crammed to over-flowing with threaded stems of fat, wedge-shaped leaves. They are a lovely sea-green colour, stained faintly with purple. Just now each string of jade-like 'beads' carries upturned heads of tiny yellow flowers to form an aureole of light around the pot.

After weeks of delaying tactics on my part, I am pinned down by Rosie, my long suffering secretary, to make a start on revising the catalogue. Once we have made the decision to leave undone all the other things we would much prefer to do, and have put our backs, and our minds, into it for a day, we know we have begun a task that will last on and off for the best part of January, and will still haunt us in February when the printers' galleys come flopping onto our desks.

First there are plants to be discontinued, seldom because they are unsaleable, usually because they are slow or difficult to propagate and so the supply is always behind the demand. Then we make a list of plants we feel should be included and are not. At this point I am sent off to write seductive descriptions, since as yet we do not use illustrations. On my return we go through every word, hyphen and comma of the previous catalogue trying to sort out inconsistencies, making sure we have translated measurements correctly from imperial to metric, checking for the umpteenth time unlikely-looking spellings of Latin names. Occasionally we find one we have spelt incorrectly for years without being aware of it. This year the packhouse girls were delighted to discover *Zigadenus*, instead of *Zygadenus* as I had written it from the beginning of time. The constant changing of names is a worry. We try to be accurate, as we sit surrounded by the works of Graham Stuart Thomas, the RHS dictionary, and other authoritative works, but we do not always have the very latest information. By the time we have caught up the plant has sometimes reverted to its original name or spelling. I remember we went through a phase when words ending *-iense* came to have *-ense*, so that *Chrysanthemum hosmariense* became *Chrysanthemum hosmarense*. This lasted a few years and now we are back to inserting the 'i', but the genus has now changed to *Leucanthemum hosmariense*! Fortunately the plant remains its enchanting self, smothered in spring with short-stemmed, bold daisies over low cushions of grey leaves. It is worth noticing the fat buds: tightly clenched grey calyces outlined with black.

When we think we have corrected all the mistakes we can find, the catalogue is cut and pasted onto clean sheets. Unwanted plants are removed and the new additions are inserted in the correct places.

The next job is to revise the price list. It might surprise some people to know how much we deliberate new prices. We are reluctant to put on too high a figure, yet in some cases we have to remind ourselves of the years it has taken to produce enough stock to sell. At one fraught moment, when one particularly rare plant was being considered, Rosie

reminded me of the cost of an ounce of French perfume. We did not immediately add an extra nought to the price in question, but it gave us a sense of proportion – and 'French Perfume' gave us a laugh and a reminder, whenever we became bogged down again, that we are dealing with a plant in the luxury class. It would be very nice to leave the prices where they are, but I am reminded by my practical assistant of the rise in price of everything we pay for to keep the nursery running. We carefully review each plant. In some cases we do not change the price if we have good stocks; or if the plant is easily propagated; but we also have to remember that all plants will require care and attention and will take up valuable space. This year, for the first time, we set a minimum price for all plants at the one pound mark. It is pointless to look back, but in one of my early catalogues, in 1969, the lowest price was three shillings, while much further back I remember shopping as a schoolgirl in Woolworth's with my mother, finding plant treasures for threepence and sixpence. Several of those actual plants (maintained by cuttings) are still in my garden today.

Finally we tackled the ex-directory catalogue. Here are listed many unusual plants, generally available to personal visitors, but not in sufficient quantities to be entered in our postal catalogue. The catalogue is contained in a loose-leaf file with every sheet protected in a plastic envelope. There are several copies of this 'catalogue' on the nursery, available for staff with muddied hands to look up prices for customers. We are sometimes asked why we do not print copies for the public, but it runs into many pages and as it represents a shifting population, we cannot guarantee availability.

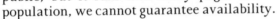

Spreading bark on the stock beds

Several other good things come out of this somewhat academic exercise. My attention is drawn to every plant we propagate and sell – outside on the nursery it is easy to overlook something. I am reminded to make lists of plants which need to be increased for stock, and of others not yet planted in the garden. By the end of it all I have guidelines for the propagating staff and classified lists for myself in the garden – all written in bold black pen on sheets of waste cardboard. These are a great help when, having found a day free to plant, I can see exactly what I meant to plant and where to put it.

As a diversion from such weighty matters, late one afternoon, as I was about the leave the office, I noticed that a large shallow bowl of pot-pourri on top of the filing cabinet had been spilt. 'Never mind,' I said to Rosie. 'It can be thrown away now, it has probably lost its scent.' As I said this, I swirled around the remaining contents of the bowl with my free hand, the other being full of correspondence needing my attention. 'Oh dear!' I said, lifting out my hand. It was dripping wet. Everyone collapsed with laughter. Resourceful Emma. If no one thinks to provide a cat box on a cold night she will not foul the office but will find something eminently suitable. Madge had come in to share the fun. 'Oh, I'll soon sort her out,' she said, and off she went to make a cat tray, lining a tomato box with a sheet of plastic and filling it with spent compost.

On my table is a little pewter jug filled with snowdrops. They are not *Galanthus reginae olgae* as I had long thought they were, but are *Galanthus caucasicus* var. *hiemale*. (*Hiemale* means of winter flowering; they usually open in November lasting well into December.) In the warmth of the room the snow-white petals have opened wide over prim, closely-folded petals, each bearing a green heart-shaped mark at the tip. In the garden the broad grey leaves are just appearing at ground level, rolled round the base of each flower stalk. They will lengthen throughout the winter but the flowers will be over long before February and March when *Galanthus caucasicus* will be at its best.

I have added to my small bouquet a few early leaves of *Arum italicum* 'Pictum' and three sprays of an unusual form of ivy called *Hedera helix* 'Purpurea'. In summer the leaves are green, but after the first cold spell they deepen to purplish black, prettily netted with green veins.

In the garden we all look out for the first blooms of *Narcissus minor* 'Cedric Morris'. There are two or three little trumpets opened already on the edge of the Wood Garden, with many more buds coming up strongly through the short turf. *Helleborus atrorubens* is in full flower. What will be left for January when we usually expect to see it? Before the leaves, it thrusts through the soil short stems carrying three or four open-faced nodding blooms. They are not a rich colour, being light plum, marked inside with dark veins. Overall, there is a greyish bloom-like tinge to the flowers.

286

I am disturbed to see how advanced are many of the forms of *Helleborus orientalis*. Most of them show clusters of bud at ground level when they should be tucked safely below ground.

I have waited for short days and bad weather to sort out my basket of vegetable seeds, to see which would still be viable, which must be reordered. It is a soothing job on a raw cold day, when I am comfortably settled by the office fire. As I take the seed packets, looking at pictures of fat corn cobs or crisp scarlet radish, it seems no time at all since spring when I was handling these seeds. The thought of doing it again wipes out, for the moment, the thought of the bleak mean winter still to come.

It is useful to know how long seeds can be kept before they lose their power to germinate. Here is a list showing those you are most likely to need:

Aubergine	6 yrs	Cucumber	7 yrs	Pumpkin (Squash)	4 yrs
Beans (all)	2 yrs	Endive	5 yrs	Radish	4 yrs
Beetroot	4 yrs	Fennel	3 yrs	Spinach	2 yrs
Brussels Sprouts	4 yrs	Leek	4 yrs	Spinach beet	4 yrs
Cabbage	4 yrs	Lettuce	3-4 yrs	Sprouting broccoli	4 yrs
Carrot	4 yrs	Marrow		Swede	2 yrs
Cauliflower	4 yrs	(Courgette)	7 yrs	Sweetcorn	2 yrs
Celeriac	6 yrs	Onion	1-2 yrs	Swiss chard	4 yrs
Celery	6 yrs	Pea	2 yrs	Tomato	3 yrs
Chicory	6 yrs	Sweet Pepper	4 yrs	Turnip	2 yrs

I was surprised when I first saw some of these figures, and somewhat peeved, too, when I realised how much good seed I had previously thrown away assuming it was always best to sow fresh. It can also be quite a saving to know which you can keep. A good pinch of most of the brassicas (cabbage family) will provide plenty of plants for a small family, the rest can be kept for another year – or longer if you have plenty. Why sow a hundred seeds when you need only ten plants? Sow a few more than you think you will need, in case of accidents, or to give a few to your neighbour, then fasten the packet securely with a paper clip or a rubber band and store it in a safe place. It is a good idea to put the date on the packet if it is not stamped by the supplier or if you have torn it off.

This year I have sorted my seeds, then packed them into two large cake tins. In one I keep packets of hardy vegetable seeds such as carrot, lettuce, radish, etc., in the other I put the seeds of tender plants – sweet corn, courgettes, tomato and basil. This saves a good deal of searching around when suddenly you discover it's time to put seed of the half hardies into pots to start them off in the warmth of the greenhouse or later in a frame.

I like to start broad beans in small, individual pots. Recent hard winters, followed by cold springs, have delayed sowing them outside. It is very satisfying to carry out trays of young plants, hardened off in a cold frame (not drawn up and weakly), to know you will have a complete block undamaged by frost or mice.

When the old seed packets are sorted I write a list of each, then put seeds and lists into their labelled tins. Then it is a fairly simple matter to go through the catalogues to order those I still require. I say 'fairly simple'; in fact it can be as time-wasting an occupation for me as it might be for some people walking round boutiques. Every year there are 'new' varieties, with packet pictures perhaps more tempting than ever. But by experience I have learnt which vegetables and salads suit my soil and way of gardening. My enthusiasm for unusual vegetables has been rejuvenated by Joy Larkcom, first by her articles in the RHS journal, and her book *Salads the Year Round*, and then by meeting her both here and in her own garden where she is endlessly experimenting with seed she has collected on her travels. Generously she has given me little twists of rare seed to see how we liked it, and to see how it reacted to our conditions. Joy also gave me a book I treasure, *The Vegetable Garden* by Mme Vilmorin-Andrieux. It is a gourmet's treat to sit and read the minutely detailed descriptions of vegetables familiar and unknown. Many different varieties of each individual vegetable or salad are described, far more than are available today. Can you imagine fifteen different kinds of endive or twenty-seven pages on lettuce? Many are illustrated with beautiful line drawings. There are lettuces curled, crimped or speckled – and not only green, but 'Brown Batavian', 'Chavigny White', and 'Red Besson' Cabbage Lettuce. 'The full grown plant is stout and rather thick-set and of rapid growth. Head roundish and slightly flattened on the top where it is deeply tinged with bright red, which contrasts in a striking manner with the very pale tint of those parts of the plant which are not exposed to the sun.' The seeds of both brown and red-tinged lettuce have crept back into the seed lists recently, but they are not so 'new' as we might have been led to believe.

If you are interested in unusual vegetables you should write to the Henry Doubleday Association, Ryton-in-Dunsmore, Coventry CV8 3LG. Another firm which lists unusual vegetables and herbs and wild flowers is 'Suffolk Herbs' run by John and Caroline Stevens, Sawyers Farm, Little Cornard, Sudbury, Suffolk CO10 ONY. Joy Larkcom's books are both inspiring and practical. She has travelled extensively in Europe with her husband, looking for plants, cultivated or wild, eaten by country folk. Recently she has done the same in China and Japan where a wide range of salad vegetables are extensively cultivated.

Many people have little choice in the food they eat, the selection offered by the commercial growers, but some of these unusual saladings take very little room, can be grown in boxes and cut, again and again, to provide fresh unsprayed leaves and shoots. Not only lettuce, but quick-growing salads like Pak-choi with crisp dark green leaves and the finely-cut Mizuma can be used when the leaves are quite small, cutting again and again from the same plants.

Among the less well-known vegetables I have ordered is scorzonera. This is a root vegetable, not sweet like carrot or parsnip, but with a delicate flavour and texture that puts it into the luxury class. Sometimes it is called the Vegetable Oyster. As with oysters, the pleasure of eating it comes only after a certain amount of effort, even discomfort. First scrub the long black roots free of soil, then steam them in shallow water, making sure it does not boil dry. When tender, strain them and prepare to peel them while still hot. This is not too difficult if you rest them on a board or tray, rolling them over as you lift the black skin with a sharp knife. Before you have finished, the remainder will be cool enough to slip the skin easily between your fingers, the smooth tender white flesh slipping out like a baby wet from the bath. Serve warm with melted butter or use as a salad with a mild French dressing or home-made mayonnaise.

Before dark, I collect a basket of vegetables and fruit for the juicing machine. Bright orange carrots, yellow or white beetroot, red-skinned apples with creamy-white flesh, crisp celery with rose-tinted stems, all scrubbed and shining wet they make a glowing pattern of shapes and colour piled onto a tray – sunshine colours brought in from the cold dark garden. Juiced onto ice cubes, with lemon or orange juice added for zest, they make a refreshing drink very different from processed juices sold in cardboard boxes.

This is our last working week of the year. Everywhere that can be has been swept, all the buildings made tidy. Tools have been cleaned and hung on their proper hooks, or else put to one side to be repaired or sharpened when it is too cold to work outside. Water pipes have been relagged with split sleeves of polystyrene. Short lengths slip easily over the pipes and are then taped together. Taps not required are discon-nected but some must be well protected in order to have a supply of water for the tunnels using hosepipes instead of the overhead sprinklers. In the plastic tunnels plants can die more easily of drought than frost during the winter months.

Shrubs and trees prone to attack by bullfinches have been sprayed with something distasteful. All plants in covered places have received their routine protective spray against moulds and mildew. The pack-house floor is piled with trays of plants well covered over to provide work splitting and potting if the New Year finds everything outside frozen solid. The heaters have been checked.

Christmas is close at hand. The staff dinner party has become a very pleasant tradition. All members of staff are invited, including the girls from the neighbouring fruit farm who have spent six months of every summer working with us for the past ten or fifteen years. Husbands, wives and sweethearts come too, making a very large family party. I feel a little glow of pride as I look round to see so many familiar faces closely involved with the fortunes and future of the garden. But on the last day before the two week Christmas break, the winter staff and I slip off along to a little local pub to have a simple lunch and drink together. It is end of term; we exchange cards and presents, then we part. We have weathered the past year together; together we are hopeful for the year to come.

For me the garden is never closed. On Boxing Day morning I made my usual daily round. Low rays of winter sunlight dazzled my eyes so I was often obliged to turn my back to the sun to see individual colours and shapes. As I walked I picked a flower of every plant in bloom until I had a basketful, astonished to count eighty-five different kinds. Some were seasonal, most were quite out of season. Back at my desk I piled them onto two trays, the better to enjoy them but also to sort them out. Each tray had a different colour scheme, each was a perfect gift for Boxing Day. One tray held flowers from cool shaded parts of the garden, lime-green and white, purple and flushed pink, while the other was vibrant with clear yellows, scarlet and pink of flowers picked in the drier, open parts of the garden. Suddenly I realised I had gathered together in this last week of the old year flowers representing every month. I cannot remember seeing such a time-span encapsulated so exquisitely in one moment. If such a large collection has been possible in the garden before, I have been unaware of it. This can only be the result of an unusually long spell of mild weather, with autumn lasting almost until Christmas. But (typical of gardeners I suppose – we can always find something to moan about) my pleasure in finding all these old friends celebrating the kind conditions, was marred by my concern for the safety of others. Many plants, normally well out of winter's harm, are showing too much new growth. Bulbs of all kinds are several inches through the soil, buds are exposed which would normally be tucked deep into nests of protecting crowns. Many plants look as I would expect to see them by the end of February rather than at the end of December. What will happen if we have severe frosts during the next two months as we have had these past two winters? These forward creatures will collapse, apparently limp and lifeless, frozen to the iron-hard soil. Will they, I wonder, have the capacity to rise, to carry on their life-cycle when the thaw comes as do some of the truly winter flowers? Without a blanket of snow I shall fear for them. This flat, open part of the country receives the full blast of icy winds out of Russia, but seldom deep falls of snow caught usually by higher ground, both to the north and south.

Many hellebores are as advanced as if it were March. The Lenten Roses, *Helleborus orientalis*, have buds on stems several inches tall.

Some are in bloom. On my tray are perfectly formed specimens – plum, purple and white. Even if they could be pollinated, they are unlikely to have weather kind enough to let them set seed. It will be interesting to see how all these plants behave in the perilous weeks ahead.

It is the last day of the old year. I have just pulled back the curtains letting in half-light as dawn slowly pushes aside the dark of a long winter night. Beneath my hands I feel the comforting warmth of the tea pot as I stand waiting for the breakfast kettle to boil. The wide kitchen window is filled with a view of the garden; beyond lies the recently made wet nursery. Successive screens of bare branches and warm tinted twigs fill the frame like a painting. The dun colours are relieved by emerald grass and fresh young corn glimpsed on the field beyond our boundary. Closer to the house are protective groups of evergreens, *Garrya elliptica*, with catkins small and tight; bold shining fig-like leaves of *Fatsia japonica* are sheltered against the house wall.

At the base of a group of tall upright junipers billow blue-grey masses of my favourite *Euphorbia wulfenii*. The curving heads of flower buds are already well advanced. Variegated forms of common ivy, with small leaves edged white or centred with yellow, make bright patches as they scramble up and over a retaining wall onto the level of the gravelled drive above.

My gaze travels back to the little paved and cobbled square on the lower level, just below the kitchen window, protected by the wall and screen of trees and shrubs. Suddenly, from among the privacy of the great euphorbias, there appears a fox, a fine great fellow, his tawny coat matching the russet of oak leaves huddled into corners. Quite unaware he pauses a moment, then passes me by majestically on springy feet, to disappear beneath a huge *Rosa moyesii* and into the garden beyond. I dash to the sitting room window hoping for another glimpse, but he has vanished, as at home in the garden as I am. My heart thuds with excitement to have seen him so closely exactly where, last winter, I watched the fieldfare gulping down the orange seeds of *Iris foetidissima*, and later the grey squirrel holding in dainty black hands an apple thrown out onto the snow. I run to find Andrew to share the thrill with him.

POSTSCRIPT

THIS notebook has taken longer than I had hoped to put into readable form. Since I began, changes on the nursery have inevitably taken place. Perhaps the most surprising has been the installation of a computer. Only a short while ago we were hesitant to take this step, yet within a few months we are delighted to see how time and talent are being saved, both in the office and in the packing-shed. Skilled people are released from boring, repetitive jobs, leaving more time to deal with matters requiring personal attention and skills.

We have been surprised at the ease with which the transition has been made, and grateful for the encouragement of Jack Gingell of Rampart's Nursery, Colchester, whose experience in introducing a computer into his nursery was an important deciding factor for us. He introduced us to Ray Skeet, Associate Director of Orwell Data Services, who supplied our equipment. Already experienced in devising programmes for several other nursery firms, Ray was familiar with the kind of service we would need; but naturally every business has its own special requirements. Once the initial programmes were set up Ray could not have been more helpful in guiding us through the first few weeks, until now the daily routine has become as familiar as was that of the typewriter. While the office staff obviously make most of the new machine, some of the outside staff have also been involved, so they understand how and when it can help them.

Sometimes I am asked, what are my future plans? How much bigger will the nursery grow? These are not easy questions to answer, but I feel the atmosphere of the nursey and garden would change (possibly not for the better) if we became very much larger. My aim is to consolidate what we have achieved; to continue to improve the range and quality of our plants and service. We are involved in the conservation, propagation and distribution of unusual and rare plants as well as demonstrating ways of using them when we show them established in harmonious settings in the garden.

Although I shall continually assess new methods of work and production, I have no intenton of turning the nursery into a factory for best-selling lines. Sometimes I think our enterprise resembles a jeweller's shop where people come to search around for a particular treasure they may have been seeking for years. If they come across it and tell us so, we share their pleasure and feel great satisfaction in being able to supply that need.

In the coming years I shall look forward to seeing new members of staff grow in character, as well as ability. As certain of our plants take many years to mature, so it takes a long time to grow a genuine plantsman. Those of us who have been at it longest know that one lifetime is not half enough, once you become aware of the limitless art of gardening.

Our Japanese student, Kazu, was followed by an American student, Jack Henning, who came and captivated everyone by his enthusiasm, abilities, and warmth of character. 'Why can't we adopt him?' said Madge, when all efforts failed to extend his work permit. We all learnt and gained from Jack and made, I think, a friend for life.

Our next student is a young girl from Germany, Mechthild Soergel. She may become part of another story.

The computer installed and working

Italic numbers indicate pages on which illustrations appear